D1632597

Illustration

Related study material is available on the Laurence King website at
www.laurenceking.com

For Kelly, Taylor and Robin.

Published in 2011 by Laurence King Publishing in
Association with Central Saint Martins College of Art
& Design

The content for this book has been produced by
Central Saint Martins Book Creation, Southampton
Row, London, WC1B 4AP, UK

Laurence King Publishing Ltd
361–373 City Road
London EC1V 1LR
United Kingdom
Tel: +44 20 7841 6900
Fax: +44 20 7841 6910
e-mail: enquiries@laurenceking.com
www.laurenceking.com

A catalogue record for this book is available from the
British Library.

ISBN-13: 978-1-85669-710-1

Designed by Unlimited
Series designer: Jon Allan

Printed in China

Front cover: *Cubik,* by David Foldvari.
Mixed media, 2010.

Back cover: *The Wall (Sister Morphine)*, by Neal Fox.
Ink on paper, 2008.

Frontispiece: Branding for Nike Jordan,
by McFaul Studio. Digital, 2008.

LAURENCE KING

1.

Training to be an illustrator

'There is nothing to stop anyone from making art. The problem is what you do with it, and in what way it's recognized. You'll ultimately have to engage with the business of either applied art or fine art.' Peter Saville, graphic designer

'There's applied art and fine art. The tools are irrelevant. It's either applied: applied to somebody else's problem or product, or it's fine art: standing alone. The difference is really defined. It's not a grey zone, in my opinion, it's black and white.' Peter Saville, graphic designer

As with any creative enterprise, perhaps it is best to start this one with a blank space. Be it on screen or paper, the blank space is a place for the illustrator to think, to imagine and to form thought. It is a powerful entity, a force to be reckoned with, a nothing that can become a something. It can fill the illustrator with hope and with fear; it can fill them with frustration and even despair. It can also, time and again, serve as a portal for the illustrator to enter a creative world where an image can be rendered, where a subject can be explored and where a solution to a client's problem can be found.

This blank space is not an entity that people working in other professions engage with on a daily basis. The accountant, the lawyer and the doctor are not expected to find a 'new' answer to problems that they face regularly in their areas of expertise. On the contrary, they are expected to have an extensive knowledge of existing accounting, legal or medical systems, knowledge that they skilfully apply to their work. Although innovation does take place within their fields, it is essentially an isolated, risk-averse activity that may or may not lead to fruition. By contrast, the illustrator, who earns a livelihood by making specific types of imagery, has no rulebook, no right or wrong way of doing things, no set answers, and faces the real risk of failure on a daily basis.

The illustrator's job is to create a something from a nothing, to encapsulate an idea that communicates to an audience in an innovative way that is also articulate. Though systems surround visual language, and theories define the process of communication, it is not enough to have an extensive grasp of these systems and theories – simply regurgitating them will not do. The training for an illustrator requires that they explore key areas of their subject, both practically and intellectually, until they can competently reassemble them in a fashion that is peculiar to them, that carries their authorship and that is imprinted with their own particular artistic and intellectual vision.

The writer, too, has an intimate knowledge of the blank space, be it the white surface of the paper or the luminous glow of the computer screen. They too must find their way into this space, to map their thoughts and ideas, but with a different system – the system of written language. It is no surprise,

Above
Images of our world are used to convey messages to global audiences. In this simple sign the idea of a male and female toilet is instantly communicated.

ABCDEFGHIJKLM
NOPQRSTUVWXYZ
abcdefghijklm
nopqrstuvwxyz

Above
The Western alphabet, formed of 26 characters, is a formidable system of communication.

therefore, that these two professions, one using pictures and one using words, have been intertwined for so many years; these two, born of the same starting point, have forged a union that, when functioning properly, becomes a force far greater than the sum of its parts.

This union between picture and word is called 'graphic design'; it is arranged, ordered and conceptually driven by graphic designers. This subject, vast in reach, has saturated all areas of culture. We see graphic design in newspapers, books, adverts and corporate literature; we see it accompanying the music that we buy, on television and in film; we see it within the physical environment that we inhabit, on the clothing we wear and on our navigational signage systems. It is very hard to imagine a world without graphic design; it has become integral to the way in which we communicate, function and organize ourselves as human beings.

Contextualizing illustration within graphic design

As a subject, and as a defined profession, the term 'graphic design' has existed for a relatively short time – since the end of the Second World War. Prior to this, scribes, religious personnel, printers, fine artists and, most recently, commercial artists, had dealt with the arrangement of pictures and words for mass public consumption. After the war, and due to the breadth and depth of its reach, the business of 'communication design' fragmented into distinct areas of specialism. Illustrators appropriated the territory of the constructed image (be it drawn, painted, printed, collaged or computer-generated); typographers appropriated the letterform; advertising art directors controlled the generation and formation of the publicity concept for products and services; photographers monopolized the photographic image; and of course graphic designers were in charge of orchestrating (and in many cases, generating) any and all of these elements, both intellectually and artistically, into dynamic and articulate messages for the purpose of 'identification,

Think small.

FRANK SINATRA · ELEANOR PARKER · KIM NOVAK

THE MAN WITH THE GOLDEN ARM

A FILM BY OTTO PREMINGER · FROM THE NOVEL BY NELSON ALGREN · MUSIC BY ELMER BERNSTEIN · PRODUCED & DIRECTED BY OTTO PREMINGER

information and instruction, presentation and promotion'. These messages have appeared ever since in print, on television, in the cinema, on books, in the environment, on packaging and, most recently, on the internet via the desktop computer and the digital phone.

Chapters 4 to 7 cover the use of illustration within all of these areas – editorial, publishing, corporate design and advertising, and light entertainment. As we shall see over the course of this book, the continuing history of illustration exists within the history of graphic design; it is embedded, intertwined and co-reliant.

Pictures and words – similarities and differences

We have ascertained that there is a powerful connection between word and image, facilitating the creation of 'graphic design'. Pictures and words possess particular qualities, both apart and in common, that assist in their power to communicate together within such a diverse arena.

The picture has the power to:
- Communicate instantaneously.
- Communicate to a global audience, regardless of age, location or era.
- Locate the viewer within the image.
- Represent literally the human experience of seeing.
- Visually delight, again and again.
- Be arranged sequentially to communicate narrative.
- Connect instantaneously with emotion, memory and experience.
- Delight through shape, colour and form.

Above left
Volkswagen Beetle advert by Helmut Krone and Julian Koenig. Lithograph, 1960. This poster from New York advertising agency Doyle Dane Bernbach employs a central concept that is displayed in a light and playful way.

Above right
The Man with the Golden Arm by Saul Bass. Poster, 1955. Commissioned by Otto Preminger Films. The work of American illustrator Saul Bass, who was particularly famed for iconic film posters such as this, pervaded many areas of contemporary communication design discourse.

[handwritten note:] Sketch of an army of people in a line with same cameras but different age race height

Left
Esquire cover, art direction by Henry Wolf; photography by Ronny Jaques, 1953. Commissioned by *Esquire*. This magazine cover shows the dominance of the concept in 1950s American art direction.

Below left
Illustration by Arpi Ermoyan for the story 'Heart's Ease', written by Sarah-Elizabeth Rodger, in *Woman* magazine, 1952. The new-found liberation of the postwar years is clearly visible in this illustration from one of the numerous romance magazines available.

Below right
Without My Cloak, written by Kate O'Brien, cover design by Jan Tschichold. Penguin, 1949. The work of renowned German typographer Jan Tschichold for Penguin Books shows the development of typography as a powerful stand-alone element that, coupled with a colour-coding system, also serves to identify the genre of the writing.

Bottom
Photograph of Marilyn Monroe, 1948. This image of the film star Marilyn Monroe shows how the photographic image came to be recognized as an art form in its own right.

The word has the power to:
- Communicate specifically.
- Communicate with great accuracy.
- Communicate to localized and specialized audiences.
- Engage an audience over a prolonged period of time.
- Reveal things slowly to an audience.
- Be arranged sequentially to communicate narrative.
- Connect with emotion, memory and experience.
- Delight through shape, colour and form.

Both have their strengths, their weaknesses and points of similarity. You may
want to add your own thoughts on image and word to this list. What is certain,
however, is that when combined, when working together, they have the
ability to endorse each other's strengths and to compensate for each
other's weaknesses.

Similarities and differences between fine art and applied art

It is tempting to think of 'fine art' and 'applied art' as being one and the same. They can look the same, they can share the same visual language, and they can be made by the same person. However, as tempting as this supposition may be, it is important to clarify their differences in order to understand the role of illustration (an 'applied art') more exactly. We can achieve this by asking questions about the intentions behind the picture, the *object* that we are looking at:

1 What is the primary, intended origination point of the object?
2 What is the primary, intended function of the object?
3 What is the primary, intended fabric of the object?
4 What is the primary, intended worth of the object?
5 What is the primary, intended numerical edition of the object?
6 What is the primary, intended audience of the object?
7 What is the primary, intended context of the object?

By using these questions as a framework, we can try to tease out the main criteria for a picture that is 'fine art' and a picture that is 'applied art'. You can always add criteria to this list as you work through the questions.

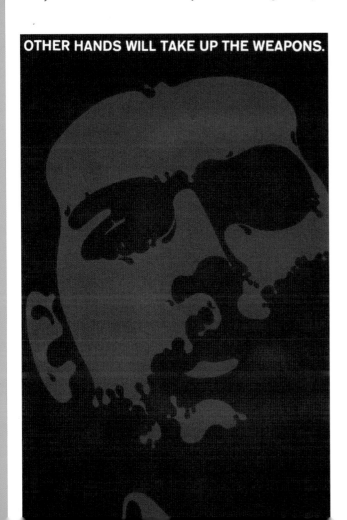

Left
Other Hands will Take Up the Weapons by The Cuban Institute of Friendship with the Peoples, c. 1967–80. This poster harnesses the glamorous figure of the Marxist revolutionary Ernesto 'Che' Guevara with the implication of a constant and ongoing state of world revolution.

Image A

Q: What is the primary, intended origination point of the object?
A: It is an editorial piece commissioned by the London department store Fortnum & Mason.
Q: What is the primary, intended function of the object?
A: It is an image supporting an article in an in-house Fortnum & Mason magazine for their exclusive range of environmentally friendly products.
Q: What is the primary, intended fabric of the object?
A: Mass-produced print (ink on paper).
Q: What is the primary, intended worth of the object?
A: £250 ($500).
Q: What is the primary, intended numerical edition of the object?
A: Approximately 10,000.
Q: What is the primary, intended audience of the object?
A: Fortnum & Mason customers and staff.
Q: What is the primary, intended context of the object?
A: Set next to an editorial article in a mass-produced magazine.

Image B

Q: What is the primary, intended origination point of the object?
A: It is a self-initiated piece of work.
Q: What is the primary, intended function of the object?
A: It is a piece of art.
Q: What is the primary, intended fabric of the object?
A: Acrylic on paper.
Q: What is the primary, intended worth of the object?
A: £500 ($1000).
Q: What is the primary, intended numerical edition of the object?
A: One.
Q: What is the primary, intended audience of the object?
A: For a private collector.
Q: What is the primary, intended context of the object?
A: Displayed on the wall of a private residence.

Image A
Illustration promoting laundry products by Sion Ap Tomos. Ink on paper, 2007. Commissioned by Fortnum & Mason. This drawing, of a glamorous lady hanging out her washing aided by cherubs, can potentially be read as fine art or applied art.

Image B
Somewhere Between Bethnal Green and Hackney Downs by Sion Ap Tomos. Acrylic on paper, 2008. Personal work. This painting, a poetic description of a run-down area of London, can potentially be read as fine art or applied art.

Clearly, Image A is applied art ('applied to somebody else's problem or product'), and Image B is fine art ('standing alone'). Though fine art and applied art are clearly different pursuits, they also share similar properties. These key areas of similarity are 'Visual Language' and 'Communication Language'. We will explore both of these areas in great depth in Chapters 2 and 3 of this book.

So, now that we've found a structure to identify the subject of illustration as an 'applied art' rather than a 'fine art', let's move on to look at key methodologies, processes and procedures that you'll need to understand when working as a practitioner.

Developing your product: problem-solving processes

Most adult employment involves the practical challenge of how to solve a problem (be it a simple problem or a supremely complex one), and illustration is no exception. The illustrator's problem is a visual problem, requiring the employment of artistic, intellectual and organizational skills in order to achieve success within their profession. Visual problem-solving is an exciting challenge, a task that, when complete, gives immense satisfaction as well as financial reward. In order to complete this task, the illustrator has to engage in a process – a consecutive, interlinked series of steps that takes them on a journey to find a visual solution to a problem that they have been paid to solve. Management consultants also use these steps in order to help businesses solve some of the problems that they face on a daily basis.

Along with many other skills, precise ways of thinking are needed along the journey. One person in particular has made a substantial contribution to articulating the way that we can think: Edward De Bono. He invented the term 'lateral thinking' in 1967, and is well known for his problem-solving methodologies, especially 'The Six Thinking Hats'. This clarifies six different methods that can be used individually or in unison in the problem-solving arena. The six hats, defined by colour, represent the following types of thinking:

The White Hat   To gather information.
The Green Hat   To explore and generate ideas without criticism.
The Yellow Hat To assess the strengths and benefits of each alternative.
The Black Hat   To assess the weaknesses and dangers of each alternative.
The Blue Hat   To maintain an overview of the progress and focus on the whole process.
The Red Hat   To express intuitive and emotional views that have no defined rationale.

Edward De Bono also focused on the idea of 'cutting out', 'sticking together' and 'shaping' information – he used the analogy of a carpenter, but this can be applied to the work of an illustrator with equal relevance. Lastly, De Bono invented the term 'operacy'. He used this word to encompass the many practical skills that work alongside creative skills, each one crucial for people to achieve solutions to problems. Without these operacy skills, creative skills can at best be compromised, at worst amount to nothing. We will look at these operacy skills in Chapter 9. Though Edward De Bono's work merits extensive study in its own right (see Further Reading, p. 222), we will respectfully use him as a mentor in this section, to guide us through our discussion of the various ways to approach the stages of the creative process as applied to the task of solving problems.

Stage 1
Defining the problem

For the illustrator, the problem is referred to as 'the brief'. Generally speaking, this is written by the client (the paymaster). It outlines background information, an explanation and summary of the visual problem, specific details and requirements, timescales and fees. This stage involves the gathering of information. For De Bono, this is '**White Hat Thinking**' – it encourages you to ask: 'What information do I have? What information do I need? What information is missing?' Asking these detailed questions of the brief (and the client) will help you to clarify the task in hand; to avoid any pitfalls (remember that wise old phrase 'the devil is in the detail'); and to ensure that both you and your client are thinking along the same lines and can proceed accordingly.

Stage 2
Gathering the relevant information

Having clarified what is being asked of you, you move to Stage 2. This is a continuation of the information-gathering stage ('**White Hat Thinking**'), but this time it is driven by your own knowledge, intellect, experience and intuition. Generally speaking, this first information-gathering exercise is called 'primary research' (initial research). Research can be carried out in many different ways – for example, consulting the visual reference collection in your studio, reading books, visiting a museum to record information, talking to an expert, visiting and recording a physical location, watching a film, listening to a radio programme, watching television, carrying out a focused internet search. The main point of engaging in research is for you to achieve a broader and deeper understanding of the subject of the brief you are tackling. It allows you to choose and 'cut out' selective and specialized information before you start to formulate possible solutions to the visual problem. Primary research needs to be carried out with an attitude of open-mindedness; if you are merely seeking to confirm what you *think* you already know, thereby closing your mind to alternative ways of thinking about a subject, then little can be achieved by this process.

Stage 3
Generating options

Having carried out your analysis of the brief (Stage 1) and initial research (Stage 2), clarifying your understanding of the problem, you now enter the creative phase of generating options. In De Bono's Six Hats model, this is '**Green Hat Thinking**', signifying 'growth, energy and life'. Using your primary research, you begin to generate ideas, you propose solutions, you let your mind wander off the beaten path, you explore parallel approaches to the same problem, you avoid being critical or overly logical, you think in different ways about the same thing. In essence you are beginning to 'stick together' potential solutions in a number of different ways. This can be achieved using work sheets, sketches, diagrams, collage – all speedy, fluid ways of working that can be used to communicate your ideas while still allowing room for further development and change.

As previously mentioned, De Bono invented the term 'lateral thinking' to encapsulate this approach. His key observation was that we establish certain patterns in the brain – ways of thinking and doing things that coalesce into set ways of thinking and behaving. Though this is useful when driving a car, when it comes to being creative, De Bono suggests that we need to 'jack knife' ourselves out of these patterns, to veer off the well-trodden path, to experiment and explore with information and ideas. We can either do this by using one of his strategies or by inventing our own strategies. One method he suggests is prefixing any new idea with the word 'Po' in order for the participant to be empowered to float (potentially) outrageous ideas/solutions into the creative melting pot.

After this period of uncritical and broad exploration and discovery, we need to evaluate those discoveries, to find their inherent worth, and return with those of value in our metaphorical knapsack, back on to the road to finding a solution to the brief.

Stage 4
Evaluating the options

Having allowed yourself to explore a subject, informed by your primary research, you now have to make decisions, to extract the value or worth of those explorations. For this stage, you generally need to use a 'positive' and 'negative' discussion, essentially '**Yellow Hat Thinking**' and '**Black Hat Thinking**'. The Yellow Hat helps you focus on the positive aspects of an idea, the benefits, whereas the Black Hat helps you to focus on the negative aspects of an idea, the downside and the potential problems. You might also use '**Red Hat Thinking**' – this allows you to respond to ideas in an intuitive, emotional way that does not have to be underpinned by rational explanations. After considering your ideas using these very different ways of thinking, you may wish to draw up a shortlist of ideas that still might be appropriate as a solution to your brief. You may wish to engage in a small amount of secondary research for each of these ideas, ways in which they can become better informed and firmed up; this will prepare you for the next stage, where a final choice needs to be made.

Stage 5

Selecting the best option

When selecting the 'best' option, usually by using '**Black Hat Thinking**', you might wish to generate criteria by which you can objectively judge your shortlist. Criteria will vary from person to person, as well as from job to job, but generally speaking they will encompass some of the following areas:

• Is it original?
• Does it answer the brief?
• Is it achievable within the timeframe?
• Is it achievable at reasonable cost?

This framework will immediately discount one or more of your proposed solutions. However, if all or some of your proposals fully meet the criteria, then the criteria will have to be toughened up:

• Is it the most original idea?
• Does it best answer the brief?
• Is it the most achievable within the timeframe?
• Is it the most achievable at reasonable cost?

From this stringent process, one solution will emerge that merits further development.

Stage 6

Implementing the chosen solution

Now that you have made your decision, stick to it. Don't be tempted to return to Stage 5, or worse, Stage 3. Your decision has emerged through a stringent and critical process. Although you still face the challenge of implementing your proposal (the 'shaping' phase), the illusion that a better solution is around the corner is just that, an illusion. Implementing your solution will employ many of your skills, artistically, intellectually and technically. Your final outcome may be a print, a painting, a collage or a three-dimensional piece. At this stage, it is worth checking again the factual information provided on the brief: size(s), colour(s), physical or digital form and deadline. Continue to be critical even at this late stage – employ 'Black Hat Thinking' and 'Yellow Hat Thinking' – further detailed thinking and visual refinement will still be necessary. Don't allow your thinking to be dominated by stylistic possibilities (which are endless); return again and again to the original concept that is driving the idea. As the architect Louis Sullivan famously said, 'Form follows function'.

Stage 7

Monitor and evaluate outcomes

This stage involves a process of reflection and evaluation after the work has been realized. There are always things that you can learn from a job, even the most successful ones. You can ask yourself whether the client was pleased with the result, whether there were things that you would do differently a second time ('Yellow Hat Thinking'), whether any improvements could be made to your process ('Blue Hat Thinking'). Without reflection and evaluation, and being able to think of possible improvements, you may make the same mistakes again and again, which is neither helpful to you nor your clients.

It is also worth mentioning that employing '**Blue Hat Thinking**' is useful at any point along the creative journey, to help refocus on your task and to check that you are applying the right type of thinking to the right part of the problem. 'Blue Hat Thinking' is particularly useful when working in groups – people can quickly generate irrelevant tangents to the main discussion, which in turn can lead to a huge amount of time and energy being wasted.

From this rigorous process, you can solve any job, be it for editorial illustration, publishing, corporate identity and advertising work or light entertainment. All of these commercial areas of the applied image are covered in this book. We also outline who you need to approach for commissioned work, the people you will be involved with in the creative decision-making process, and the means by which a satisfactory solution is achieved for every brief that you engage with.

Problem-solving in practice: Jessica Jane Barlow's *The Rake's Progress*

It may be useful to study a live example of this problem-solving process. The brief here, set in Stage 2 of a Graphic Design degree course, was to re-tell Hogarth's eighteenth-century graphic story of 'The Rake's Progress'. This series of eight images tells the tale of a young man who inherits his father's money, which allows him to make a series of disastrous choices that set him on the road to ruin. Although in the new version the main character could change, as could the world in which the character existed and the events that unfolded, the students were asked to stay true to the spirit of the original and to retain the inherent narrative structure of Hogarth's series. The response featured is that of Jessica Jane Barlow.

3

Generating options

'As Michael Alig had an outrageous persona and the club-kid scene was full of costume and glamour, I wanted to tell his story without the obvious colour outcome. I veered into science and medicine while looking at drug-addled Alig's story. I began to experiment with telling his story of growth, spread and collapse. I was looking for a visual language that could carry this story. I first turned to the molecular structure of drugs, then modular origami, using ink splats, and finally crushing and photocopying paper.'

Initial reactions to the brief.

Michael Alig.

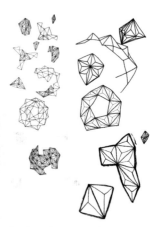

Sketches of modular origami options.

Photocopy of crushed paper.

1

Defining the problem

'I understood we were to take the existing narrative of Hogarth's "The Rake's Progress" and find our own replacement for the Rake. Much like how David Hockney re-positioned himself as the Rake in his print edition, we were to put a figure in the Rake's role and take the audience through each of the eight stages of his life.'

2

Gathering the relevant information

'Having chosen the infamous club kid, promoter and murderer Michael Alig as my rake, I began to expand my knowledge of the man by first turning to the biography Disco Bloodbath. Then I reviewed Party Monster: The Shockumentary and the Hollywood re-telling of his story, Party Monster. After this I spent time trawling the internet for information on him, finding his presence on YouTube, Wikipedia, The New York Times archive, his official website, and many fan pages. I also drew from personal experiences of the London equivalent of the New York club-kid scene with club nights such as Boombox.'

1.

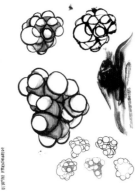

Sketches of ketamine.

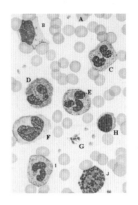

Molecular structure research.

4

Evaluating the options

'At this point I was championing the modular origami option, thinking that the sculptural forms would be ideal to tell Alig's story. However, at a crit, my peers were drawn to the molecular drug option and made me see the potential that it had. I carried out secondary research at this point, visiting the Science Museum and the Wellcome Collection in London and looking into pharmacology.'

5

Selecting the best option

'Having found out the molecular structure of the drug ketamine and looked into white blood cells, I found that the molecular forms were the best option for telling this story. Alig's rise to fame, his addiction and the murder that he committed mirror the organic process of growth, spread and collapse of the drug's infiltration and elimination of the blood cells.'

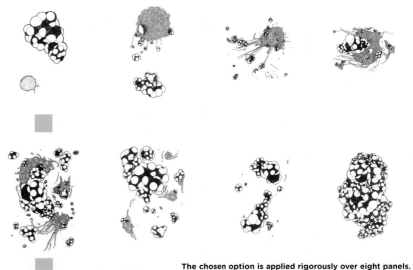

The chosen option is applied rigorously over eight panels.

6

Implementing the chosen solution

'I had three outcomes at this point. The first was eight framed detailed drawings (with a key) that documented interaction between white blood cells and the drug ketamine. The second outcome was a zine, created with the drug imagery, very erratic and with a grungy element. This did not show narrative quite as well as the first outcome.

For the third outcome, I created a set of 3D lettering spelling out "Alig" scattered with the drug molecule and with pink neon highlights – this helped to bridge the gap between the man, lifestyle and persona and the narrative. However, in the end, the original framed drawings were the final outcome chosen.'

Conclusion

Solving visual problems within this subject is an evergreen, fascinating challenge. The answer to one problem is not the answer to another, and the illustrator needs to muster new ideas and creative approaches with each brief, even if the structural process of problem-solving remains constant.

So let's return to the start of our discussion – the blank space. To begin the journey of how you can fill that space, the first thing that we will look at is visual language – and this is probably why you started looking at this book in the first instance.

2.

The mechanics of visualizing

The mechanics of visualizing

'I don't want to avoid telling a story, but I want very, very much to do the thing that Valéry said – to give the sensation without the boredom of its conveyance.' Francis Bacon, artist

As an illustration student, you are sure to be interested in the technical aspects of your subject: the visual systems artists employ to construct powerful and convincing images. This practice involves the artistic composition of visual elements together on the two-dimensional picture plane and includes traditions in depicting space, form, tone and light, composition and colour. These conventions, which can be utilized in the activities of drawing, painting, printmaking and assemblage, have been arrived at over hundreds of years by pioneers of the visual arts and are integral to the evolution of the subject.

During the twentieth century alone, many artistic movements were responsible for changing the public's perception of art. Each new movement had its own particular conceptual positions and visual language, its own common approach that in turn can be referenced by new generations of artists and illustrators. These movements include Fauvism, Cubism, Expressionism, Vorticism, Abstraction, Constructivism and Suprematism, Futurism, Dada, the Bauhaus School, the School of Paris, De Stijl, Surrealism, International Abstract Art (Geometric Abstraction, Semi-Abstraction, Action Painting, Calligraphic, Expressionist), the Australian School, Figurative Revivalism, Pop Art, Graffiti Art… the list goes on.

Although only a proportion of these artists sought to create specific artistic movements (many, if not all, should be viewed primarily as individual artists in their own right), these groupings provide a useful framework for understanding the history of illustration. Historically, the commercial brief has limited the illustrator's freedom to experiment far more than that of the fine artist, but artistic innovation has undoubtedly facilitated commercial artists in progressing their own work within the marketplace.

The reasons for the creation of artistic movements (and their eventual demise) are rich and varied: political and social upheaval, advances in technology, travel and the free transfer of ideas, and the influence of other expressive art forms have all played their part in changing the direction of the visual arts. Perhaps, though, the link between each of these movements is the artists' desire to pursue the original, to investigate fresh lines of enquiry to understand the world they inhabit. You too will need to harbour this inquisitiveness in relation to your own illustration work; you should be keen to experiment with the tools that your subject offers and to grasp the technical aspects of your subject. Through this, you will see the development of your own work during a lifetime of experimentation, enabling you to find your own voice or style, an identity to your artwork that has been arrived at through trial and error between media and the discovery of a visual language that can carry your concepts.

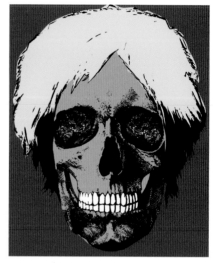

Above
Warholes by Paul Baines. Digital vector, 2008. Personal work. This illustration works as a striking contemporary image that refers to the screenprints of the Pop artist Andy Warhol.

Above
Space: Cosmic Hair by Andrew Clark. Pencil and graphite, 2009. Personal work. In this drawing, elements of the figurative and abstract artistic traditions are combined in an innovative way.

Opposite
China by David Foldvari. Mixed media, 2008. Personal work. This image, with its extensive use of layering and paint drips developed on a vertical picture plane, shows the influence of street art and graffiti on this illustrator.

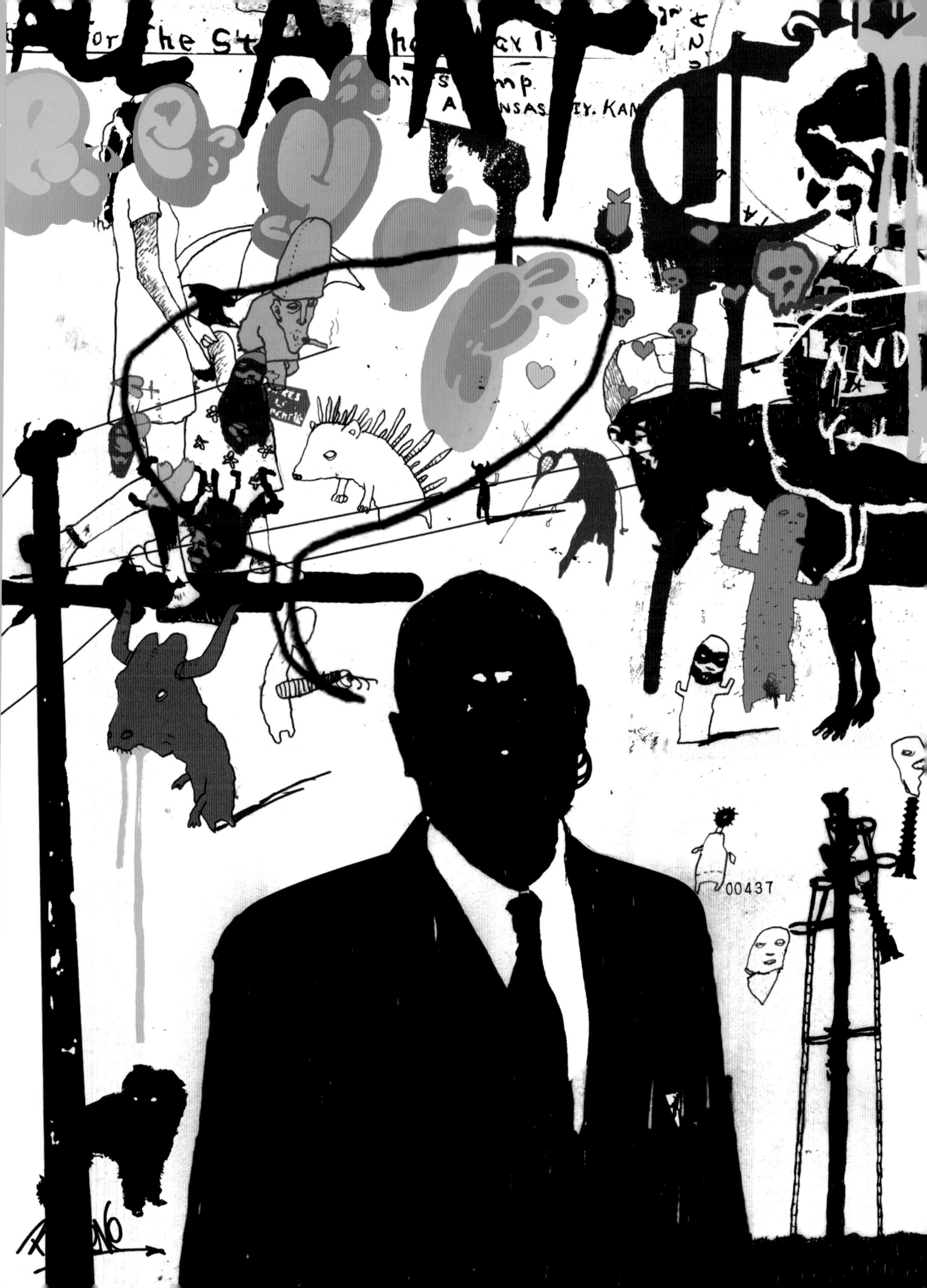
AND
00437

In this chapter, we look first at the activities of drawing, painting, printmaking and assemblage, before looking at artistic systems from various traditions in the depiction of space, form, tone and light, composition and colour.

Although it is useful to artificially isolate these subjects for the sake of discussion, in reality they are interconnected (for instance, colour cannot be isolated from form) and can be employed sparingly, in selected combinations or, sometimes, all together. It is important to remember that it isn't necessary to employ all of these methods, all of the time. On the contrary, constraint and selectivity in employing these techniques will determine the identity of your work and will afford your audience the mental space to engage with it whole-heartedly. It is often economy, wit and deftness of description that the audience appreciates in artistic work, far more than images that leave little or nothing to the imagination.

You should also be wary of an over-emphasis on technique. Remember that the message is everything. These systems are merely tools by which you can communicate your message – tools that the audience may not even be aware of. At the same time, you don't want technical ineptness to hinder the audience's appreciation of your work and undermine its authenticity. Familiarize yourself with these tools, use them every day, and they will empower you to extract images from your mind and successfully commit them to paper or screen.

Drawing

Drawing is the keystone of the visual arts; the tool most commonly used in drawing is the pencil, which is popular because of its versatility. Different leads, ranging from 9H (the lightest) to EE (the darkest), allow the artist to create many different types of mark on the paper – from light, subtle marks through to thick, heavy marks – all down to the way that the pencil is held in relation to the paper (from point-on to side-on) and the pressure that is applied.

Other materials, such as chalk, crayon and pastel, are softer than graphite; these create a broken line on the paper and produce a blurred effect. They also need to be 'fixed' (using a fixative spray in a ventilated booth or outside in the fresh air) in order to prevent smudging when the work is complete.

Paper, too, is integral to the quality of the finished drawing; your choice of paper is as important as your choice of drawing implement. Made from the pulp of wood or other fibrous substances, and formed of a thin layer, paper is available in many different weights and surface treatments, as well as in different colourways. Your choice of paper directly affects the quality of your pencil mark; it is worth picking up a sample pack from a local paper manufacturer to get an idea of the range of papers on offer.

Your next key drawing tool is the rubber or eraser. Again, there is a wide variety of rubbers available, from hard to soft and from coarse to fine. When using ordinary pencils, a standard rubber will be suitable when making your

Above
Study of a Woman by Oliver O'Keefe. Pencil, 2007. Personal work. The use of two pencils within this drawing, each with different leads, creates variety, focus and depth.

Opposite, top
Afghanistan 3 by Howard Read. Charcoal, 2009. Personal work. This sketch is made by applying charcoal to the whole surface of the paper and removing it with a putty rubber in key places to create a surprisingly sophisticated and detailed figurative image.

Opposite, bottom left
Afghanistan 1 by Howard Read. Pencil, 2009. Personal work. This sketch is made using a rough-textured paper, thereby fragmenting the line and the tone work in the image.

Opposite, bottom right
Afghanistan 2 by Howard Read. Pencil, 2009. Personal work. This sketch is made using a smooth paper – note how the drawn line remains unbroken.

And that will be England gone.

corrections. However, when using softer drawing materials, such as charcoal or graphite stick, a putty rubber will be most suitable. This material, although bought as a rectangular block, can be massaged into almost any shape and is capable of lifting a great deal of graphite or charcoal off the surface of the paper. There is even a method of drawing where the paper is covered in a layer of, say, charcoal, and drawn into using the putty rubber – a 'negative' drawing method.

In addition to your pencil and rubber, you will need a sharpening tool. A standard pencil sharpener will suffice with the harder leads, but a craft knife is more useful to fashion a softer lead into a point without breaking it.

Pen and ink and brush and ink are also commonly used for drawing. The former pairing can produce strong graphic lines, where even the ink splatters contribute to the visual feel. The latter pairing can produce work that has a calligraphic feel and is reminiscent of work from East and South-east Asia.

The computer is also a possible drawing tool, of course. Using a mouse or a drawing tablet, a 'drawn' image can be generated on a screen and further embellished or printed off. The technology is improving in terms of translating the nuances of the pressure of pencil on paper and the way that the pencil is held. This in turn is reliant on having a choice of papers to print on to, which can greatly improve the quality of the printed line. Although cheap printers are limited in paper choice, more expensive models are now capable of printing on to a good range of high-quality papers.

Drawing can take many different visual forms, from the naïve to the photo-realistic, from the crude to the complex. This appearance is commonly referred to as the 'visual vernacular' and is determined by your own artistic intentions. It can also be artificially divided into two main categories: the sketch and the finished drawing.

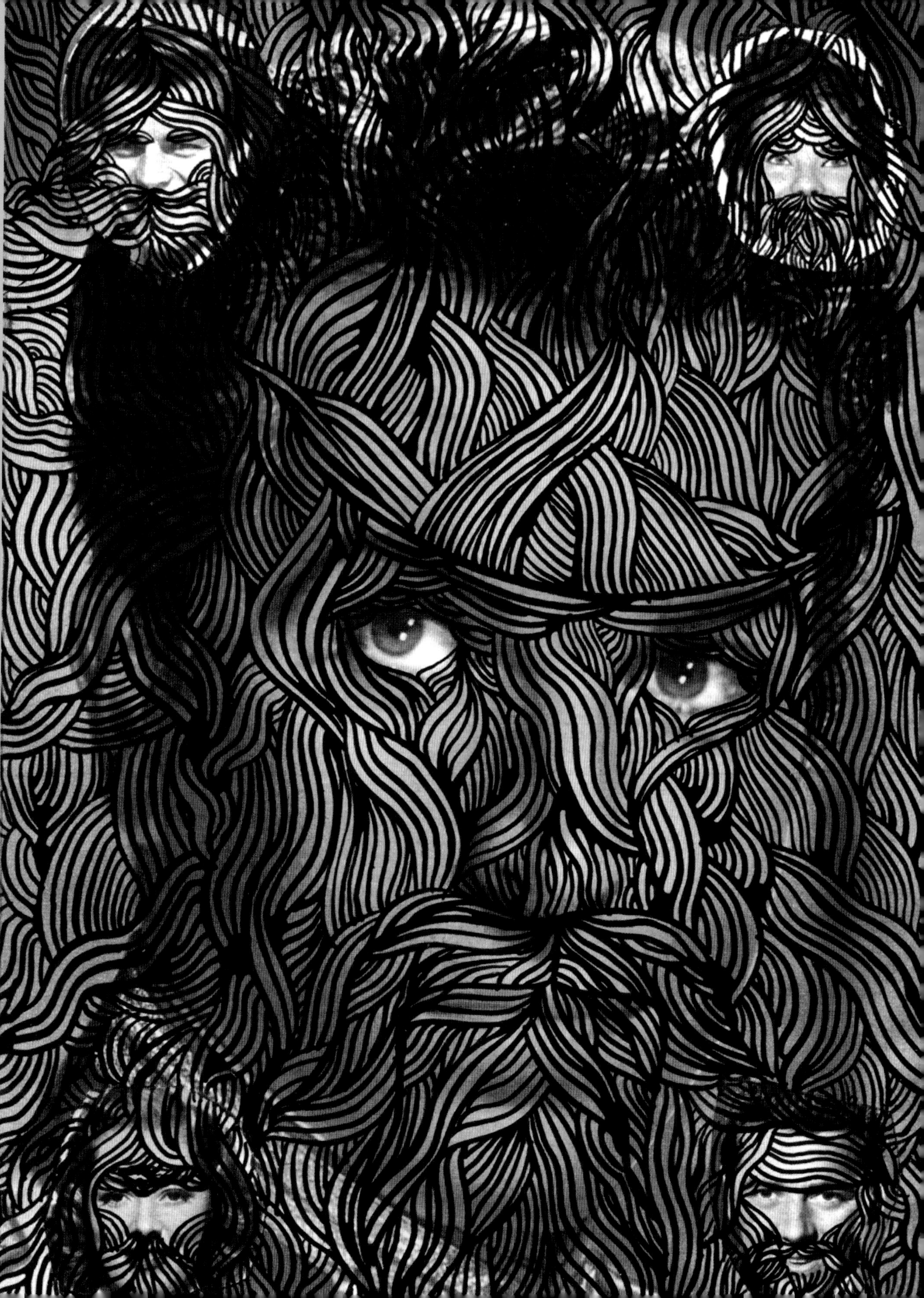

The sketch

The sketch is one of the most valuable tools within the business of visual communication. It is approached without self-consciousness, is not intended to be a complete statement in itself, and allows you the freedom to initiate, develop and refine ideas in a fluid and flexible way. Although an idea for an image might appear perfectly formed in your mind, it will rarely survive the transition from mind to paper without needing corrections and further development. Rather than being frustrated by this process, embrace this activity as a necessary part of your journey to achieving a strong piece of finished work that communicates clearly and answers the brief successfully.

Especially within the field of commercial art, the sketch is a fundamental tool with which to communicate, criticize and progress your work in discussion with your peers and tutors (and eventually your clients). A sketch is there to be argued over, added to, moderated and improved, without risk of wasting much time in implementing the necessary changes. Even visual communicators who work in more mechanical-based media, such as photography, film and e-graphics, often use sketches as a fast and economical way to develop and communicate their concepts visually.

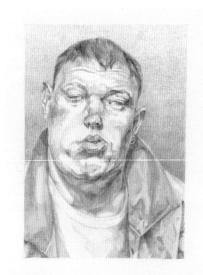

Of course, the sketch can also be used to record the world around you, providing a reference point for later visual development. This method of image-making was particularly important before the invention of photography, when, for example, artists would accompany explorers on their voyages and record land masses, natural flora and fauna, and indigenous peoples.

The finished drawing

A finished drawing can take many different forms, from the apparent simplicity of a portrait by Matisse, to the meticulous (though ironically inaccurate) detail of Albrecht Dürer's rhinoceros. The similarity is that the drawing appears complete, without need for addition or subtraction, and contains both accuracy in observation and authenticity – the audience is convinced that the artist knows their subject intimately. In the case of Matisse, this one image may be

deceptively simple, and may have been arrived at through the destruction of 99 others, each one similar though not as successful as the one ultimately chosen. Within the field of illustration, the finished drawing can be broadly split into two main categories: the observed and the imagined.

The observed

Observational drawing is generally executed in situ (at least at the outset) – drawn from life, in a specific environment, and recorded mainly within the timeframe of the visit. Any number of drawing tools can be used, and there is often a great deal of energy and dynamism to this kind of work, because the illustrator is reacting directly to life as it unravels around them – people moving past, cars driving down the street, minor dramas taking place. The skill with observational drawing lies in choosing what to include and what to leave out, and in remaining in control of the creation of the image. Minor additions and subtractions can be made afterwards – figures added (possibly from another sketch), words added, details refined, or washes of colour applied. However, there is a raw energy to this kind of drawing that could be spoilt (or lost completely) if too much intervention and refinement occur afterwards.

This approach to drawing is used in many different areas of illustration where the element of recording is necessary – for example, the interior of a new restaurant, a couple chatting on mobile phones, a prisoner in his cell, a street in a capital city or even a war zone.

The imagined

The creation of the imagined drawing presents a different set of challenges for the illustrator. Although this type of image contains visual information gathered from the outside world, the illustrator alone orchestrates the assembly of the image. In order to create a convincing unity to this world, you not only have to carry out thorough research, sourcing visual information from different civilizations and historical eras, but you also need to have a powerful and highly inventive imagination.

Although not necessarily realistic in character, these imagined pictures form the majority of work commissioned for commercial illustration, since they are doing the work that a camera cannot: they elucidate ideas, show us the future, take us to places that we can never go to, and visualize our interior worlds. The exciting aspect of this type of work is that it is your world; rather like a film director, you are in charge of everything present within that world – you choose the locations, the characters and their costumes, the furniture and the lighting.

Drawing is usually rendered in monochrome; we will now move our discussion on to the colour image. Within illustration, the colour image is usually rendered by painting, by printmaking techniques (which, when developed on an industrial scale, have played a major part in the use of the image for commercial purposes) and also within the digital environment of the computer.

Above
Empire State by Patrick Vale. Pen and ink, 2009. Commissioned for the 'Taste Of The Nation' event, New York. This sketch of the Empire State Building in New York City, complete with ink spots and smudges, has a vitality inherent in its execution that implies the drawing was realized within a particular timeframe and in situ.

Opposite, top left
Growth Assembly (development sketch) by Sion Ap Tomos. Ink and brush on paper, 2009. Commissioned by Sascha Pohflepp and Alexandra Daisy Ginsberg. The act of sketching allows mind and hand to form thoughts on paper.

Opposite, right
Asbo by Craig Boagey. Pencil on paper, 2008. Personal work. The high level of detail contained within this portrait allows us to contemplate the characteristics of the subject for far longer than a photograph would normally allow.

Opposite, bottom
Rembet by Alex Spiro. Indian ink on paper, 2007. Personal work. A face can be rendered with supreme economy of line, while still giving the audience a surprising amount of detail about the character depicted.

Union Square
A blues singer, Alice Tan Ridley was sitting on a chair singing up a storm. People would stop and not move on for hours. Some took off their coats and started to dance. **ALICE SEEMED TO BE WELL-KNOWN BY MANY**

I SAW PEOPLE WHO WOULD NOT TALK TO EACH OTHER UNDER REGULAR CIRCUMSTANCES TALK AND DANCE TOGETHER UNDERGROUND. I RECORDED HOW SHE SANG AND THE VOICES OF THE PEOPLE THE CLAPPING, THE SOUNDS OF THE TRAINS THE DOORS CLOSING THE COMMENTS. IT IS A SHAKY RECORDING BUT CAPTURES THE MOOD DOWN THERE IN THE SUBWAY STATION.

I WAS QUITE TIRED THAT DAY COMING FROM SCHOOL AT 9 PM AFTER TEACHING FOR 3 HOURS. I WANTED TO GET HOME. I CALLED ADAM TO TELL HIM THAT I AM ON MY WAY. AT THE ENTRANCE I SAW THE CROWD AND THERE WAS MUSIC. WHEN I WENT CLOSER I SAW THIS TALL, HEAVY SET BLACK LADY IN A JUMPSUIT OF BROWN VELVET STANDING BY A SUITCASE FILLED WITH DOLLAR BILLS, A CHAIR AND AN MTA ARTS FOR TRANSIT MUSIC UNDER NEW YORK BANNER. SHE DID NOT LOOK CHARISMATIC BUT WHEN SHE SANG CHILLS WERE GOING DOWN MY SPINE. ALICE TAN RIDLEY USED TO BE A PUBLIC SCHOOL TEACHER TEACHING SPECIAL EDUCATION KIDS. SHE SAID SHE LIKED TO SING IN THE SUBWAY BECAUSE SHE SAW PEOPLE WHO WOULD ORDINARILY NOT TALK TO EACH OTHER TALK AND DANCE TOGETHER I STAYED THERE FOR WHAT IT SEEMED LIKE HOURS ARRIVING HOME AT 11 PM 2009 APRIL 22 NYC

GREED

SWINE FLU EPIDEMIC

W.H.O.
LATEST DEVELOPMENTS
APRIL 30 2009

Experts on the global movement of flu say the world must accept that swine flu cannot be contained and that closing borders would not fail

H1N1

M. CHEN

possibly ADD TO THE DEATH RATE...

PANDEMIC
MEXICO: 170 DEAD 2,500 SICK
NEW YORK: NOW 49 CASES SICK
USA: 11 STATES 91 CASES SICK

YOU CAN — NOT — GET IT FROM PIGS

PRESIDENT BARACK OBAMA CALLS IT H1N1 VIRUS NOT SWINE FLU. ADAM THINKS THAT'S GOOD BECAUSE WHY BLAME THE POOR PIGS. BUT WE CALLED THE BIRD FLU BIRD FLU NOT A VIRUS SO WHAT ABOUT THAT?

THIS LITTLE PIGGIE WENT TO QUEENS THIS LITTLE PIGGIE WENT TO TEN OChTITLAN

⑤ **WIDESPREAD HUMAN INFECTION**

IT'S BECAUSE PEOPLE ALWAYS DO SOMETHING STUPID & GREEDY & UNLEASH A CALAMITY THEN

MEXICO

CANNOT CONTAIN.

YOU CAN NOT GET IT FROM PIGS...
EGYPT: PIGS ARE SLAUGHTERED. WHAT ARE PIGS DOING IN EGYPT ANYWAY?
BEIJING: THE CHINESE AUTHORITIES HAVE CONFINED DOZENS OF MEXICANS TO HOTELS AND HOSPITALS DESPITE HAVING NO SIGNS OF THE HUMAN SWINE VIRUS. MEXICAN CONSULAR OFFICIALS SAID MONDAY, LEADING THE MEXICAN GOVERNMENT TO ACCUSE CHINA OF UNFAIRLY QUARANTINING ITS NATIONALS AND ACTING WITHOUT REGARD

MEXICO OBJECTS TO

QUARANTINES IN CHINA

Above
Cover image for *Not This World* magazine by
Jim Stoten. Pen on paper, 2009. Commissioned
by *Not This World*. This illustration suggests an
imagined world for the viewer that sits outside of
the realms of agreed conventions of reality.

Opposite
New York Sketchbook by Andrea Dezsö. Pen, ink
and watercolour on paper, 2009. Personal work.
This visual diary, which contains both thoughts
and observations, has an immediacy that is
almost impossible to achieve without direct
experience of a subject matter.

Painting, printmaking and assemblage

Artists have used colours found in the natural world (including powdered stone, plants and oils) to make paints and inks for many hundreds (if not thousands) of years. They have applied these to wall surfaces, paper, animal skin, wood and canvas by using brushes (initially made from animal hair and wood), rollers, squeegees, their hands and even the whole of the human body. This long heritage of image-making has come to be representative of a more 'final' piece of artwork than the drawing or the sketch. In the case of painting (as opposed to printmaking, where an image may be reproduced in a limited edition or in vast quantities over and over again), it is also considered more valuable (artists have long released limited editions of prints to sell their work for less and in larger quantities).

Illustrators have tended to favour water-based paints over oil-based colours (which, although rich in depth and allure, can take a very long time to dry). These materials include:

- Gouache paint, which produces consistently flat areas of colour, but can be used as a wash when higher volumes of water are added.
- Acrylic paint, which is thick in texture, much like oil paint, and has a plastic sheen.
- Watercolour paint, which produces an expressive, textured and translucent area of colour.

These paints are applied to paper, art board and stretched canvas. It is worth experimenting with each of these media (and with good-quality brushes that suit each medium) to find a paint that you feel comfortable with and that also suits your purposes. You will also need to experiment with different types of paper. Watercolour paint, in particular, which is combined with a good deal of water, benefits from the use of a dedicated watercolour paper that is highly absorbent; this needs to be stretched on to a wooden board using clear water and gum arabic tape prior to painting. Once stretched, the paper will retain its flatness when dry.

Opposite, top
Miss Smilla by Somang Lee. Gouache, 2009. Personal work. This image is made with gouache paint, which can be used to create uniform, opaque areas of colour. Adding generous amounts of water to gouache can also achieve the textured and translucent washes more reminiscent of watercolour paint.

Opposite, bottom left
Tourists And Locals: Memphis by Mat Williams. Acrylic, pencil and pen, 2008. Personal work. This image shows how acrylic paint can be used to create consistently flat areas of colour. Acrylic also has the advantage of drying rapidly, allowing the overlaying of new colour on old in rapid succession.

Opposite, centre right
Tiananmen Square by Ying Ping Mak. Watercolour and pencil on paper, 2009. Personal work. Pencil work, overlaid with watercolour washes, is used with great effect to convey the tragic events of the Tiananmen Square uprising of 1989.

Opposite, bottom right
A Darker Side Of Me by Owain Thomas. Acrylic on paper, 2008. Personal work. This image, painted with acrylic, shows how the illustrator can create a textured surface on the picture plane with acrylic that is reminiscent of oil paint.

Above

Head by Mus Mehmet. Drypoint, 1999. Personal work. This portrait shows how a drypoint print, where lines are gouged out of a metal plate and inked up before printing off, produces an image that transmits the energy of that physical activity.

Above left

The Diving Bell and the Butterfly – The Beach by Mat Williams. Etching, 2008. Personal work. Etchings can be hand-coloured by the illustrator after printing, in this case by using colours that add to the seaside narrative of the image.

Left

Magnificent Desolation by Mus Mehmet. Inkjet print, 2009. Personal work. This image captures the influence that fine-art practitioners have exerted over the ways in which digital printing technology is used.

Below

Panorama by Anne Desmet. Wood engraving, 1995. Personal work. This composite composition of nine wood-engraved prints contains a remarkable amount of detail that is created by gouging out areas from a block of hardwood before inking up and printing off.

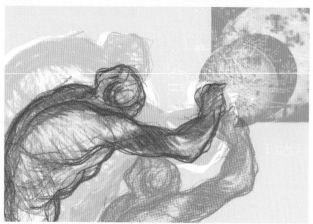

Printmaking

In terms of printmaking, which is essentially a range of mechanical techniques that can be employed to reproduce an image again and again (the exception being monoprinting), there is a wide choice for the illustration student:

- Wood engraving, where the image is carved out of a piece of hardwood, before being inked up and printed off on a press or by hand.
- Linocut, where the image is gouged out of soft linoleum, before being inked up and printed off on a press or by hand.
- Drypoint, where the image is scratched out of a soft metal plate, before being inked up and printed off on a press.
- Etching, where wax is applied to a rigid metal plate, scratched away and put into an acid bath to eat away at the exposed metal. The plate is inked up, pushing ink into the grooves, before being printed off on a press.
- Engraving, where a line is cut into the metal plate (like bank notes), inked up and printed off.
- Lithography, where a wax-resist technique is used by applying wax on to stone tablets. The tablets are inked up (the ink will not stay on the wax, thus producing a 'negative drawing'), and a drum is rolled across the tablet before transferring the ink (and therefore the image) to paper.
- Screenprinting, where masks are made up (thus stopping the ink from reaching certain areas of the paper) before coloured inks are pushed through a fine silk screen using a rubber squeegee, past the masks and on to the paper.
- Monoprinting, where ink is drawn on to a plate of glass and printed off without need for a press.
- Digital printing, where digital printing technology is used in an innovative way to produce limited-edition, digital fine-art prints.

Your ability to experiment with these types of printmaking, some of which have been central to the production of the mass-produced printed image, relies on access to specialized training and to supervised workshops. If your college does not offer these facilities, then it is usually possible to gain access to commercial workshops that can be booked on an hourly rate at reasonable cost.

Above
Oak by Helena Ivins. Linocut, 2005. Personal work. This image shows the supremely graphic nature of the linocut print, with its dramatic inter-play between areas of black and white.

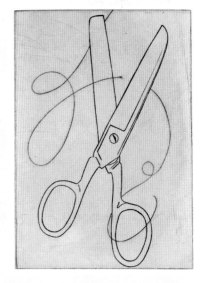

Above
Untitled by Douglas Bevans. Engraving on copper, 2009. Personal work. This image shows the delicacy of line that can be achieved with the engraving process.

Above
Two Heads by Mus Mehmet. Lithography, 1991.
Personal work. The lithographic printing process
is used to build up images by overlaying different
coloured layers one on top of the other.

Left
Big Belly by Sroop Sunar. Screenprint, 2009.
Personal work. Inspired by Aravind Adiga's novel
The White Tiger (2008), this image is from a four-
part series that explores some of the book's
themes. The big bellies of rich, fat politicians
symbolize the corrupt, indulgent lifestyles of
India's elite. This illustrator has intentionally
used inaccurate registration to imply an aesthetic
inherent in the industrial printing processes that
are used in India to make matchbox labels.

Opposite
Eat Me, Drink Me by Amy Carter. Monoprint, 2008.
Personal work. This image combines monoprinting
techniques in a strikingly contemporary way.

Assemblage

Assemblage (or collage) is quite a different type of image-making, where the artist/illustrator uses fragments of 'found' imagery and assembles them in a new way. This type of work can create rich collisions of visual elements that one would not necessarily expect to see in the same space. This method of image-making was popular with the Surrealist and Dada movements, and has also been used by prominent writers (such as William Burroughs) and musicians (including David Bowie).

The digital environment

As we have already mentioned, illustrators also use computers to construct images. Employed in conjunction with a scanner and a printer, almost any drawn, printed or painted image can be originated, further developed or refined within the digital environment using such programs as Adobe Photoshop, Adobe Illustrator and Adobe Flash (for animation). With the arrival of computers in the late 1980s, illustrators began mimicking the feel of printed material solely by using the computer environment, presumably in order to give their work a more human feel and to sidestep issues of time and money in gaining access to printing workshops. Some of the most interesting illustration work produced today defies its origins, and is a successful mixture of 'old' technology with 'new' technology.

    The next focus for our discussion is the key elements inherent within all of the forms of image-making discussed above. First, we'll look at some very different visual approaches to depicting space, from Africa, India, East Asia and the West.

Above
Walls by Sergei Sviatchenko. Collage, 2008.
For *Rojo*'s limited-edition poster collection.
The collisions of different subject matter, which also allow for dramatic shifts in scale, can produce powerful results that evoke the internal world of the human being.

Opposite
Heart, a collaboration between Von and Justin Maller. Hand-drawn and Photoshop, 2008.
Personal work. This image combines the power of traditional drawing with the digital environment to produce dynamic results.

2.

Traditions in depicting space

One of the key elements within visual language is the depiction of space. Essentially an illusion, it transfers a three-dimensional image on to a two-dimensional picture plane. Each region of the world has its own artistic tradition in depicting space. The fact that these traditional approaches sit side by side suggests that the artistic depiction of space, like colour, is a perceptual entity – that is to say, that the decoder of the information (the viewer) is as important as the code-maker (the artist) in creating the convention. For example, an image in which parallel lines diverge as they move farther away might seem right to a Chinese viewer, whereas the same image observed by a Westerner might appear wrong, because Western convention is the opposite – that parallel lines converge as they move farther away. In truth, neither convention is accurate – in the physical world, parallel lines stay parallel. Neither artistic tradition is right, and yet both are right.

As we have already noted in this chapter, artistic ideas travel as people travel – many Western illustrators have successfully embraced Mogul, African and Asian artistic traditions and used them with great flair to communicate to a Western audience. Likewise, contemporary East Asian illustrators have ignored the artistic traditions of their own country and employed Western artistic conventions to communicate their own messages.

Each of these systems has its own merits and idiosyncrasies – it is your job as an illustration student to explore these systems in isolation as well as

Left

Cowboys in Madagascar by Chris Corr. Gouache on paper, 2000. Commissioned by UNICEF. This image is employing systems of depicting space that are present in the Asian artistic tradition in which objects that are different distances from the viewer are depicted at the same size.

Below

Muhammad – Messenger Of Allah by Ruh al-'Alam. Digital canvas print, 2007. Personal work. By using textured colour, pattern and calligraphy, this artist has successfully evoked the Eastern artistic tradition.

combining them in interesting ways. Start to get a sense of the visual identity that harnessing these systems will give to your work, mix them up, take your time in understanding their guiding principles and you will feel empowered; you will literally be able to render anything that you wish to.

Outside of these dominant traditions, there are hundreds (if not thousands) of spatial traditions that relate to the specific artistic cultures of indigenous peoples. Although outside the scope of this book, these traditions are worth researching.

The Indian tradition

In the Mogul artistic tradition, drawing is used mainly as preparation for painting. Each pictorial element within the image – people, buildings, animals, vegetation and landscape – is depicted using standard stylistic conventions.

In terms of space, relationships are depicted by employing a simple system: forms nearest to the viewer are placed at the bottom of the image, forms in the middle distance to the viewer are placed in the middle, and forms farthest from the viewer are placed at the top of the picture. Usually there is no variation in scale between similar-sized forms – for example, human figures will not reduce in size as they recede. Instead, recession is described by one form being partially obscured by another – the partially hidden form is read by the viewer as being the one that is farthest away. The exception to this is when a figure within the image has special significance – for instance, a deity, a mythical hero or a member of the aristocracy.

The East Asian tradition

In this artistic tradition there is a very close relationship between calligraphy, drawing and painting. Chinese and Japanese art might be more accurately described as drawing. There is normally one colour and thickness of line that is employed to depict and express different qualities within the subject. Minimalism and economy of line are celebrated here, conventions of depiction are adhered to, with a single brushstroke being used to convey a great deal of information.

In terms of space, parallel lines diverge, and there are links to the African and Indian traditions in the depiction of human beings and more important characters, and also the use of partial covering of forms to depict their relationship. Picasso and Braque (and other Cubist artists) adopted some of these approaches (in particular, using the idea of diverging parallel lines) in their development of a Cubist approach to painting.

The African tradition

In early Sumerian and Egyptian civilizations, drawing was used as preparation for sculpture and painting. Stylized forms were employed to embody religious ideas, practices and rituals within the community.

In the Egyptian artistic tradition, different viewpoints of the human figure are assembled to emphasize the most recognizable features of a character:

Above
Black Antoinette by Olaf Hajek. Acrylic painting, 2008. Personal work. This image draws on the African artistic tradition but also points towards methods of adapting it in conjunction with the Western tradition.

Above
Aoyama Flower Market by Wabisabi. Hand-drawn and Photoshop, 2003. Commissioned by Aoyama Flower Market. This poster is in a monochrome, calligraphic style that is evocative of East Asian artistic tradition.

the head is depicted in profile (side-on), the torso is shown from the front, and in female characters, one breast is seen from front on, the other in profile. Also, interestingly, a front view of the eye is combined with a side view of the head.

The Western tradition

Until the Renaissance in Western Europe (where a scientific understanding of the world began to challenge the existing religious doctrine), artists described space in similar ways to their Eastern counterparts. Placing one figure in front of another denoted spatial recession, and important characters were depicted much larger than the lesser players within the drama.

Though certain elements of the perspective system that we are familiar with today can be observed in imagery that pre-dates the Renaissance, it was not until the Italian architect Filippo Brunelleschi (1377–1446) put forward his own theories of perspective that a coherent system of ordering space in imagery evolved. The key to Brunelleschi's work was that he developed a method of depicting space that accurately reflected how every human being on the planet saw the world. This had eluded artists for centuries, and though 'seeing in perspective' had always existed, Brunelleschi's discovery of its rules and guiding principles, culminating in a perspective-based drawing system (sometimes called 'mechanical perspective'), made it possible for artists to render the world in the way that they (and everyone else) actually saw it.

Today, perspective-based imagery surrounds us in such abundance that we take it for granted that most of these images comport with human sight. When perspective is exaggerated or ignored by artists and illustrators, it is usually for artistic or dramatic effect.

Full mechanical perspective (a very time-consuming process) is rarely used today, since the tracing of photographs or the modification of images in the digital environment means that artists no longer have to engage in hours of laborious draughtsmanship in order to achieve accuracy in their images. Nevertheless, understanding some of the guiding principles and key terms of perspective can be invaluable when constructing your own images.

Right
Baltimore Docks by eBoy. Photoshop, 2008. Poster. This image is executed using an isometric perspective system, favoured by Western engineers and architects from the Industrial Revolution onwards, although it is thought to have originated in China many centuries before.

Perspective

Guiding principles

- Parallel lines appear to converge when viewed obliquely (at an angle).
- Equal dimensions become foreshortened as they move off into the distance.
- Objects of a similar size appear to diminish as they recede into the distance.
- Overlapping by foreground objects obscures the view of more distant objects.

In addition:

- Atmospheric perspective (or aerial perspective) denotes distance, where atmospheric effects will diminish the intensity of colours and diminish contrast.
- Texture and pattern appear more detailed when seen closer up than when seen from a distance.

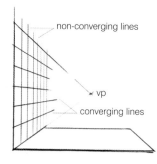

Parallel lines appear to converge as they move away from the viewer. Those not oblique to the viewer remain parallel.

Equal distances appear to diminish the farther they are from the observer.

More distant objects appear smaller and may be obscured by closer objects.

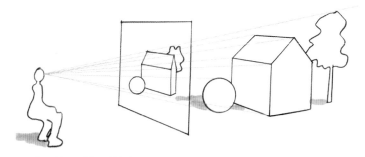

Perspective drawing imagines a 'picture plane' between the viewer (the 'fixed viewpoint') and the subject. Sight lines passing through this plane plot a two-dimensional image of what is seen.

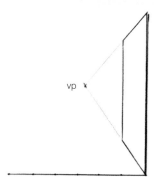

Establishing equal measurements along a receding surface or line: **1.** Plot equal measurements (dots) along a non-receding line.aa

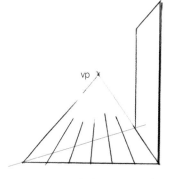

2. Project lines 'back' from the dots towards a vanishing point.
3. Lay a diagonal across the resulting field.

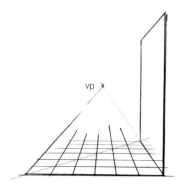

4. Using the crossing points of the diagonal and receding lines, complete a grid. The result is receding equal measurements.

Key terms

- Fixed viewpoint (or station point): this is the chosen position from which the object is to be drawn – the closer the viewpoint, the more distorted the object will be. It is 'fixed' because it is important that the relationship between objects remains constant.
- Cone of vision: although the human eye can 'see' 180 degrees, only 60 degrees of that is clear vision (the rest is called 'peripheral' vision). For this reason, it is usually best to draw no more than 30 degrees to either side of your central line of sight.
- Picture plane: this is an imaginary vertical plane on which the drawing is plotted – it is always perpendicular to and at right angles to the central line of vision. The farther away the picture plane is from the object being drawn, the bigger it is. Distance also reduces distortion.
- Vanishing points (VP): parallel lines converge towards a given point.
- The horizon line: this is where an imagined horizontal line going through the eye meets the picture plane. This is also the point at which the ground plane ends; therefore, the vanishing points for all lines, which are parallel to the line of the ground plane, will be located on the horizon line (where earth and sky meet).

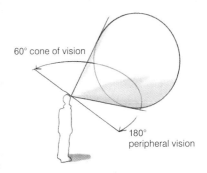

60° cone of vision

180°
peripheral vision

Generally speaking, artists can describe what is in front of them using a 60-degree cone of vision.

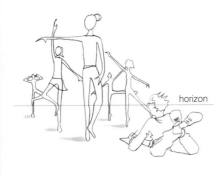

horizon

If your vantage point is knee high, all knees will align (given a horizontal surface and similarly sized figures)...

horizon

If your vantage point is head high, and you and your subjects are the same height, all heads will align.

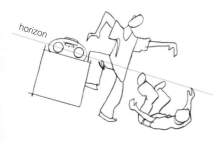

horizon

A sloped horizon results from the 'viewer's head' being tilted. This can add dynamism, or even chaos, to a drawing.

Close proximity of a foreground element heightens its prominence.

One-point perspective

If you are drawing a box or a room, and your central line of vision meets one of the end planes at right angles, all of the apparently converging lines will meet at the same, single vanishing point (all other lines will remain horizontal or vertical).

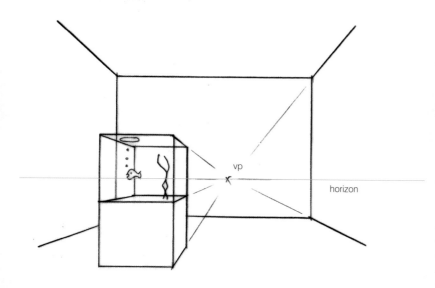

One-point perspective is used when major surfaces or lines are flat to the viewer. Parallel lines oblique to the viewer converge at a single vanishing point (VP). It is applicable to both spaces and objects.

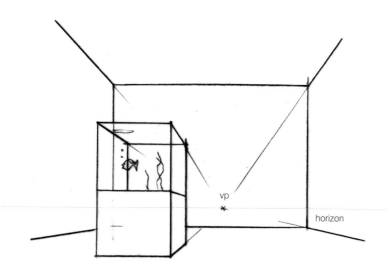

A lower horizon occurs when the viewpoint is lowered. Vanishing points of lines parallel to a horizontal ground plane will always lie on the horizon.

Two-point perspective

If you view the same box or room obliquely, you will have two sets of parallel lines – each set of parallel lines has its own vanishing point (both located on the horizon line).

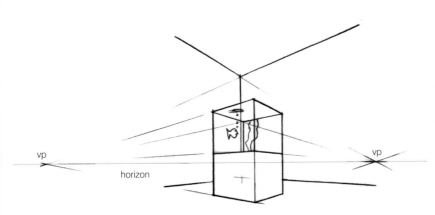

vp

horizon

vp

As the viewpoint swings to the right or left, it is necessary to switch to two-point perspective.

Three-point perspective

When much nearer an object, an additional vanishing point must be added above or below the object to allow for distortion; this in turn can lead to a greater sense of drama within the image.

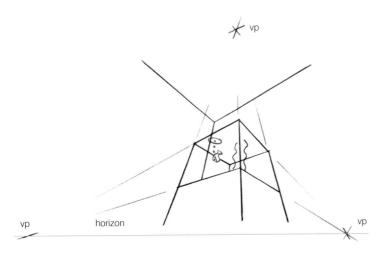

vp

vp

horizon

vp

If the viewpoint is low and looking up, a third vanishing point is required for the convergence of vertical lines as they appear to taper upward.

Form, tone and light

We perceive the world around us by differentiating between the apparent lightness and the apparent darkness of visual areas (be they in monochrome or full colour), which in turn gives objects a shape. We immediately compare the shape we see with a visual memory of an object, recorded after an encounter with that object. For instance, we look at a 'jug-shaped object', compare it with the memory of a jug stored in our brain, and say 'yes, it's a jug'. Of course, this process happens at lightning speed.

The simplest units of shape in two dimensions are the square, the circle and the triangle. Everything that we see is essentially made up of one or more of these units. When we translate these shapes into three dimensions, we have the cube, the sphere and the pyramid or cone.

The opposite poles of the monochromatic world are black and white, essentially non-colours (black being a complete absence of light, and white being a mixture of the seven components of the colour spectrum). All other tones lie somewhere between these two poles.

The tonal values that we see are created by light, be it from the sun or from man-made sources, which in turn leads to our perception of the world in three dimensions (in a blacked-out room, for instance, we cannot visually perceive the world in three dimensions). Planes advance or recede in relation to how much light is cast upon them; objects cast shadows on to the plane on which they sit. On a much smaller scale, shadows create the impression of texture – for instance, on a piece of fabric, tiny shadows inform us as to the make-up of that fabric.

Materials also reflect light – plastics, for example, have a glossy appearance, often creating highlights (intense areas of white light that can help create focus within an image). The depth of shadow and the shape of the shadow also rely on the intensity and position of the light source. A high light source casts short shadows, whereas a low light source casts long shadows.

When tone is combined with colour (this is essentially how most people see, unless they are colour blind), it becomes more complex. The key to tone is to believe what you see. Although this seems simple, your brain often makes assumptions that are in fact inaccurate. For example, if you look at a very dark area of yellow and a very light area of blue, your brain might tell you 'yellow is a very light colour, lighter than blue, which is a very dark colour, therefore…'. In fact, if you look more closely, possibly even by squinting, you will see that your yellow is much darker than your blue.

If you wish to work in full colour, producing monochrome sketches of your subject will help you clarify tonal relationships in an image and serve as an invaluable reference point before you bring full colour into your image.

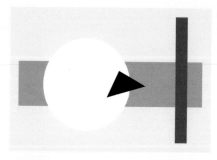

Above
Shape is essentially differentiated by tone.

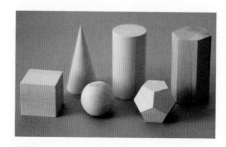

Above
The nineteenth-century French artist Paul Cézanne pointed out that the cube, the pyramid and the cone were inherent in all natural forms.

Below
Qualities of 'lightness' and 'darkness' are categorized by a bandwidth of different tonal values.

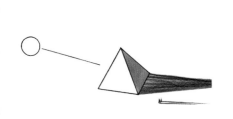

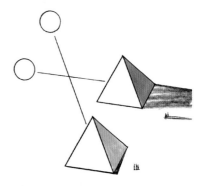

Above
A high light source and a low light source generate different lengths of shadows, thereby implying different times of the day.

Above
Squint, and you will see that the yellow square has a darker tonal value than the blue square.

Left
Film still from *Blue Velvet*, directed by David Lynch, 1986. The design of the lighting in this classic film contributes greatly to its sinister and macabre atmosphere.

Fine artists and illustrators use light to create real depth and atmosphere in their paintings, for instance in the work of the Italian painter Caravaggio (1573–1610), who used what is termed *chiaroscuro* – the interplay of light and dark in an image. This work in turn has inspired lighting designers and directors for film, television and theatre (as well as photographers). It is worth looking at film (and photography) in order to see how these practitioners actively use light (and of course darkness) to create mood, atmosphere, tension and fear. There is even a Hollywood film genre that specifically names the use of darkness in its title: film noir.

Composition

Composition is the ordering of shapes on the picture plane. These shapes may be figurative or abstract, they may be in colour or monochrome, they may employ perspective systems or be naïve, but they need to be ordered in a coherent way that is pleasing to the eye. Generally speaking, there will also be a variety of shapes and a variety of scale – variation is the key to creating images that sing.

Format

When planning a composition, your first choice will be connected to the format of your image – this relates to the dimensions of the image. In terms of commercial work, each country has its own integrated sizing system for mainstream printing (for example, the US uses 'Imperial' sizes, whereas Britain uses 'A' sizes). When you work on commercial projects, you will mostly find that the size of image is stipulated in your contract and you will need to adhere to this. You will also be told whether the image will be 'landscape' or 'portrait'. In most cases, common sense prevails – there's no point trying to squeeze a very long, horizontal object into a 'portrait' image or a very thin, vertical object into a 'landscape' image. Outside of commercial constraints, or when you are working with a book designer, for instance, it is worth experimenting with format – squares, circles and triangles can produce interesting results.

Main elements

Composition is generally dominated by four main elements. These are contained within the basic shapes of the square, the circle and the triangle.

- The vertical element: deriving from the square, this element moves the eye from the top to the bottom of the picture plane in a broken or straight line.
- The horizontal element: deriving again from the square, this element moves the eye from the left to the right of the picture plane in a broken or straight line.
- The diagonal element: deriving from the triangle, this element moves the eye from one corner of the picture plane to the other – for instance, from the bottom left-hand corner to the top right of the picture plane (or vice versa).
- The circular element: deriving from the circle, this element moves the eye around the picture plane in a circular or curving movement.

Compositionally, these elements work well together, but can also be used to great effect when one element becomes dominant within a composition.

Dominant theories within composition

Though there are no set rules regarding composition, there are certainly

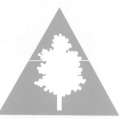

Above
Although the tree icon remains consistent in shape and size, its shifting context changes how the audience perceives it.

Left
Focus by Géraldine Georges. Mixed media, 2008. Personal work. This image invites the viewer's gaze to travel in a vertical direction.

Below
Glamorama by Marianna Rossi. Collage, 2007. Personal work. This image invites the viewer's gaze to travel horizontally.

Bottom left
Head Planet by Franz-Georg Stämmele at Projekttriangle Design Studio. Pencil drawing, 2008. This image invites the viewer's gaze to travel in a circular motion.

Bottom right
Purplevolute by Florence Manlik. Ink on paper, 2004. Personal work. This image invites the viewer's gaze to travel diagonally.

defined approaches to composition. These have been generated over many years by artists, theorists, mathematicians and philosophers, and can be useful to you, especially if you wish to instil your image with a certain quality. Here we look at four approaches: the golden section, symmetrical composition, asymmetrical composition and cropping.

The golden section

The Ancient Greeks produced a good deal of valuable work on composition, which they synthesized in the theory of the golden section. This was a broad-ranging, mathematical theory that could be related to natural forms (the most noticeable being the shell) and its aesthetic goal was to find a method of composition that was most pleasing to the eye. The Greeks divided the picture plane roughly into thirds, avoiding the central area of the image. They located the focal point of the image on one-third or two-thirds into the picture (usually on the dividing line between the 'thirds'), and one-third or two-thirds from the top (again, on the dividing line). This helped the eye to locate the focal point within the image, before allowing it to travel around the picture in an extended spiral before returning to the focal point. Employing the golden section helps create a classical and ordered composition.

The symmetrical composition

This type of composition locates the main focus of the image within the centre of the picture plane, and is reliant on each side of the image being similar. Though the eye tends to remain at the centre of the image (symmetry does not encourage the eye to ramble), this approach has been used by artists to great effect, especially in the field of portraiture, where a symmetrical composition increases the intensity of the subject's gaze. Shields, too, which (like targets) have very little time to communicate their message, generally employ a symmetrical composition to create maximum impact and to direct the eye straight to the most important area of the image. Employing symmetry helps create a direct and static composition.

The asymmetrical composition

Attempts have been made to abandon an ordered approach to composition completely, in favour of a more intuitive one. For instance, when developing their ideas around Cubism, at a time when photography was firmly established, Picasso and Braque fractured their compositions in order to try to reflect the nature of how we see. They pointed out that we gather information at lightning speed – a look into someone's pupil, a close-up of hair texture, moisture on the lips, as well as taking our time in walking all around an object. From these details, viewed over time and space, we compose an overall impression. Enveloping a very broad range of approaches to image-making, an asymmetrical composition is simply any composition that does not use symmetry. Employing an asymmetrical approach helps create a dynamic and vibrant composition.

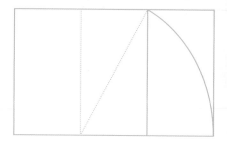

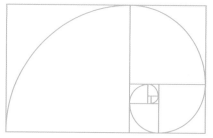

Above
The golden section is a useful compositional theory that breaks down the picture plane into a pleasing series of co-existing relationships.

Above
Untitled by Géraldine Georges. Digital, 2008. Personal work. This image employs a symmetrical composition (with minor aberrations) that makes for a very direct form of communication.

Left
Elevator Fakeout by Matthew Vescovo. Animation for MTV spot, 2004. Cropping can contribute to a filmic quality that allows events to be deconstructed into precise moments.

Below left
Untitled by Nick White. Collage, pen and ink, gouache, pencil and crayon, 2008. One-off piece for the 'Joyful Bewilderment' exhibition, Rough Trade East, London. By placing the balloon off-centre, this illustrator encourages his audience's gaze to move around the picture plane.

Cropping

Cropping is essentially a way to 'zoom in' or 'zoom out' of an image, in order to create focus and drama. By not showing the whole of an image, cropping often works as a stimulus to an audience's imagination and helps intensify the part of the image that they can see. It is used extensively in comic-book art, as is the notion of 'point of view' – the depiction of the drama from one particular person's point of view. This expressive art form played a major part in the development of early film language, and in many ways references that language whenever it is used now.

Colour within the image

Much valuable work, both artistic and scientific, has been devoted to the study of colour. The pioneering scientist Sir Isaac Newton (1642–1727) split a beam of white light into its seven individual colours by using a glass prism, thus revealing the individual components of light. In the early nineteenth century, German writer Johann Wolfgang von Goethe (1749–1832) published the *Theory Of Colours*, which attributed each colour a numerical value in relation to its visual intensity, thus developing a system that enabled artists to arrange colour in their 'correct' proportions in order to achieve visual harmony (green and red, for instance, share the same numerical value). Later in the nineteenth century, French chemist Michel-Eugene Chevreul (1786–1889) wrote *The Principles of Harmony and Contrast and their Application to the Arts*, which greatly influenced the Impressionists and Post-Impressionists in France and also some of the key tutors at the Bauhaus School in Germany (including Josef Albers, Paul Klee and Johannes Itten). It has come to form the basis of the colour theory taught in art schools ever since. Chevreul's work (which began with his observation of the relationship between coloured threads in a tapestry) was central in focusing on the behaviour of one colour in relation to the colour or colours that surround it. In essence, he developed the theory of 'simultaneous contrast'. As an illustrator, your main concern when working with colour is to understand the shifting relationship between colours as they sit together on the picture plane.

Guiding principles

- Primary colours: these are red, yellow and blue, and are indivisible.

- Secondary colours: these are the result of mixing the primaries – red and yellow make orange, blue and yellow make green, and red and blue make violet.

- Tertiary colours: these are the result of mixing primary and secondary colours – red-orange, yellow-green, blue-violet, and so on.

Key terms

- Hue: this refers to the intrinsic 'colour' of a colour (i.e., red, yellow, blue).

- Value: this refers to the 'lightness' and 'darkness' of a colour. (In addition, a lighter version of a colour than the pure hue is referred to as a 'tint'; a darker version is referred to as a 'shade'.) Colours can be arranged in a value chart.

- Chroma: this refers to a combination of hue and saturation. 'High chroma' describes a saturated colour in its purest strength; 'low chroma' describes colour in its most muted, greyish form. Colours can be arranged in a chroma chart.

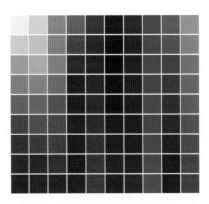

- Colour wheel: this is a systematic mixing guide, based on Newton's Colour Spectrum. The three primary colours (red, yellow and blue) are plotted at equal distance around the wheel, before even increments between the colours are carefully plotted.

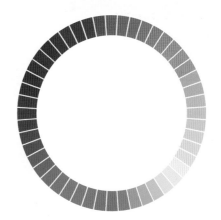

- Complementary colours: these are colours that are opposite to each other on the colour wheel (for example, red and green) and are visually harmonious and of equal value.

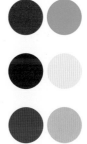

- Colour solid: this is a three-dimensional mixing system that combines a colour wheel, a chroma chart and a value chart.

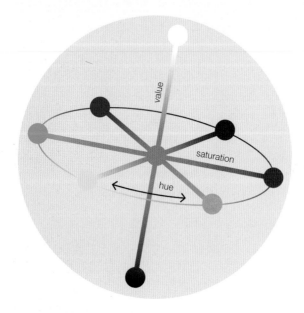

- Colour scheme: this refers to the use of a restricted colour palette.

- Monochromatic: this refers to a colour scheme that only uses variations (in tone) of one hue.

- Perceptual transparency: this refers to an illusion of transparency (or overlapping) created with flat, opaque colours, using two colours and their exact midway colour.

- Simultaneous contrast: this refers to the way that a particular colour is changed by its neighbouring colour, the most extreme example being two complementary colours that highlight their neighbour's hue.

Although these ideas may appear complex, the best way to understand colour is to explore it creatively. Whether you are trying to record colour as you see it, or using a limited colour palette, developing familiarity with colour on a day-to-day basis will help you use it skilfully in your work.

BROADSIDE 3 FREE WITH THIS ISSUE

ARCHITECTURE, DESIGN, CULTURE | JULY 2005 | N°232 | £4.25

BLUEPRINT

THE PRODUCT DESIGN FORGOT
WHY SOON EVERYONE WILL WANT A HEARING AID

ROALD DAHL:
THE MUSEUM AND THE MOVIE

LIGHTS OUT IN LOS ANGELES' THEATRES

REFINING THE WORKPLACE AT DESIGN PRIMA

Perfume

Above
Cover illustration for Patrick Süskind's novel *Perfume* by Warren Holder. Pencil drawing, 2005. This illustration, for a self-initiated college project, already points to the identity of Holder's work.

Left
Cover illustration for *Blueprint* magazine by Warren Holder. Pencil drawing and Photoshop, 2005. This illustration accompanied the main feature article on the designs and technological innovations of the future of the hearing aid. The addition of colour to the intricate drawing work makes for a commercial style that can compete amid the plethora of magazines for sale.

Below, far left
Cover illustration for *Diplomat* magazine by Warren Holder. Pencil and Photoshop, 2009. This illustration was for the main feature on the G20 and global economic crisis. Editorial work is still a crucial area of work for the graduate illustrator.

Left
Morgan le Fay by Warren Holder. Pencil, ink and Photoshop, 2009. Personal work. This detailed image is an example of the illustrator experimenting with the editorial format.

Below
Dream of the Fisherman's Wife by Warren Holder. Pencil, ink and Photoshop, 2006. Personal work. The addition of colour to artwork is crucial in offering potential clients visual flexibility.

DIPLOMAT
ESTABLISHED 1947

MAY 2009 £10

G20 SUMMIT: SORTING THE REALITY FROM THE RHETORIC
DIPLOMATIC EXPULSIONS
INTERVIEW WITH THE PRESIDENT OF THE MALDIVES

Conclusion

We have covered a great deal of technical information in this chapter, information that cannot be absorbed in a day. However, by being patient and exploring these ideas with help from your tutors and alongside your own ideas, your work will start to form into an entity that has its own identity, a fusion of the visual language you employ and the content you wish to show.

It is tempting to assume that once you have completed your illustration course, you will leave college with a product that will afford you an income for the remainder of your working days, but this is rarely the case. Just as the world around you changes, fuelled by innovation, so too must your illustration work evolve in relation to the zeitgeist ('spirit of the times'). To explore the zeitgeist, we turn next to communication theory and semiotics.

3.

The mechanics of communication

'Possession of natural language and the sign systems constructed upon it is the specific particularity of man.'
V.V. Ivanov, writer

Communication is central to our lives. It manifests itself in many different forms, from the aural, to the written, to the drawn and painted, to the non-verbal gestures and expressions that we make with our bodies. We experience it when making a baby smile, when cheering on our favourite football team to victory and when talking to our loved ones. Communication is the very glue that binds human societies together. Without it, we would become completely isolated and incapable of working together.

What is communication?
Communication can be defined as:

'A process whereby a communicator or sender directs a message through a medium/channel with some effect.'
(David Gill and Bridget Adams, *ABC of Communication Studies*, 1999)

Alternatively, it can be seen as:

'A social activity, where people in a given culture create and exchange meanings in response to the reality they experience.'
(David Gill and Bridget Adams, *ABC of Communication Studies*, 1999)

Within the study of communication, there are two main schools of thought, the Process School and the Semiotic School.

The Process School
The Process School aims to differentiate between the various separate elements and also the various interrelated parts of the communication process in order to see how the process as a whole functions. American political scientist Harold Lasswell (1902–1980) famously summarized this as:

'Who says what to whom in which channel with what effect?'

Other commentators within the Process School have looked at the notions of 'purpose' and 'context' within the communication process. This focuses on the aim(s) of a communicator and the way that their surroundings and social standing influence the way that they create their messages and also how an audience receives these messages. In addition, the Process School focuses on the fact that a message needs to be converted into a code that is appropriate for the channel being used to transmit it.

The Semiotic School

Although there are similarities between the two schools, the Semiotic School (from the Greek word *semeiotikos*, an interpreter of signs) has a slightly different focus: semioticians concentrate on 'text' (which can mean a painting, a photograph, a film, a dance and so on), on the signs and codes that text is comprised of, on the people who decode them and on the social context within which both text and audience exist.

The Semiotic School is a broad church – as demonstrated by Paul Cobley in his book *Introducing Semiotics* (first published in 1999 under the title *Semiotics for Beginners*):

'At the last International Association of Semiotic Studies, panels took place on: gesture, artificial intelligence, theatre, cognitive science, cinema, design, politics, time, music, space, biology, "firstness", painting, advertising, law, the Grateful Dead [a 1960s/1970s rock band], narrative, aesthetics, religion, architecture, the body, humour, calligraphy, dance, didactics, history, regimes of verisimilitude, marketing and others.'

Below left
Air Kiss from *Instructoart – Travel Edition*, written and illustrated by Matthew Vescovo. Digital, 2005. Published by Union Square Press. Communication theory and semiotics facilitate an understanding of many aspects of our existence, including human behaviour.

Below right
Face Of New Generation by Matthew Vescovo. Digital, 2009. Personal work. Today's generation has been given unprecedented access to portable, functional and affordable communication technology.

The communication process

As an illustrator, why is this important to you? In order for you to communicate your message to your audience successfully, you need to focus on the four key stages of the communication process:

1 **You: the originator of the message, the communicator.**
2 **Message: the 'thought' to be encoded by you and the code used to encapsulate that thought.**
3 **Channel/medium: the physical means and media type by which your code is carried.**
4 **Destination: the decoding of your message and the intended destination of that message.**

Your understanding of these four components, and their relationship to each other, will be crucial to your success as an illustrator.

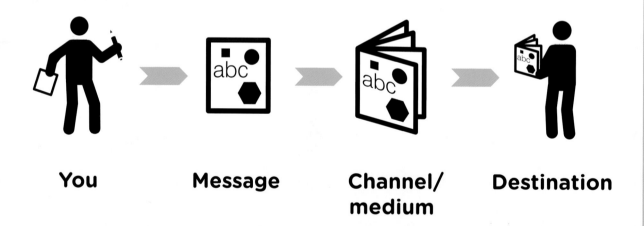

You   **Message**   **Channel/ medium**   **Destination**

Above
This diagram demonstrates the four key stages of the communication process, as cited by the theorist Harold Lasswell.

1 Thinking about you

Let's start by thinking about the person who is encoding the message: you. As a communicator, your style of communication will depend on many factors – personality, age, habitat, interests, family group, cultural background, education (especially in art and design) and experience – in fact, everything that has contributed to the forming of your identity as a human being.

Place, time, social context and dominant culture will also be central to the way in which your illustrated messages will be received. Your audience will have a strong notion of their own particular culture, their own ways of doing things and the values of their community, which are expressed around them through various different codes. This large group of people can also be broken down into smaller sub-groups that have an even more specialized idea of their particular culture.

As an illustrator, it is worth remembering that change or development within your own life, be it permanent or temporary, will continually feed back into your illustration work, allowing it to grow and develop over the span of your career.

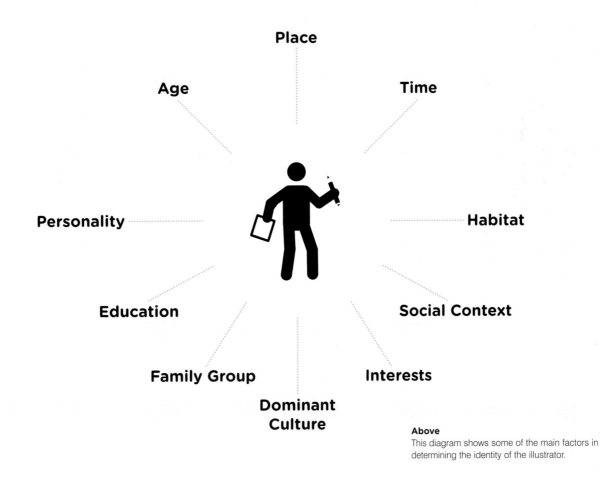

Above
This diagram shows some of the main factors in determining the identity of the illustrator.

2 Creating the message

In order to formulate your message, you will need to employ a code. A code is a system or group of signs, governed by an overall collection of rules shared by both sender and audience, that is used to transmit a message over time and space.

The code that illustrators use is a visual code. As we discussed in Chapter 2, there are a variety of artistic conventions (i.e. the 'rules' or 'grammar') when depicting space, texture, light, tone, colour and so on, as well as the formal way in which these factors are arranged ('composition'). These elements all contribute to an overall code, which, although to some extent reliant on the specific creators and recipients of the code, has the potential to communicate to every human being on the planet.

If a code is a system of signs, what is a sign?

The Swiss linguist Ferdinand de Saussure (1857–1913), commonly thought of as the father of modern semiotics, expressed the idea of a 'sign' in this simple dyad (a two-sided equation):

Sign = signifier + signified

In our case, the signifier is drawn (i.e. a drawing of a chair), and the signified is the meaning (the idea of a three-dimensional chair) that the signifier (the drawing of the chair) evokes in the mind of the receiver (the audience).

Saussure sees the general phenomenon of language as constituting two main factors:

Langue: a system of differences between signs
Parole: individual acts of speech

As described by Paul Cobley and Litza Jansz in their book *Introducing Semiotics*, 'langue' is the 'store cupboard' containing a whole collection of signs (for example, the Western alphabet) that are given individual meaning by nature of their difference, whereas 'parole' are individual units of communication. When applying this idea to visual language, 'art' is the langue, the whole store cupboard of visual language, whereas Van Gogh's image of a pipe placed on a chair is a parole, an individual unit of communication where he has employed individual signs from the store cupboard and arranged them in a particular way.

Saussure was also concerned with syntagm (in written language, this is referred to as syntax) – the way in which meaning is altered by the arrangement and ordering of signs. What precedes a sign and what succeeds a sign inevitably changes that sign, leading to what is termed 'unlimited semiosis' – a chain of associations that unravel from an initial signifier, taking the

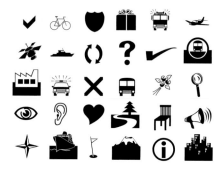

Above
This grid of dingbats shows some of the many elements of visual grammar that illustrators have at their disposal to arrange and order in images as they see fit.

Above
Van Gogh's Chair by Vincent van Gogh. Oil on canvas, 1888. The Dutch artist Van Gogh took three key elements – a tobacco pouch, pipe and chair – to create an atmospheric image that paradoxically suggests both a human presence and an absence.

audience farther and farther away from the original symbol. In other words, their sequential relationship and interdependence is of vital importance.

Take a simple image of a small girl looking at a tiger. In the first image, the girl looks at a tiger through the bars of its cage, while surrounded by the open spaces of the zoo. In the second image, the same small girl is looking at the same tiger, but this time she is waking up in her bedroom to be confronted by the tiger looking directly at her. Though both images contain the same key elements, the reordering of those elements (in addition to some others) radically alters their meaning: in one scenario, the girl is safe and happy; in the other, she is in danger and (presumably) terrified. From these two starting points, these images can start to unravel all sorts of associations in our minds, leading to 'unlimited semiosis'.

Are there different types of signs?

Charles Sanders Peirce (1839–1914), an American philosopher and semiotician, built an alternative to the dyad model of the communication process and originated a modified semiotic interpretation. He proposed a triad (or three-sided equation) model:

Representamen (the sign), which relates to an object (that which the sign represents), which relates to an interpretant (the 'proper significate effect').

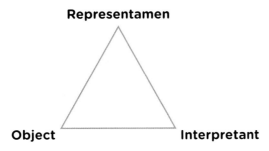

Representamen

Object　　　　　　　　**Interpretant**

In Peirce's model, it is the interpretant that is crucial to understand. Not to be confused with the word 'interpreter', the interpretant is that part of an interpreter that informs the meaning of the sign. In the simplest of terms, this refers to 'the sign in the mind that is the result of an encounter with a sign' (Cobley and Jansz); it is also referred to as 'the proper significate effect'.

Peirce classified signs in three distinct categories: firstness, secondness and thirdness. The triad of sign types he used most frequently was icon, symbol and index.

Icon
This iconic sign of a car is a simple visual rendition of the vehicle itself.

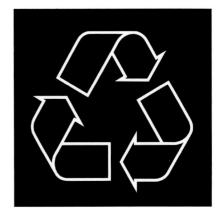

Symbol
This symbolic sign, although it does not figuratively depict the act of recycling, succeeds in implying and encapsulating that process.

Index
This image of storm clouds illustrates the idea of a naturally occurring index sign that, to the viewer, indicates that it may be about to rain.

Icon

This is a sign that closely resembles the object it is signifying; for example, a drawing of a car, signifying the object 'a car', a sign so simple that even a toddler can understand it.

Symbol

This is a sign that is culturally agreed upon but has no (visible) connection with what it signifies, such as a letterform that has no visible connection with the sound (termed a 'phoneme') it signifies. For example, we often use green as a symbol of jealousy, although the colour green clearly has no connection with the mental state of being jealous. This lack of connection between signified and signifier is often described as an arbitrary relationship.

Index

This is a 'natural' sign, which has a physical connection between the sign and what it signifies. For example, a grey cloud indexically signifies that rain is on its way, because it is carrying a substantial quantity of water molecules that appear grey and will physically produce rain. Sometimes, an illustrator will turn an index sign back into an iconic sign: depicting the grey cloud in a painting could suggest the same thing as encountering the cloud on a walk – that rain is on its way.

The iconic sign

As an illustrator, you will work primarily with iconic and symbolic sign types. The first, the icon, is the type of sign that communicates most effectively to the broadest number of people. As mentioned above, it is the first type of symbol that a small child understands.

In John Berger's classic text *Ways of Seeing* (1972), he states that:

'Seeing comes before words. The child looks and recognizes before it can speak.'

The iconic sign is not reliant on any specialized knowledge; in order to be fully understood it simply needs to have been encountered and remembered by the interpreter (thus forming Peirce's 'interpretant' in their mind).

For this reason, figurative art is one of the most populist forms (that is, it speaks to the widest possible audience about their own lives) of coded visual information. For example, it has consistently been used as a code to deliver propaganda, and has been used by Fascist and Communist governments alike to deliver their ideology to the masses – this artistic code is called 'Social Realism'.

Further simplified, iconic symbols are used in international signage systems, in order to convey important information with speed and clarity to the broadest possible audience (for example, the symbols of a man and a woman are used worldwide to denote a male and female toilet respectively).

Above
Illustration for the book *Clean* by Walter Baumann. Digital, 2006. Final-year project at California College of Arts. This image implies the variety of signs that surround us all in our daily lives.

The Chinese written language employs an iconic sign system, comprising literally thousands of individual characters.

The symbolic sign

The symbol is a more complex form of sign than the icon. As such, it has little or no visual connection to the object it signifies (its connection is therefore arbitrary); for this reason, the meaning of symbols must be learnt. Once achieved, this gives people the necessary knowledge to operate effectively within their own culture. When children learn to read and write in their native language, they start by learning to 'sound speak' and write individual letters; next they learn to 'sound speak' and write groupings of letters (in spoken English, there are 45 different sounds, otherwise known as phonemes), before proceeding to form sentences, groups of sentences and so on.

Examples of symbolic signs are letterforms, words (apart from onomatopoeic words that sound like the object they signify, such as 'bang') and national flags (a combination of shapes and colours). An interesting example of the transition between iconic and symbolic sign is the Egyptian (Sumerian) hieroglyph – the signs employed in this code started out as iconic signs and mutated into symbolic signs.

Interestingly, in the field of fine art, abstract art has often confounded the public for a very simple reason – when approaching an abstract painting, some people expect the signs that the artist has used will be iconic, when in fact they are symbolic. Flummoxed, they turn away, muttering 'I could have done that' under their breath. The irony is that those people who find abstract art (an art form that seeks to articulate the 'unseen') baffling use the symbolic signs of the alphabet code every day, without ever questioning the validity or accessibility of that system.

When working as an illustrator with symbols, the last part of Peirce's triad, the 'interpretant', is worth bearing in mind. Because people have different experiences in life, as well as living in very different cultures, the interpretant ('the sign in the mind that is the result of an encounter with a sign') will also differ. This phenomenon is often termed 'perceptual'.

For instance, let's take two identical twin sisters, Robin and Taylor. Robin has been bitten by a dog when leaving a taxi; Taylor has not. Though they are physically identical, and may well have left the same taxi at the same time, they will each have a different interpretant when encountering the sign for a dog. For Robin, her 'interpretant' will be negative, reminding her of the unpleasant encounter she had with a dog, whereas Taylor's will be positive, since her dominant interpretant will be of a different (hopefully) peaceful encounter with a different dog.

The index sign

The index sign is a sign that occurs naturally. For instance, tracks made by wild animals were used to great effect by the North American Indians when out hunting. Though not commonly used by illustrators, fine artists such as

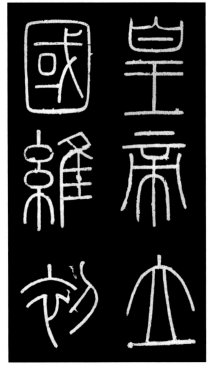

Above
One of the Chinese written languages uses individual iconic signs to describe the world that we live in.

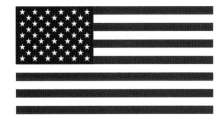

Above
The flag of each country of the world is a symbolic sign that is used to represent that specific territory.

Richard Long, Andy Goldsworthy and Antony Gormley have employed and intervened with the index sign in their work with great effect. In his 2007 show at the Hayward Gallery, London, Gormley filled an interior space within the gallery with simulated clouds.

How do artists arrange signs into codes?

Artists within different cultures, at different times in their evolution, have developed their own signs and codes to make art. The presence or absence of spatial and perspective systems, political or religious conventions when depicting the human form, subject genres and so on have all contributed to the particular ways in which the thoughts, beliefs and experiences of a specific culture have been encoded by groups of human beings. What is particularly interesting about art (and therefore illustration) as a code, with its employment of the iconic, symbolic and index signs, is its interpretability across great distances of time and space. Long after a particular civilization has vanished, the remaining visual code of that civilization is accessible for interpretation by future civilizations (think of the Egyptians, the Ancient Greeks or the Aztecs).

This is among the reasons that art has become a highly valued commodity within today's global culture (at present, Jackson Pollock's painting *No. 5, 1948* is reputed to hold the record for the 'most expensive painting', having, it is claimed, been sold for around US$142 million in 2006).

Building the code

In terms of a general visual code, housed under the term 'Art', we can artificially separate out various key elements that contribute to the formulation of meaning, be it in a single image or in a series of images (called a 'sequential narrative'). In spoken and written language, we can employ adjectives and adverbs to bolt additional description on to nouns and verbs; visual language can also carry description. These elements can have semiotic value signifying status, emotion, material wealth, period, location and spiritual values. In fact, so many meanings can be generated from one sign that we end up with the aforementioned phenomenon that Saussure termed 'unlimited semiosis' – an endless chain of associations generated by an audience, spiralling outwards from an original signifier.

Above
Blind Light by Antony Gormley. Installation at the Hayward Gallery, London, 2007. © The artist. The *Blind Light* project involved this British artist recreating clouds (an index sign) within a public exhibition space.

Key elements within iconic visual systems

Setting

The space, be it natural or man-made, inhabited by the characters and the location where events take place – the setting will denote period, wealth, status and location.

Costume

The clothing that characters wear – costume will denote period, profession, wealth, social group, status, age, character, gender and situation.

Character

Specific, recognizable types of people, depicted in a naturalistic or in an exaggerated manner – character denotes race, age, profession, demeanour and personality.

Composition

The formal arrangement of key characters and events within an image – composition denotes the hierarchy of people and places within the image; the most important being the most prominent, the least important being the least prominent.

Colour

Though perceptual (of different semiotic value in different cultures), colour denotes location, status and hierarchical importance, as well as having symbolic value.

Properties

Objects belonging to characters – properties denote profession, character, personality, situation, location and period.

Body language

The facial expressions and physical gestures of character (known as 'phatic' communication) – body language denotes state of mind, intention, physical prowess, character, psychological state, status and age.

Drama

Actions that take place or the situations that people find themselves in, all contributing to plot progression – the key components of drama are a series of actions and reactions (in the classic Hollywood sense) that create a significant shift in the storyline.

Above
Film stills from *Through A Scanner Darkly*, directed by Richard Linklater; animation by Bob Sabiston, 2007. We can tell a great deal from looking into the top still, an animated depiction of the face of Keanu Reeves, who plays the main character in this film. All eight main narrative elements are incorporated into the middle still, suggesting to the viewer that these two people are relaxed in each other's company and are enjoying a meal in a modern American diner. The cropping of the final frame creates a composition that is dramatic and intense, intimating that something malevolent is about to happen.

Sequential narratives

Visual stories that employ more than one image are called sequential narratives. Elements of narrative – scenes, if you like – are bolted together to form a much larger narrative. This phenomenon will be familiar through reading comic books and graphic novels.

When studying certain 'primitive' tribes, the anthropologist and semiotician Claude Levi-Strauss (1908–2009) looked closely at the relationship between separate elements within a culture and their relationship to a larger system. From this work, he focused on narrative; in particular, the nature of myth within society, which he felt was roughly the same story being retold again and again with minor alterations in the ordering of key elements.

In analysing the structure of myth, Levi-Strauss reduced the story to its simplest possible constituents; he called these 'mythèmes'. Levi-Strauss saw mythèmes as bundles of relations. Disregarding the phenomenon 'narrative', where one action flows from another, Levi-Strauss rearranged the perception of myth so that types of mythèmes are placed in groups with one another.

Myth can be arranged into columns of grouped mythèmes (single events and interactions) and rows of narrative – this arrangement results in a syntagmatic axis (horizontal narrative sequence) and a paradigmatic axis (vertical bundles of relations). In other words, as the narrative moves along, it also moves up; each stage becomes a new hurdle that has to be overcome by the protagonist(s).

Most narratives work in this way. For instance, a book can be broken down into individual chapters. Each chapter is made up of a series of events and descriptions that, when grouped together, form a significant unit of narrative. For example:

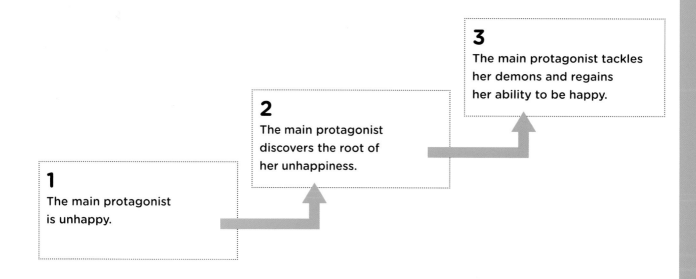

1
The main protagonist is unhappy.

2
The main protagonist discovers the root of her unhappiness.

3
The main protagonist tackles her demons and regains her ability to be happy.

These units (the groups of mythèmes) follow on, one from the other, until the author leads us to a point where we cannot imagine anything further happening – in other words, 'The End'.

Levi-Strauss's focus on the relationship between elements within narrative led to Structuralism, as represented by the Paris School in the 1960s. One of its main proponents, Roland Barthes (1915–1980), wrote prodigiously on text in such classic theoretical books as *Mythologies* (1957) and *Image, Music, Text* (1978). In the latter, Barthes talks of narrative as having a vertical axis as well as a horizontal axis:

'To understand a narrative is not merely to follow the unfolding of the story, it is also to recognize its construction in "storeys", to project the horizontal concatenations (links) of the narrative thread on to an implicitly vertical axis; to read (to listen to) a narrative is not merely to move from one word to the next, it is also to move from one level to the next.'

As well as sequential narrative being governed by rules regarding story structure, it is also governed by visual conventions. This is especially important in the execution of comic books and graphic novels, where there are conventions in regards to time (the spatial breaks between images), in the treatment of text, in the visual framing (close-up, long shot and so on) and in the hierarchical arrangement of images on the page. It is interesting to note that early filmmakers appropriated the visual language of comic books.

Before undertaking the task of writing and illustrating your own story, be it a children's book or a graphic novel, it is worth studying story structure and the visual conventions surrounding sequential storytelling. This will help you understand the general genre of storytelling and make you aware of the audience's expectations when reading your story.

As well as using description and narrative when building codes, illustrators also use the conventions of metaphor, allegory and humour.

Metaphor

The concept of metaphor is employed in many forms of communication as a way to draw comparison (often in a poetic way) between one thing and another. For instance, a fine silk thread wrapped around a rough piece of wood could be used as a metaphor for the liaison between Lady Chatterley and her gamekeeper, a love affair between an upper-class woman and a working-class man, in D.H. Lawrence's novel *Lady Chatterley's Lover* (1928).

Illustrators also often use metaphor as a way of summing up a large, complex situation in a simple and direct way that an audience can easily grasp. For instance, the artist El Lissitzky summed up the armed struggle between the Whites (the Russian Tsarists) and the Reds (the Russian Bolsheviks) by drawing a wedge driving into a circle.

Above
The Complete Persepolis, written and illustrated by Marjane Satrapi. Random House, 2007. This graphic novel tells the story of a young woman growing up in Iran after the 1979 Islamic revolution. It has proved so popular that it has been turned into an animated feature film.

Metaphors can also be used to represent place. For instance, 'the Big Apple' is a visual and word-based metaphor often used in connection with New York. Although this type of metaphor can lapse into cliché, it is often the case that the over-used cliché is ripe for reinvention.

Allegory

Allegory is employed to make a message more palatable and/or accessible to its audience. In particular, allegory is often employed when telling stories to a young audience. For instance, if George Orwell had written an academic treatise on the problems connected with Communism, few people would have read it. However, by turning this complex subject into the allegorical novel *Animal Farm* (1945), Orwell succeeded in communicating his doubts about Communism to many millions of people. The story had such popular appeal that it was turned into a feature-length animation in 1954.

Humour

Though humour or wit is almost impossible to define, from the physical mishaps of Buster Keaton and Laurel and Hardy to the absurdist comedy of *Monty Python's Flying Circus*, humour in the image is primarily based around situation. In cartoons, we see familiar characters, such as politicians and celebrities, in unfamiliar surroundings and humorous predicaments – they are being boiled alive, caught with their pants down, seen doing various crazy things that undoubtedly will make us laugh, and all a far cry from the carefully constructed images that they present to us in public. These satirical images are popular because they are designed to dispel illusion and promote truth within our cultures in a humorous way.

Wit is also inherent in the accuracy with which illustrators describe things – be it something physical (for example, a person, animals or place) or a phenomenon (for example, our current predicament regarding global warming). If it is well observed, and therefore well communicated, the audience will respond to that accuracy.

Top
New York and Texas by Felipe Fatarelli and Lia Penteado, Estúdio Manjericão. Digital collage using Photoshop and Illustrator, 2008. Illustration for *Fortune* magazine. This assemblage reinvents various clichés that are representative of New York and Texas and weaves them together to produce a new image with fresh meaning.

Centre
Film still from *Animal Farm*, directed and animated by Halas and Batchelor, 1954. This film, based on the George Orwell book of the same name, translated well into an animated feature that used the writer's allegorical approach to explore the problems of putting political ideology into practice.

Bottom
Still from *Gay Straight* by Matthew Vescovo. Animation for MTV spot, 2006. This illustrator uses humour to express the paradoxes inherent in the interpretation of tactile male behaviour.

How do we change existing codes?

In each of the expressive arts, there are pioneers who seek to develop new codes. These innovators respond to changes in the world that they live in and formulate new codes to reflect those changes. This kind of progress is normally referred to as having six main, sometimes interdependent, components: political-led change, economic-led change, social-led change, technological-led change, legal-led change and environmental-led change (known as 'PESTLE' for short).

Historically, these innovators have either been located at the fine-art end of their discipline, or they have existed outside the mainstream of popular culture. In both cases, this has allowed them a high degree of freedom to explore new coding systems, without experiencing concerns of alienating existing audiences.

In other practitioners, there is evidence of transitions between codes, where part of the old code exists alongside a new code. This can often be an astute way of maintaining contact with an existing audience while simultaneously taking them in a new aesthetic and intellectual direction.

Example of a new code in art

The beginning of the First World War (an example of political-led change), and the human tragedy that followed, prompted the birth of Dadaism. Started by an international group of artists, its premise was that since the war made no sense, art's role was to reflect the insanity of the world. To this end, Marcel Duchamp (1887–1968), one of the movement's leading protagonists, displayed a urinal as an exhibit in an art gallery, wittily titling it *Fountain* (1917).

At the time, the Dadaists met with much hostility:

'*The Dada Philosophy is the sickest, most paralyzing and most destructive thing that has ever originated from the brain of man.*'
American Art News, 1921

Dada has since proved to be a lasting influence on the direction of contemporary art and illustration, as can be seen in the work of the artist Damien Hirst and the illustrator Russell Mills.

Example of a transitional code in art

Surrealism, established by André Breton (1896–1966) and other artists and writers, gathered momentum as a dominant artistic force in the 1930s. Influenced by the writings of the Austrian psychoanalyst Sigmund Freud, Surrealist art sought to reveal the internal human landscape without compromise:

Above
The Glass Box, designed by Peter Buchanan-Smith and Josef Reyes, 2008. Nonesuch Records. A ten-disk retrospective of work by contemporary American composer Philip Glass, who created a radical new approach to the composing of classical music. Each side of the cube portrays an image of the composer as rendered by the artists Annie Leibovitz, Francesco Clemente, Chuck Close, Robert Mapplethorpe and Robert Wilson.

Above
DVD artwork by Jonny Halifax and John Rambo Stevens for *The Sex Pistols – There'll Always Be An England*, directed by Julien Temple, 2008. This design for a film about the legendary British punk band The Sex Pistols evokes the anarchic visual language and contentious subject matter of the band's creative outpourings.

Left
The Physical Impossibility of Death in the Mind of Someone Living by Damien Hirst. Mixed media, 1991. British artist Hirst's notorious shark encased in a glass cabinet filled with formaldehyde pointed fine art in a new direction.

'Surrealism (noun): Psychic automatism in its purest state, by which it is intended to express either verbally, or in writing, or in any other way, the true functioning of thought. Thought expressed in the absence of any control exerted by reason and outside all moral and aesthetic considerations.'
André Breton, *Manifeste de Surréalisme*, 1924

In terms of Surrealism's transitional nature, the Surrealists employed a figurative artistic code and rearranged it in an extraordinary way:

'Disrupting the senses by inverting traditional modes of communication… the more conventional the language, the greater the derangement.'
Richard Calvocoressi, *Magritte*, 1984

One of Surrealism's main proponents was the Belgian artist René Magritte (1898–1967), who worked intermittently in a wallpaper factory as a draughtsman and within the fields of publicity and advertising, as well as being a fine artist. In his work, typified by a neutral, impersonal visual language that often played with scale, he explored the relationships between objects, images and names (Peirce's triad of representamen, object and inter-pretant), as well as displaying:

'An urge to challenge our preconceived ideas about reality, to break our habits of thought and behaviour and force us into a new and heightened awareness of our surroundings.'
Richard Calvocoressi, *Magritte*, 1984

Surrealism's influence on illustration, on the commercial image-maker's ability to express the metaphysical world visually, cannot be emphasized enough in terms of providing a reference point for contemporary illustration.

3 Channel/medium

A channel is the physical means of directing communication between a communicator and an audience. In television and radio, aural and visual messages are encoded into electronic signals and sent through the airwaves before being decoded by a receiver at the other end – in this case, a radio or television set.

In terms of mass-produced visual material, information is prepared on computers, before being sent in electronic code to the print works, where it is decoded and printed on to rolls of paper. This is assembled (as a newspaper, a magazine, a book or a pamphlet), gathered up and carried by air, road and rail to distribution outlets, ultimately to be 'received' by an audience through purchasing the product in a shop.

Above
Cover illustration for the Nine Inch Nails album *The Downward Spiral* by Russell Mills. Mixed media, 1994. Interscope Records. Mills employed Dadaist methods to communicate the visceral and nihilistic content of this album by the Los Angeles band Nine Inch Nails.

Above
After The Flood by James Marsh. Acrylic on canvas board, 1991. Single cover and promo for the band Talk Talk. Polydor Ltd. Surrealism is still a key tool with which illustrators communicate their clients' messages.

The most recent channel to be invented is the internet, which, like television and radio, has the advantage of arriving directly into our homes. This is proving to be an extremely valuable employment growth area for the illustrator in the form of still and sequential image-making (including animation).

Whichever channel you are commissioned to produce illustration work within, you will be presented with certain technical requirements. When working within printed media outlets, these requirements will be connected with image size and colour palette. When working within transmitted media, these requirements will be connected with dpi (dots per inch), the software that the work is created in, the amount of compression and so on.

To reiterate, channels are the physical means by which messages are sent, and to this end are primarily looked after by people with specialist technical skills.

A 'medium' is the communication system that is used to carry encoded information – 'the message'. John Fiske, a writer on communication studies, categorizes 'media' in three groups:

Above
Icons of methods of communication. Channels include phones, radios, televisions and satellite communication systems.

- **Presentational (for example voice, face or body).**
- **Representational (for example writing, drawing, painting).**
- **Mechanical (for example press, radio, television).**

The influential 1960s philosopher Marshall McLuhan famously stated that 'the medium is the message'. In his 1967 book of nearly the same name (*The Medium Is The Massage* – the final word the result of a typographical error that McLuhan liked and kept), he discussed the idea of the 'global village'. He thought that the very fact that we had such unprecedented access to information was of more significance than the information itself – a forward-thinking statement in light of the unprecedented amount of information that is now available to us on the internet.

Who controls the medium?

People called 'gatekeepers' influence the type of information that enters various forms of media. These people shape and control the representation of information within the channel before transmission. Their decisions are informed by knowledge of the identity of the channel, commonly termed 'house style' or 'brand identity'. They also have a clear perception of the intended recipients of the code, their audience.

Channels and media generally work as hierarchical structures. As an illustrator, your first point of contact will be with an art director or art buyer. These people are responsible for commissioning illustration work for the channel and will be expert in controlling the visual appearance of that channel and creating unity from the different visual components. Ultimate responsibility for the messages carried within a channel lies at the editor's door – if they make the wrong decision, and in the process affront public taste, they may lose their job.

4 Destination

This term refers to the people who decode the messages – in other words, the audience. As we have seen, communication is a two-way process: the audience is expected to share the particular code of the message. Decoding information is an active process and commentators on communication have suggested that the process of receiving messages is just as important as the creation of the messages themselves.

Much time and money continues to be invested in ascertaining the tastes of particular audiences by categorizing them in terms of age, economics, socio-economic status and so on, in the hope that a greater degree of accuracy can be attained in designing specific messages for the consumption of these particular groups.

In all of the fields where illustration is applied – be it advertising and corporate work, editorial, children's fiction and non-fiction, adult fiction and non-fiction, entertainment and music – the code is influenced by the intended recipients of the message.

In general, creative directors and art directors are the people responsible for honing and shaping the messages of illustrators for these particular destinations. When being briefed by an art director, you will almost certainly be asked to consider the particular characteristics of your target audience – the group of people who will receive your illustration work – to ensure that the content and visual language of your work is appropriate for that group.

Conclusion

The language of semiotics is a shifting, academically complex landscape, constantly reshaped and influenced by the main forces of change previously mentioned: political, economic, social, technological, legal and environmental.

What is so exciting about illustration as a subject, in relation to this semiotic landscape, is that the relationship(s) between communicator (the illustrator), message (the illustration), channel/medium and audience is constantly changing, redefining the physical nature of illustration and its function within society. Your job as a working illustrator is to keep abreast of change, and in so doing, to maintain the relevance of and commercial demand for your work.

4.

The editorial brief

'As life grows more complex, it requires a greater and greater extension of language. Graphic presentation is that extension, that synthesis of art and science now urgently demanded by contemporary life.' Will Burtin, graphic designer

Newspapers and magazines have long been a key part of global culture, providing their audiences with topical news, political comment, lifestyle features and extensive arts and sports coverage. Firmly connected to the present, their editorial content reflects all aspects of the politics of life – people's concerns and desires, their aspirations and interests, as well as their constant requirement for up-to-date national and international news coverage.

Traditionally, words and pictures (a mixture of symbolic and iconic codes) have been used to deliver editorial content via the relatively inexpensive information channels of the newspaper and the magazine (both appearing in the West in the seventeenth century), though further significant technological developments occurred in the twentieth century in the form of radio and television.

The internet, too, has joined the editorial fray, conveying information to mass audiences on an unprecedented global scale. Developed originally by the US military in the early 1970s as a secure communication resource (a network of transatlantic cables allowed participating factions to encode and decode information in total secrecy), it became widely available to the global populace in the 1980s.

Since this significant event (coupled with an equally important and simultaneous revolution in home computing), the internet has proved to be an editorial medium with far-reaching potential, combining many of the advantages of print, radio and television within one technological environment.

Now, with the advent of third-generation mobile phones that have internet capability, coupled with the rapid improvement of broadband technology (delivering better and better sound and vision at higher and higher speeds), we may see the internet eclipse its main competitors in the near future and become the primary conduit of editorial information. Built on the same economic model as newspapers and magazines (that is, funded by advertising revenue), future mass audiences may prefer to use the internet exclusively to browse for information, to seek out specific pieces of writing, imagery and film, and to deliver their own comments in relation to a particular editorial news item or feature.

The most consistent approach to web-based editorial content has been to adopt print-based formats and apply them to the new digital media. In some ways this makes perfect sense – if people are already dealing with new and complex technology, why make them grapple with new information delivery formats as well? In other ways, it remains an open-ended question – how can we develop a universal web-based format that exploits the editorial medium to its full potential as well as proving useful to its users?

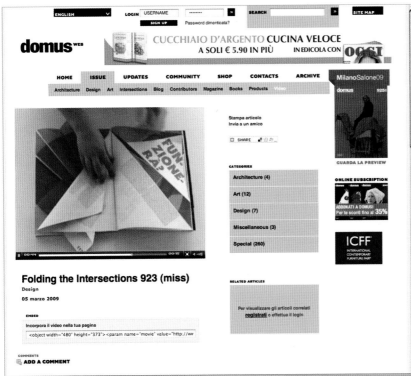

Above

Intersections – The New Web for *Domus* magazine, 2009. Creative direction and concept Nicolas
Bourquin and Sven Ehmann; graphic design
Nicolas Bourquin, Thibaud Tissot, Maike
Hamacher and Barbara Hoffman; illustration
Tobias Krafczyk. As a format, the magazine can
carry image and word in a myriad of different
graphic arrangements. The innovation in this
issue is contained within the playful use of folds
to create illustrated portraits.

Left

Intersections – The New Web for *Domus* maga-
zine, 2009. Creative direction and concept Nicolas
Bourquin and Sven Ehmann; graphic design
Nicolas Bourquin, Thibaud Tissot, Maike
Hamacher and Barbara Hoffman; illustration
Tobias Krafczyk. The magazine format is now
rapidly migrating to the internet, as this video
animation that illustrates the folding system on
Domus's website shows.

While this process continues, a great deal of innovation is in progress. Young entrepreneurs have created ways of using the web that have proved popular and that have commercial potential (YouTube, Facebook, MySpace). Illustrators too have found their way into this territory, and have used the web both as a marketing tool and as a way to generate new areas of commissioned work.

In terms of established newspapers and magazines, we are seeing a synthesis between print-based delivery and web-based delivery. Most national newspapers have established their own websites, utilizing the long-established credibility of their brand. In the most successful cases they have seen a national, print-based audience of perhaps half a million transformed into an international, web-based audience of 10 million. This in turn has attracted the attention of advertisers, who now spend much more money on digitally delivered advertising than on print-based advertising. They are especially attracted to the precise nature of the web, which can tell them exactly how many people have clicked on their advertisement link. Journalists, too, are now working across both media within the same organization, and the print-based newspapers and magazines they write for often contain links to areas of the website where sound and vision can be accessed.

Nevertheless, people are still buying newspapers and magazines. This is primarily because they are cheap, portable, easy to read, broad in content, commentary and opinion, familiar as objects, interacted with in silence and navigated with supreme ease. For these reasons, and others integral to the individual readerships of certain newspapers and magazines, they continue to hold their place within society, communicating word-based and image-based messages (created by journalists, graphic designers, illustrators and photographers alike) to mass audiences, who in turn attract advertisers, who in turn provide the funding for the majority of the newspapers and magazines that we buy.

Editorial illustration is the most likely starting point for the young illustrator just out of college; the outlets are broad, from national to in-house publications; the fees are reasonable; and there is a healthy level of commissioning.

Illustration and the evolution of newspapers and magazines

Although the concept of movable type had its origins in China and Korea in the eleventh and twelfth centuries, it was not until the invention by Johannes Gutenberg (d. 1468) of an alphabet of foundry-cast metal characters (coupled with a significant advance in the production of paper) that the mass production of pages of type (and later images) became possible.

The world's first magazine was *Erbauliche Monaths-Unterredungen* ('Edifying Monthly Editions') and appeared in Germany in 1663. The world's first newspaper, *The London Gazette*, appeared in 1666. Both publications catered to a privileged, educated elite (few people outside of the Church and the aristocracy could read or write) and were more akin to books (they had linear narratives with no pictures) than the newspapers and magazines we are familiar with today.

Above
Illustration by Luke Best for the *LA Times* book review section. Mixed media, 2009. Modern editorial illustration provides a colourful visual counterpoint to columns of text.

Opposite, top
The London Gazette, 19–22 September 1687. A layout with two columns of text, written as a linear narrative, was a standard format for early newspapers.

Opposite, centre
The Illustrated London News, 14 May 1842. The title of this publication points to the fact that including illustration to accompany text was a groundbreaking innovation within the newspaper format.

Opposite, bottom
Leipziger Neueste Nachrichten, 8 May 1937. Half-tone reproduction techniques meant that photographic imagery displaced engraved images in twentieth-century news coverage.

Typographic and illustrative innovations in the eighteenth century included the typographic point system, invented by Pierre Fournier (1712–1768), and the method of image transfer known as lithography (see p. 33), developed by Alois Senefelder (1771–1834). These developments paved the way for the mass-media revolution that took place in the nineteenth century. This happened within the wider context of the Industrial Revolution, a social and technological revolution that saw the populace shift in vast numbers from the country to the town, where they were employed by the new landed gentry in factories to produce goods that were marketed across the globe. This shift, although detrimental to the quality of human life in many ways, signalled the beginnings of formal education for all, including, most importantly for newspapers and magazines, the advent of mass literacy programmes.

During this era, *The Illustrated London News* (established in 1842) introduced weekly woodcuts and engravings into the printed editorial medium for the first time, setting a precedent for the growth of the illustrated journal over the second half of the nineteenth century. Commercial artists became crucial to the new media in sketching newsworthy events – their drawings would then be translated into engravings suitable for printing. This type of illustration work continues today in the form of reportage illustration, where the direct recording of subject matter by the illustrator is crucial to the process of making an image for a particular publication.

By the end of the nineteenth century, advances in photography, which in the minds of the audience came to be representative of truth, displaced these reportage engravings. However, rather than extinguishing the use of the drawn and painted image in newspapers and magazines, photography simply redirected illustration away from the reporting of current events and into the more thoughtful and discursive areas of publications.

By the early part of the twentieth century, mass media had truly arrived, with an economic model built exclusively around advertising revenue (which dramatically reduced the unit price), with production speeds that allowed for 10,000 complete newspapers to be printed and assembled per hour (heralding the first circulation figures of over a million copies per edition), and with efficient and speedy distribution networks via road and rail to retail outlets.

Essentially this is the format of newspapers and magazines (and now, broadly speaking, editorial websites) familiar to us today: a mixture of headlines, copy (or text, delivered in broken narratives), illustration and photography. Now, too, the norm is full-colour printing (this first appeared in the 1930s), and there is a distinct visual differentiation between advertising content and editorial content, though both continue to vie for the reader's attention. There is also continued subsidization of the basic unit of the publication by advertisers, who continue to exert their influence over the presentation and subject matter of editorial content.

Illustrating for the modern newspaper brief

Contemporary editorial illustration utilizes the superior speed with which the image communicates over the word. It breaks up potentially daunting walls of text for the reader and tells a story far more incisively and succinctly than a stock photograph (an image not exclusively commissioned to illustrate a particular piece of writing). It also serves as an overall invitation for the reader to engage with the page.

To this end, as cited by Sarah Habershon, an art director at *The Guardian* newspaper in London, editorial illustration has to fulfil certain criteria:

- The illustration should serve as a visual 'hook', the first thing that the reader's eye is drawn to by virtue of its visual boldness, its wit or for the intriguing story that it tells. Once this has been achieved, the reader will take in the headline, the 'standfirst' (or introductory sentence) and the article itself.
- The illustration should summarize the idea at the heart of the story and it should take literally seconds to comprehend – further detail within the illustration can emerge as the reader engages with the article.
- The illustration should work as a stand-alone picture, as well as working in conjunction with the headline and article.

Above
McCain Republican Elephant by Jimmy Turrell. Mixed media, 2008. Illustration for *The Observer*. This image successfully reveals some of the problems connected with John McCain's American presidential campaign.

Below
Petworking by Paul Blow. Mixed media and digital, 2009. Illustration created for a feature on animals interacting in cyberspace for *The Independent* magazine. An unusual feature story has given this illustrator the chance to create a witty image to accompany the text.

Pets issue

Petworking (noun)
Animals interacting
in cyberspace

Does your guinea pig want to tell the world what music he likes?
Does your cat need to share the story of her most
embarrassing moment? If so, a new generation of internet sites- from Facedog to
Fishbook - has been designed just for
you and your loved one. Clare Dwyer Hogg reports

P rudence from Edmonton has a lot to say for herself. "I like to stretch, jump around like a maniac, and chew on newspaper and toilet paper rolls," she says. She is quick, however, to qualify her last hobby. "The days of me trying to stick my head into them are over... because of a certain 'toilet paper roll incident'." She doesn't go into details, but given that Prudence is a Peruvian long-haired guinea pig, they're not hard to imagine. No matter, she moves on, unhampered by a speech impediment, breezily announcing she likes to 'eat lettuce and guinea pig pellets, drink water, grab lettuce from giant hand with lime green nail polish... oh and I like to violently clean myself.' Prudence is enjoying the luxury of Rodentbook – a social networking site for eloquent pets who want to move up the food chain.

Illustration by Paul Blow

84 The Independent Magazine

Left
Illustration by Katherine Streeter for an article on women bullying other women in the workplace. Mixed media, 2009. For *The New York Times* business section. Editorial illustration often deals with controversial contemporary issues.

Centre left
Illustration by Mick Marston for article on adopting SWOT analysis approach for school education. Vector illustration, 2009. For *TES* magazine. The illustrator has used humour here to draw in the reader.

Below
Illustration by Jimmy Turrell. Mixed media, 2009. For *The Observer Music Monthly*. This illustration for the music supplement of a British Sunday newspaper uses figurative visual language to depict up-and-coming young musicians.

GET WITH THE PROGRAMME

How come bands like the Gossip owe their big break to teen drama Skins? Johnny Davis reports on the TV shows now breaking the hottest new acts. Illustration by Jimmy Turrell

You're breaking my arm! You're breaking my fucking arm!" Closing time at the Paradise Inn and a riot has broken out. A dozen policemen are losing their battle to contain the lagered-up lads and bullet-headed locals. Pint glasses rain down, a chair goes through a window, there's blood everywhere. Earlier this evening, nine underage teenagers had walked into the grim Croydon boozer and straight up the patrons' noses: pointing at the woman with the ponytail doing karaoke, snorting cocaine off a credit card, getting off with one another in the toilets and pouring beer down each other's throats. Then 16-year-old Cook climbed on a table and lit a flare. Then it all kicked off.

Ah, the youth of today. Or, at least, the youth of *Skins* – the gritty E4 drama, now in its third series, that has earned both a nod from Bafta and a shake of the head from Middle England for its lively portrayal of British teens. Here, abortion, self-harm and coffin theft are part of the daily routine, one that inevitably ends, druggily, with an all-night house party. "That's *Skins*' job, to shock the *Daily Mail*," grins Neil Gorringe, who is directing today's pub fight, an edit of which was eventually toned down for TV.

Since announcing itself noisily in 2007 *Skins* has been noted for risk-taking. For this series, almost the entire cast was dumped and replaced by unknowns (only Effy Stonem, played by Kaya Scodelario, remains from the first two series). For the past few weeks, viewers have been ▶▶

Above left

Illustration by Yulia Brodskaya for an article titled 'Thrifty Christmas'. Cut paper, 2008. For *The Guardian*'s 'G2' section. This illustration for the cover of the Christmas edition of a British daily newspaper deftly interweaves type and image using sculpted coloured papers.

Above right

Illustration by David Foldvari for an article titled 'This Terrifying Moment is Our One Chance for a New World'. Mixed media, 2008. For *The Observer*. This illustration for the society section of a British Sunday newspaper combines imagery of establishment figures with the atmosphere of political dissent inherent in street art.

Left

Illustration by Geneviève Gauckler. Vector illustration, 2006. For the art festival supplement of *Libération*. The figurative and the abstract are combined in this colourful illustration for the arts section of a French newspaper.

Within newspaper editorial, there are distinct genres, all providing commissioning possibilities for the freelance illustrator. The invention of the Saturday supplement (which combines newspaper and magazine in the same publication) has also offered new areas of employment for the illustrator.

Components of a modern broadsheet newspaper

(This includes Saturday supplements.)

- **National news** (dominated by photography)
- **International news** (dominated by photography)
- **Feature stories** (illustration and photography)
- **Political analysis** (illustration and photography)
- **Business section** (illustration and photography)
- **Education section** (illustration and photography)
- **Media section** (illustration and photography)
- **Arts section** (illustration and photography)
- **Society section** (illustration and photography)
- **Consumer section** (illustration and photography)
- **Sports section** (dominated by photography)
- **Gardening section** (dominated by photography)
- **Food section** (dominated by photography)
- **Property section** (illustration and photography)
- **Star signs** (dominated by illustration)
- **Syndicated strip cartoons** (dominated by illustration)
- **Other strip cartoons** (dominated by illustration)
- **Weather** (dominated by information graphics/illustration)

Below left
Leo Star Sign by Eda Akaltun. Etching, 2007–08. One of a complete set of horoscope illustrations for *The Saturday Telegraph Magazine*. This arresting image for the weekend magazine of a British daily newspaper was made using the etching printing process.

Below right, top
Hunter & Painter, written and illustrated by Tom Gauld. Buenaventura Press, 2007. Originally published in *The Guardian* newspaper, these ink comic strips present a consistent cohort of characters in a variety of often humorous situations.

Below right, bottom
Illustration by Merrily Harpur for 'An Estate Agent's Diary'. Pen and watercolour, 2008. For *The London Evening Standard*. This cartoon for the property section of a London-based daily newspaper is the perfect accompaniment to a humorous weekly column by an estate agent.

The creative roles within a newspaper/magazine/editorial website

Editor

This person has overall control of the content and visual appearance of the publication. It is his or her role to ensure that the content is truthful, that it sits within the bounds of public taste and that it is attractive to the core readership of the publication. In general, the editor is not available to view portfolios.

Creative director

This person is ultimately responsible for all aspects of the visual look and feel of a publication, shouldering praise and criticism for this work in equal measure. Working closely with the editor, he or she co-ordinates the activities of the creative team (and any freelance photographers and illustrators involved), and initiates and stimulates creative approaches from within this team.

Art director

This person is responsible for commissioning illustration and photography for the publication. In the case of larger publications, there will be a number of art directors who are responsible for the different sections of that publication. They will co-ordinate the various design elements on the page, to ensure that pictures and words form a cohesive whole. They will brief the illustrator at the outset of the commission and discuss various creative possibilities in visually

Progression of a typical editorial commission

Start

1
The editor and art director meet to discuss the illustrative requirements of the forthcoming publication. Budgets will also be discussed.

2
The art director considers possible illustrators. After they reach a decision, the illustrator is contacted by phone to discuss availability, before the brief is emailed to them with size constraints, delivery times and fee(s).

3
Illustrator accepts the commission, secures a purchase order number from finance department of publication and begins work on the brief.

summarizing the article. They will also approve the roughs and the final artworks (often in conjunction with the editor). Generally, they will be available to view portfolios.

In-house designer

This person is responsible for composing the pages of a publication on a computer, utilizing the basic grid layout of the newspaper or magazine.

Picture editor

This person liaises closely with the art director, collecting, reviewing and editing photographic and illustration material for use within the publication. They will have to consider the guidelines and standards of their publication constantly, and also be aware of budget limitations.

6

Art director (and editor) approve final artwork. Illustrator submits invoice for payment, stipulating the timeframe in which payment should be received.

Finish

4

Illustrator amends work and submits roughs to art director, who will approve the roughs (often in conjunction with the editor) and return them with minor amendments.

5

Illustrator submits final artwork at correct size and resolution.

Example of a newspaper commission

The example featured here is for the Japanese national daily newspaper *Asahi Shinbun*. Although the commissioning process is slightly unusual, as there is no art director involved, it is a good example of an illustrator being prepared to be versatile and working to suit the unique requirements of a publication.

Japanese artist and illustrator Ryu Itadani is commissioned to produce an illustration every week for a column in the newspaper. The column is 'written' by a well-known Japanese comedian, Shozo Hayashiya. The process by which this column is realized is intriguing: Ryu and the editor of the newspaper meet with Mr Hayashiya once a week and listen to him talk. The topics that he discusses are usually connected with current shopping trends in Japan or foodstuffs that are seasonal.

While Mr Hayashiya talks, Ryu sketches whatever comes into his mind as he listens. He also writes down notes. After the meeting, Ryu selects the most relevant material from his sketchbook and translates this into a full-colour illustration. This is then submitted to the editor for final approval before publication.

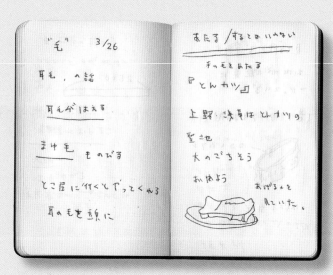

Stage 1
Examples of Ryu's sketches when listening to Mr Hayashiya, relating to 'Ton_Katsu', 12 June 2008.

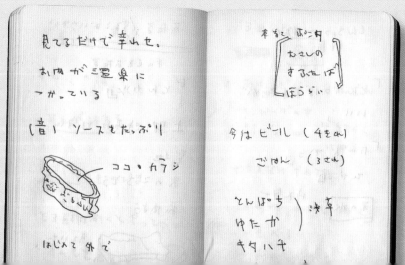

4.

Stage 2
Examples of Ryu's finished artwork submitted
for editorial approval.

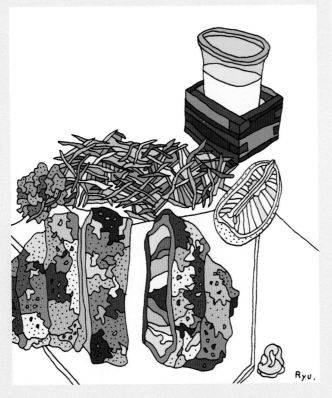

Stage 3
Examples of Ryu's illustrations, which are printed
in the newspaper at less than half of their original
size. More images for *Asahi Shinbun* can be
viewed at www.ryuitadani.com.

正蔵の **TOKYO 歳時記**

子どもの頃、トンカツは大のごちそうだった。

時おり、母が近所の肉屋から厚みのあるお肉を買ってきて、小麦粉をはたき、卵にくぐらせ、パン粉をつけ、揚げてくれた。私は「危ないわよ」と言われながら母の傍らを離れず、その手元をじっとにらんでいた。キツネ色に色づく衣を見ていると、なにか気持ちよさそうだった。これがフライパンでじかに焼かれているお肉だと、ちょっとかわいそうな気がするものだ。

揚げたてのトンカツを、まな板の上でサクサクサクサクと切られ、同じくシャッシャッシャッシャッと切

ったキャベツを添えてめいめいの皿に盛り付けられる。これもうれしかった。ソースはたっぷり。一切れを立てるようにして、断面の肉の地肌に黄色い嫌りがらしをひとすじ付けると、「痛いかな。しみるかい？」そんなやさしい言葉をかけつつ、ひと息に頬張る。白いごはんをかき込んで、ああ、たまらない。

前座になると、外でトンカツをいただく楽しみが加わった。なにしろ寄席のある上野・浅草はトンカツの聖地と言っていいほど老舗、名店が多い。上野には「蓬莱屋」「ぽん多本家」「双葉」「武蔵野」、浅草には「豚八」「ゆたか」「喜多八」などがある。それぞれ個性があって、お師匠さんごとにひいきの店が異なる。楽日になると、「この師匠がトリだから、打ち上げはこのお店だ

な」と読み、わざわざ届機ってトンカツにありついたこともあった。

メタボ？ てやんでえ

Ton_Katsu

絵・Ryu Itadani

正蔵の **TOKYO 歳時記**

シイタケ、ピーマン、ニンジンといえば、どれも子どもの嫌いな食べ物ランキング上位に入るのだろうが、私も小さい頃、苦手だった。

そういう野菜を細かく刻んでハンバーグに混ぜたりして、気がつかないうちに慣れさせる家庭も多いのだろう。親の気持ちは分からないでもないが、うちではやらない。なんかコソクな手段のような気がして、食べさせられる子どももあわれだ。

では、どうするか。旬の食材を、家族で「おいしいね」と言い合いながら食べるというのはどうだろう。

私の場合、ニンジンが嫌いだったが、ハンバーグの付け合わせがきっ

かけになった。ある日一緒に食べていた母が、「これおいしいねぇ」と言いながらニンジンを口に入れた。ほかの家族も「本当だ」と続く。別に私に食べろと圧力をかけたふうでもなかったが、自分も一つ頬張ると、あの強烈な甘さ、甘えぐい香りがなーんと口に広がった。母は私の顔を見て、「ね、おいしいでしょ」と言う。私は、「まずい」とは口にできず、頭の中で「これっておいしいのかな」と考えた。その後、付け合わせのニンジンが入っていないことがあって、意外にも「ないと寂しいじゃないか」と感じた。これですっかりニンジン嫌いが解消した。

子どもに「何を食べようか」「夕食、何にしようか」と聞いて、「なんでもいい」と言われるのも、ちょっと腹立たしい。軽くおなかを満た

そういうときでもお茶漬けがいいのか、カップ麺がいいのか、はっき

好き嫌いをなくすには

Suki_Kirai

りしてほしいのだ。関心のある人を見ると梛関心を持つというこ とを大切にするとい

私の娘は、うなのどに骨がつかえ親の私は大のらら、と思いつくう口の中でとろける。す店に連れて行きんだ。「これを生いだき、お酒をきゅあらめえんだ」とつられて娘が食べいしい」。肝焼きうな嫌いもいっ

ただ、毎び白文されたらたまっ「育ち盛りの子は分」と心の中でつ

絵・Ryu Itadani

Illustrating for the modern magazine brief

The average high-street newsagent will arrange its magazines within the following general categories:

- **Fashion** (illustration and photography)
- **Home and lifestyle** (illustration and photography)
- **Computing** (illustration and photography)
- **Men's lifestyle** (illustration and photography)
- **Sport** (illustration and photography)
- **TV and satellite** (illustration and photography)
- **General interest** (illustration and photography)
- **Business and current affairs** (illustration and photography)

Alongside mainstream publications, there are many in-house and special-interest magazines, not funded by advertising revenue and therefore more experimental in both content and design. You may be familiar with this kind of publication through your specialist interest in illustration and graphic design.

The personnel and commissioning process for a magazine are similar to those of a newspaper, although lead-in times (the time needed to assemble the complete publication before it is submitted to the printers) are longer. Normally, magazines are published every week or every month, although some specialist publications may appear only three or four times a year.

Above
Illustrations by Jim Stoten for an article on how to live in an environmentally friendly way. Pen on paper, 2009. Commissioned by *Dwell* magazine. Images like these can quickly reflect situations that readers may find themselves in and therefore instantly relate to.

Above
Illustration by Carine Brancowitz. Pen and ink, 2009. Commissioned by *Arena* magazine. This portrait of Apple boss Steve Jobs humanizes a potentially dry subject area.

Left
Illustration by Carine Brancowitz for 'The Season Story'. Pen and ink, 2008. Commissioned by *Vogue Pelle*, Italy. This illustration immediately transports the reader to the world of the chic young woman.

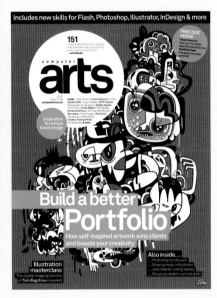

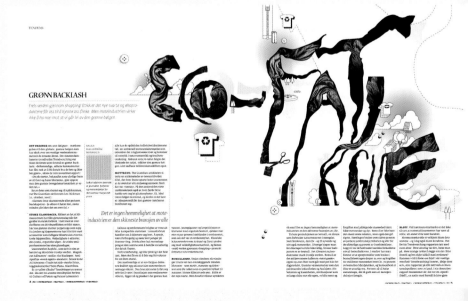

Top
Exxon Mobil by Felipe Fatarelli and Lia Penteado, Estúdio Manjericão. Photoshop and Illustrator, 2008. Commissioned by *Fortune* magazine for a feature on Exxon Mobil. This illustration shows the machinery used in oil production to convey the subject matter of the article.

Centre left
The Judgement Test by Paul Blow. Mixed media, 2008. Commissioned by *Radio Times* to illustrate a radio play of the same name. An illustration can transmit dramatic content that could potentially be unacceptable if presented as a photograph.

Centre right
Cover illustration by Jon Burgerman. Digital, 2008. Commissioned by *Computer Arts* magazine. This illustration focuses on the creative side of the computing industry.

Bottom left
Illustration by Nathan Fox. Photoshop, 2009. Commissioned by *Tennis* magazine. This image suggests the pressure that the professional tennis player is under.

Bottom right
Illustration by Grandpeople. Photoshop and Illustrator, 2007. Commissioned by *D2* magazine. This illustration uses type and image to create immediate interest in the article.

Example of a magazine commission

The example included here is a commission by the British illustrator Howard Read for *The Economist* magazine in 2007. Complex in content and scope, this magazine offers its readership in-depth analysis into global business markets and future economic trends. The art director of *The Economist* asked Howard to produce cover illustrations for eight lead stories within the magazine. Howard's job was to encapsulate these stories in a nutshell, and whet the appetite of the audience for the dense editorial information contained in each article.

Having accepted the commission, Howard receives the brief. As he reads through each article, he underlines key pieces of information within each article and notes down ideas for illustrations. From his notes and initial ideas, Howard develops rough sketches for each one of the stories. He is also aware of how they will work visually as a connected series.

Having discussed the roughs with the editor of *The Economist*, the art director asks Howard to make some corrections; these range from minor alterations to a complete rethink for one of the articles (the editor felt that the image proposed would potentially be too familiar to their audience). Notice, too, the attention to detail of the art director in ensuring that each illustration accurately reflects the drive of the article it is illustrating.

Notes

Cover

Cover idea 1

Cover idea 2

Client's comment: 'Cover: The basic metaphor is fine, but the racers need to be much closer. At the moment it looks as if Europe is winning easily, while the survey mentions how fanatically the US is performing, and Asia is certainly not bringing up the rear. If we keep this metaphor, all three need to be straining/dipping for the finishing line in a much closer, more dynamic race.'

Revised cover rough

Roughs

Client's comment: *'Roughs 1, 3, 4, 5, 7 and 8 are all OK.'*

Rough 1

Rough 2 reject

Rough 2 revised

Client's comment: *'Rough 2: needs to be redone – aside from us not quite "getting it", we need the focus to be more on the two European companies mentioned, thriving at home, without reference to China.'*

Rough 3

Rough 4

Rough 5

Rough 6 reject

Rough 6 revised

Rough 7

Rough 8

Client's comment: *'Rough 6: Does the image mean time is running out for the French 35-hour week? Could it be redone losing the stopwatch and using an hourglass/sand egg-timer, with the French man relaxing at home with his wine in the bottom half, with just a small amount of sand in the top part? Howard's style is great, so I'm sure the finished artwork will look great, but if we could see some new roughs for these by Thursday pm that would be great.'*

Howard acts upon the necessary changes and resubmits the amended roughs. Once these have been approved, Howard proceeds with the final artwork in full colour.

Howard's artwork appears in print and he submits his invoice, quoting his purchase order number, to the payroll department of *The Economist*.

Final images

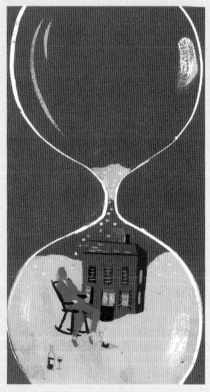

4.

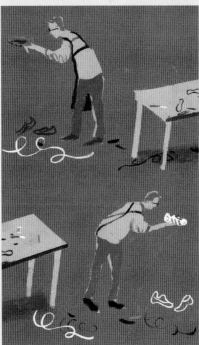

Illustrating for editorial on the web

As we have already noted, print-based editorial is in a state of transition, synthesizing with its technologically advanced web-based relative. Both share the same formats and content wherever possible, which will include copy, illustration, photography and advertising. The web does, however, have the advantage of being capable of delivering sound and vision and a genuinely up-to-the-minute news coverage service (even the most successful print-based dailies can only manage three editions per day).

There are, however, some marked differences between the two channels, which in part relate to different user behaviour. Whereas with a newspaper, there may be only three main stories on the front cover (including a large pho-tograph) – with the rest of the content set within defined areas on the following pages – in web-based editorial the homepage could more accurately be described as a synopsis of the whole newspaper. The user can seek out infor-mation very quickly, by clicking on links or using the search facility provided on the website. To some extent, this changes the way that illustration functions in this environment: the user is less susceptible to being enticed away from their purpose of reading a particular article since they already know what they are looking for. The publication might also be reluctant to encourage the user to wander, since the web itself is a vast assortment of different information that is available at the click of a mouse.

There is, however, still a need to break up large walls of type and elucidate on written content. In terms of the future, it seems that the possibilities inher-ent in the animated illustration are still far from fully realized and hold great promise for the modern illustrator.

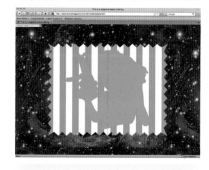

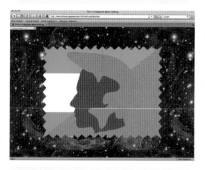

Left and above
Web animations by Andy Simionato. Digital, 2007. Commissioned by *This Is A Magazine* (www.thisisamagazine.com). The web is a multi-media environment that creates new possibilities for editorial content.

Example of a newspaper/ web-based commission

The example featured here is by the Dutch design collective Gorilla. Every day they produce a column illustration for *De Volkskrant*, a national daily newspaper produced in Holland (see www.thedailygorilla.nl for an archive of these columns). The strong, graphic style of Gorilla suits their aims in providing succinct and witty summaries of complex international news stories.

Pepijn Zurburg of the Gorilla collective explains their illustration process for this long-running project as follows:

'We respond to the day's news in words and images. This gives us a wonderful opportunity to ventilate our views on politics, the environment and all those subjects one worries about, but doesn't know how to relate to.'

Each image is created employing a journalistic approach:

'We can contact an editor for the news highlights and we make a visual reaction on one of those topics. We don't show them multiple ideas in sketch. As a "columnist" we have journalistic freedom. Of course we discuss various options among ourselves beforehand, but only one proposal is sent.'

Gorilla's work for *De Volkskrant* is only one aspect of their operations:

'Gorilla is not just a web-based editorial illustration collective. The website is part of the media mix. Gorilla is published in print magazines, online and in the public domain (posters, exhibitions, T-shirts, prints, etc.). Next to that we organize debates and happenings where our images are the starting point of many discussions.'

Screenshots from Gorilla's column for *De Volkskrant*.

Editorial illustration: summary of procedure

1

Initial research

Before making an approach to a newspaper, magazine or editorial website, make sure that you research the contents of the publication. Check if your work is suitable in terms of style, subject matter and content. If you arrive at an interview without this knowledge, the employees of the magazine (who will care a great deal about their publication) will presume that you are not serious about working for them.

2

Prospecting for work

Once you have carried out research around the publication you would like to work for, and have prepared a suitable portfolio, you need to make contact. Small publications generally have one art director or senior designer, whereas publications with larger circulations will have a separate art director for each section of the newspaper or magazine.

The art director will look at your work and decide whether they are interested in commissioning you. Make sure that you have publicity material to leave with them – a postcard on their pinboard will remind them of your skills (and may also be seen by other potential clients visiting the office).

Having had the meeting, don't expect to be called straight away – it may take six months or so for the meeting to bear fruit. If you have not heard after this period, and you left the meeting feeling optimistic about your chances, send fresh publicity material to the art director, reiterate your desire to work for the publication and state that you look forward to hearing from them in the near future. Overall, your tone must be upbeat.

3

Securing the commission

When commissioning an illustration, art directors will generally telephone to offer you the job. For this reason, it is important to invest in a mobile phone – because of editorial turnaround times, the art director can ill afford to wait for you to return their call and will readily offer the job to another illustrator.

The art director will describe the subject matter of the article (the actual article may not have been written yet), the time span of the job (including delivery points for rough sketches and final artwork), the physical size of the work (usually in millimetres) and the fee. If you accept the commission, this information will be sent to you via fax or email.

Before you agree to the job, think carefully; editorial turnaround times can be as little as a single day. If you take on the commission, and fail to deliver on deadline, the art director will not be inclined to offer you another commission. Conversely, a polite (and pragmatic) 'thank you, but no thank you' will keep you in the mind for future commissions with no harm done; your lack of availability may suggest that you are busy working on other commissions, which may even work to your advantage.

Once you have agreed to take on the commission, and have secured a purchase order number from the finance department of the publication, the brief will be delivered to you, either by fax or email. It is crucial that you take time to study it carefully, in order to understand the main thrust of the art director's brief. From this point, you will be able to start work. Highlight the main requirements of the brief to remind yourself as the job proceeds of the key elements that you need to bear in mind.

4

Starting work

Generally speaking, a pencil and paper are the best tools to start generating ideas – they facilitate the flow of thought from mind to paper with the minimum amount of interference. As you sketch, you will start to see connections between one idea and another (see Chapter 1). Often it is by combining seemingly separate ideas that something unusual and visually distinctive begins to materialize.

You may also need to carry out specific research for certain elements within your illustration – for example, a type of person, an object or a location. It is worth collecting and categorizing visual research material in your work area so it is at your disposal when required. The internet, too, is an invaluable research tool for the illustrator – by using an appropriate search engine, visual information can be accessed at great speed and with a fair amount of accuracy. Research can also take the form of a visit to your local high street, armed with pencil and paper and/or a digital camera to record the information you need.

5

Submitting the roughs

As you work through your ideas, an overall concept to communicate the thought will begin to materialize. For longer editorial jobs, you may be asked to come up with as many as three different ideas – a change of viewpoint, an increase or decrease in the number of different elements within the image, and so on. This can be a useful process, if only to help the art director come down firmly on one idea by presenting them with a choice of several.

Having drawn up the roughs, you will fax or email them through to the art director and wait for a response. Generally speaking, the corrections will be minor and will make good sense (remember, the art director will have a much bigger picture than you of how the different visual elements within the publication will relate to each other). The editor, too, will check that the illustration is appropriate for the publication and accurately reflects the contents of the journalism.

7

Securing payment

When agreeing to a commission, you will need a purchase order number and be told how long the gap will be between delivering the finished artwork and receiving payment. Once the final artwork has been accepted, submit your invoice, quoting your purchase order number and reiterating the period by which you expect to be paid. You will also need to provide proof to the commissioning newspaper, magazine or editorial website of your tax status.

6

Producing the final artwork

Having made the necessary changes, you are ready to proceed with the final artwork. Occasionally, you will be given some directions in colour use – for instance, if the newspaper uses boldly coloured headers to differentiate the sections within the publication, you may be asked to use a small amount of that colour to connect the image with the banner. Otherwise, you will know how to create an illustration that correlates closely with the work in your portfolio – the very reason for the art director commissioning you in the first place.

Conclusion

It remains to be seen whether printed editorial material will eventually disappear completely (circulation figures are now in steep decline) in favour of web-delivered editorial content. As yet, the problem of reading large amounts of text off small, handheld devices has yet to be solved, although surely at some point a solution will be found. Advertisers, too, who have no allegiance to any particular editorial medium (and who are deeply attracted to the mathematical accuracy of the web in showing them their hit rates), will, as always, follow their audience.

At present, research suggests that it is the lower social strata within society who are showing a strong move towards digitally delivered editorial content, whereas the higher social strata are showing a continued allegiance to print-based editorial coverage, mainly because they enjoy the increased breadth and depth of the discussion contained within the traditional newspaper and magazine publication. But the real key to the future of editorial lies in the hands of the younger generation – a generation that has thoroughly embraced the digital age.

5.

The publishing brief

'Digitization is here and books will never be the same again. Digitization frees books to reach new audiences in new ways. Books used to furnish a room... now they will furnish a virtual world.' Gail Rebuck, chief executive, Random House

As an object, the book has been at the epicentre of human culture for many thousands of years. Though the book was originally an object of rarity, when Johannes Gutenberg printed his first Bible in 1443 he started a revolution that would in due time make the book available to all. The book carries the printed word and image between its pages (also referred to as folios), and sits alongside oral and visual human cultural traditions as a conduit of human narrative and knowledge; for this reason, the readership of the book is immense, and it continues to be a commonplace object that we give, receive, retain and borrow.

This light, portable object, appearing both in hardback and softback format, usually carries an illustration, a photograph or a typographic design on the cover as its primary marketing point. It carries a myriad of diverse information, from the factual minutiae of the scientific world to the expansive theories of the great philosophers, from the bright and cheerful world of children's storybooks to the gritty and complex world of adult fiction. It serves as a crucial way for us attain specialist knowledge, to gain insight into the problems that we face in life as human beings, to understand our history, to understand ideas surrounding the meaning that we attribute to our lives, and, of course, to distract, entertain and amuse ourselves.

Below
'Great Loves' series. Art direction David Pearson and Jim Stoddart; illustrations by David Pearson and Victoria Sawdon. Penguin, 2007. This redesign of Penguin Book's 'Great Loves' series uses illustration to reflect the erotic content of the writing, as well as providing visual uniformity in the series as a whole.

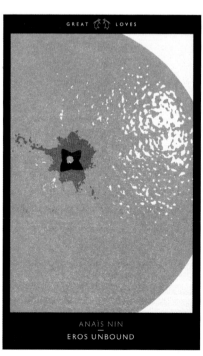

After many years of steady progress, the book has been through some radical changes of late. With the rise of the internet in the mid-1980s, Amazon, the online bookstore (launched in 1995), began to change the way that the public purchased books. Though economic progress was slow at first, by 2007 Amazon was selling over US$3.58 billion per annum in over 200 countries. They also encouraged their customers to post reviews of the books that they had purchased through the company – and word of mouth came to be recognized as a crucial factor in book selling.

Amazon's success was followed by influential television-based book clubs, particularly Oprah Winfrey in the US and Richard Madeley and Judy Finnigan in the UK. Their marketing power could be precisely measured by comparison between pre-programme and post-programme sales on Amazon. This shifted the marketing of books beyond the specialist hands of the publishers and bookstores and into the mass-audience-targeted world of daytime television.

The 1990s also saw the rise of the superstar author, a new breed of writer willing to publicly market their product and potentially make a fortune for themselves and their publisher in the process. The humble reader also gained in stature. Encouraged by the popularity of reader reviews on Amazon, the book blog became an important factor in selling books. These reader-generated sites presently have more power in shifting units of books than the once-revered review sections of the national broadsheets. In one case, the book editor of a respected US daily newspaper, the *Atlanta Journal-Constitution*, was let go in favour of book reviews from 'the common reader'. Though in some ways a laudable democratization of book criticism, this phenomenon could be detrimental to the literary world, particularly if specialist opinions on literature are allowed to disappear from the writing debate completely.

Another powerful influence within the contemporary book publishing landscape is the supermarket. These large stores have expanded their product ranges beyond foodstuffs and household goods into lifestyle commodities, and they are at present responsible for ten per cent of the book-selling market. They are known to have a direct influence over the title and cover design of new publications; if a book is not attuned to the tastes of the target audience of a supermarket, that store may demand it be changed or they will not stock it. Presumably, if the publisher chooses not to change the title and/or cover design, and the supermarket therefore does not stock the book, the outcome will be that the sales figures will suffer.

Innovation is now upon us again, in the shape of the Kindle, the first digital book to be widely accepted by readers, publishers and agents alike. This is a paperback-sized, portable, wireless object that can connect to Amazon-based Whispernet and download digital files that it displays as the pages of a book. So far, there are over 500,000 titles available. Google, too, has entered the digital book market, offering a rival downloadable, paying digital bookstore, based on the iTunes model. After the book world launched a sizeable lawsuit against them, Google started thrashing out an agreement with publishers and authors, whereby both out-of-print and in-print books could be downloaded

Above
The Kindle is a new digital hardware device that facilitates the reader in downloading e-books from a web-delivered database.

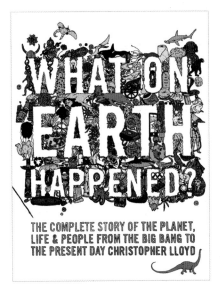

Above
What on Earth Happened, written by Christopher Lloyd; illustration by Andy Forshaw. Bloomsbury Publishing, 2008. This cover design blends type and image to create an attractive jacket that communicates the book's scientific and historical contents.

by the global populace at a price to be shared between the different book-generating factions. What is also significant about this development is that writing will be downloadable chapter by chapter, as well as book by book. In effect, this will fragment the single unit of the book into smaller units (especially in the case of non-fiction), and may challenge our perception of the book as the established format for writing, in the same way that the need for musicians to produce albums rather than songs has been called into question by iTunes.

Illustration and the evolution of the book

Since the origins of the book in antiquity, serving a need to preserve, store and promote information from a particular culture, two main elements have been employed in its making: the implement (for instance a pen and ink) by which language and image are created, and the base material (for instance paper) that carries that language and/or image.

It was the Ancient Egyptians who first developed a base material for writing called papyrus in around 2400 BCE. This they created by extracting the marrow from plants before humidifying, pressing, drying, gluing and cutting it. The Egyptians used sharpened reeds and/or bird feathers for writing on the papyrus with a form of script that differed from hieroglyphs and is now referred to as hieratic or sacerdotal. The sheet of papyrus contained columns of type and painted images (usually depicting key figures or gods) and was joined together with similar sheets of papyrus to form a scroll.

A typical papyrus scroll measured around 10 metres (33 feet), but could sometimes extend to 40 metres (131 feet) long. The scroll was attached to a pole (or axis) at either end, which the reader had to hold with each hand, and would roll out horizontally. This format for containing information was rather like a 1980s videotape; there was only a limited amount of navigability in locating an exact part of the text, with the added disadvantage that neither of the reader's hands were free for note-taking.

By the first century CE, the Ancient Greeks and Romans had adopted papyrus from the Egyptians. In Latin, the word for papyrus is *volumen*; this refers to a circular movement, a roll or a revolution. The Romans also referred to a collection of scrolls as a codex. The Greek and Roman civilizations saw the cultural status of the book grow. Authors attained public reverence and posterity, while scribes gained financially. Books were written around existing models (or genres) with authors making their own minor changes. The Greeks and Romans also paid attention to the conservation of books and to the art of literary criticism. Slowly, book production, which had developed in Rome in the first century CE, spread throughout the Roman Empire.

By the end of antiquity (between the second and fourth century CE), the idea of the codex had shifted away from a collection of papyrus scrolls and had come to represent a collection of sheets that were attached at the back (we now call this the spine of the book). The codex had distinct advantages over the scroll: it was much easier to access specific sections of the text and, helped by the clear separation of words, images, capital letters and punctuation, it could be read easily with one hand left free for note-taking. Contents tables and indices also facilitated easy and direct access to information.

As the new book (or codex) spread across Europe, it was monasteries that contributed most to its development, both in terms of design and illustration. The activity of book-making took place within a scriptorium, a room in the monastery where books were copied, decorated (a form of painted imagery called illumination) and bound. This process – the preparation of manuscripts in note form, the design and illustration of pages, copying, revision, the correction of errors, decoration and binding – is essentially the same model used by contemporary publishers in the division of labour when producing books.

By the twelfth century, universities (and university towns) had moved the book outside of monasteries, with professors using reference manuscripts for teaching theology and the liberal arts to their students. This was also the era when the book began to grow exponentially as an economic force – expanding, literate bourgeoisie initiated a demand for both specialized and general texts. The scriptoria, once the exclusive domain of the monastery, became secular, commercial ventures, and the profession of the bookseller was born.

In 1443 Johannes Gutenberg sealed the future of the book by coupling his movable type with new paper-making technology, originating in China in the first century, and spreading to Europe via Arabic traders in the thirteenth century. This joined with the rapid technological developments within the production of newspapers and magazines as mentioned in Chapter 4 (indeed, many books were serialized in newspapers and magazines first). The printed image, flourishing alongside text in the eighteenth and nineteenth centuries, also became a recognizable element within most published books; in particular, this was driven by the various religious factions publishing the Bible, who demanded mass production and distribution of their product at low unit cost. By the beginning of the twentieth century, the book jacket, too, began to rise in prominence. Originally serving merely to protect the hardcover, it slowly began to form a permanent and separate feature, culminating in the modern paperback, which carries both type and full-colour imagery on its cover.

Above
The Gutenberg Bible. Ink on vellum, 1455–56. Johannes Gutenberg's two-column Bible, printed with movable letters alongside the hand-painted initials and marginalia, was an innovation that would change the world.

Illustrating for the modern publishing brief

The main function of contemporary illustration for the book cover is to stimulate sales. It must achieve this by connecting with its potential audience, implying that this particular book, among all the others, is for them. John Hamilton, art director at Penguin Books in London, suggests that contemporary illustration for the book cover has to work in the following ways:

- The cover illustration has to attract and intrigue its potential audience, connecting with their interests and implying that the book is for them – this in turn relates to such factors as their age, values and tastes.
- The cover illustration, although it does not necessarily have to specifically convey the contents of the book, should imply an understanding of that content.
- The cover illustration has to make the book stand out against the competition, and has two 'sales lives', one face-up and one spine-out.
- The cover illustration has to imply the general category (or genre) of the book, defining where it sits within the bookshop.

Though searching for a book to purchase on the internet is a fairly specific activity, the modern bookshop categorizes books under general headings; these allow us to browse, as well as enabling us to locate specific texts. This in turn creates genres in which the contemporary illustrator can focus their talents. The books themselves are generally divided first by floor, and second under the general headings listed below.

Below

Relish, written by Joanna Weinberg; art direction and illustration by Will Webb. Bloomsbury Publishing, 2007. This cover wittily reveals the contents of the book, thereby connecting with its (potentially) hungry reader.

Bottom

Un Secreto Del Bosque, written by Jaier Sobrino; illustration by Elena Odriozola. OQO Editora, 2008. This children's book fuses type and image in a clear yet compelling way for its young readership.

the art of unpretentious entertaining joanna weinberg

Squirrel went to the river.
She heard a noise and saw Bear
scratching himself againts a chestnut tree.

- Squirrel, I´ve heard about your problem.
  When you think about him...
  your stomach goes as hard as stone,
  doesn´t it?
  That happened to me.
  I´ll give you
  some beary advice:
  tell him and offer him
  honey for tea.

- What?
  What an extravagant idea!
  - exclaimed Squirrel.

5. Components of the modern book market

- **Animals** (dominated by photography)
- **Art and design** (dominated by stock imagery)
- **Audio books** (reproduction of book cover)
- **Business** (dominated by typography)
- **Children's books** (dominated by illustration)
- **Classics** (illustration, photography and stock imagery)
- **Computing** (dominated by typography)
- **Cookery** (illustration and photography)
- **Crafts and collectables** (dominated by photography)
- **Crime** (illustration and photography)
- **Diet** (illustration and photography)
- **Drama** (illustration and photography)
- **Education** (dominated by photography and typography)
- **Erotica** (photography and illustration)
- **Fiction** (illustration and photography)
- **Games** (imagery based on visual language of game)
- **Gardening** (dominated by photography)
- **Graphic novels** (dominated by illustration)
- **Health and medicine** (illustration and photography)
- **History** (dominated by stock imagery)
- **Homes** (dominated by photography)
- **Horror** (illustration and photography)
- **Humour** (illustration and photography)
- **Maths** (dominated by typography)
- **Media** (dominated by photography and typography)
- **Mind/Body/Spirit** (illustration and photography)
- **Music** (dominated by stock imagery)
- **Parenting** (illustration and photography)
- **Philosophy** (dominated by typography)
- **Poetry** (illustration, photography and stock imagery)
- **Psychology** (dominated by typography)
- **Reference** (dominated by stock imagery)
- **Religion** (dominated by stock imagery)
- **Romance** (dominated by illustration)
- **Science** (illustration and photography)
- **Science fiction** (dominated by illustration)
- **Social sciences** (dominated by photography and typography)
- **Sport** (dominated by photography, with some illustration)
- **Teenage fiction** (dominated by illustration)
- **Transport** (dominated by photography)
- **Travel** (dominated by photography)
- **True crime** (dominated by stock imagery)

Mary Shelley
Frankenstein

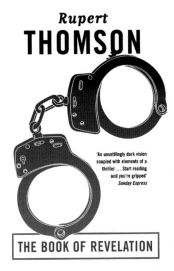

Top
Frankenstein, written by Mary Shelley; art direction by Clare Skeats; illustration by Kazuko Nomoto. Ulpius-Ház, 2007. This is an example of a classic text that is reissued by publishing houses every few years to connect with a fresh audience.

Above
The Book of Revelation, written by Rupert Thomson; art direction and illustration by Will Webb. Bloomsbury Publishing, 2006. Putting handcuffs on the cover of this novel immediately communicates the subject – a man's abduction and forced captivity.

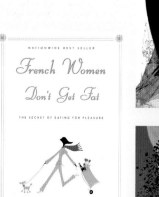

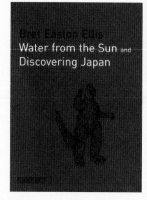

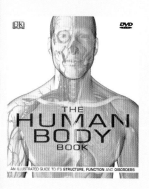

Left column

French Women Don't Get Fat: The Secret Of Eating For Pleasure, written by Mireille Guiliano; illustration by R. Nichols. Alfred A. Knopf, 2005. Dieting regimes and slimming tips have become a major commercial genre within publishing.

Water from the Sun and *Discovering Japan*, written by Bret Easton Ellis; illustrated by Roderick Mills; designed by Emma Grey and Richard Evans. Picador, Pan Macmillan Ltd, 2006. Fiction writer Bret Easton Ellis has had novels and collections of short stories (as in this case) published that predominantly centre around life in Los Angeles.

Centre column

That Face, written by Polly Stenham; design by Feast Creative; illustration by Russell Mills. Faber and Faber, 2008. A young face looking directly at the viewer not only suggests the youthfulness of the playwright but also the potency of the drama within.

Pigeons From Hell #1, written by Joe R. Lansdale; artist Nathan Fox; colorist Dave Stewart. Dark Horse Comics, 2008. The graphic novel is now firmly established as an international commercial entity.

The Eyes of the Dragon, written by Stephen King; designed by Jamie Keenan. Hodder Paperbacks, 2008. A major author's name will dominate any cover of their published work.

Right column

Candy, written by Terry Southern and Mason Hoffenberg; art direction and illustration by Will Webb. Bloomsbury Publishing, 2000. This cover, for a book that fits into the Erotica genre, implies a fairly innocent sexual journey.

The Rime of the Ancient Mariner, written by Samuel Taylor Coleridge; illustrated by Jimmy Turrell; editors/art directors Helen Osborne and Darrel Rees at Heart; design director Angus Hyland; designers Masumi Briozzo and Kyle Wheeler. Heart, 2008. The horror inherent in this classic poem is amplified by the powerful use of illustration on its cover.

The Human Body Book, written by Steve Parker; illustration by Medi-mation. Dorling Kindersley, 2007. Medical illustration uses a figurative visual language that can be much more benign than its photographic equivalent.

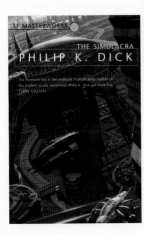

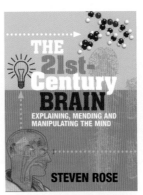

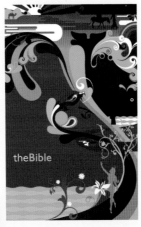

Left column

My French Whore, written by Gene Wilder; art direction and illustration by Will Webb. Old Street Publishing, 2007. The harsh title of this book is juxtaposed with an illustration and additional text that reveals to the reader that it is a romance.

Crayon Shinchan, written and illustrated by Yoshito Usui. DC Comics, 2000. Humorous narratives, such as this manga and anime, have traditionally been told using a sequential narrative structure.

The Simulacra, written by Philip K. Dick; illustration by Chris Moore. Gollancz, 2004. This cover implies the classic sci-fi vintage of a book that explores a matriarchal society of the near future.

Centre column

Baseball: The Players, The World Series, The Records, written by Ron Martirano; concept and design by John Whalen. Cider Mill Press, 2008. This witty and graphic cover instantly connects with a huge sporting fanbase.

Faerie Heart, written by Livi Michael; illustration by Rob Ryan. Puffin, 2009. This paper-cut illustration connects with a teenage readership that has not been blighted by cynicism.

Right column

The 21st-Century Brain: Explaining, Mending and Manipulating the Mind, written by Steven Rose. Jonathan Cape, 2006. This intriguing mixed-media image, collaging elements from different sources, successfully takes this book beyond the realms of the dry and dusty school textbook.

The Bible – Summer Edition, art direction by Mark Read; illustration by Steve Wilson. Hodder and Stoughton, 2009. This colourful cover attracts the reader and even surprises with its reinvention of the classic religious text.

The Idle Parent, written by Tom Hodgkinson; illustration by Nathan Burton. Hamish Hamilton, 2009. This cover reflects a humorous take on parenting.

The creative roles within a publishing house

Publishing director
This person has ultimate responsibility for the purchasing of manuscripts that the publishing house wishes to shape and merchandise as books. To this end, they co-ordinate a team of commissioning editors.

Commissioning editor
This person works closely with agents and authors in the acquisition and shaping of new written material.

Editor
This person works closely with the author and picture researcher in shaping the content of a particular book.

Sales director
This person has overall responsibility for the sales strategy of the publishing house including managing relationships with key sales accounts.

Marketing director
This person develops the pre-sale marketing campaigns for every book and co-ordinates their implementation across a broad range of media, as well as

Progression of a typical commission for adult fiction

Start

1
At an acquisitions meeting, the core team discusses potential purchases from agents/authors, citing possible marketing strategies, the literary genre of the book and potential target audience.

2
At a bi-monthly cover committee meeting (attended by the art director, picture editor, publishing director, commissioning editor, sales director and marketing director), a group of purchased books will have synopses outlined and potential cover approaches discussed. They may be prioritized if they are a publishing highlight (a publication by an established, commercially viable author), and will take precedent over less commercially valuable publications.

3
Led by the art director, the art department team discusses the visual direction of a particular cover, be it illustrative, photographic or typographic. The book might also be part of a series or connect to the brand identity of an established author. If a new author has written the book, the cover will demarcate their entry point into the market with something special. If the work is non-fiction (for example, a business or philosophy title), the cover may contain an image or be purely typographic.

4
The art director, book designer and picture editor source visual samples for the cover, spine and back, which they present to the cover committee. They may propose using an illustrator with previous experience of working with the publishing house.

ensuring the continued market presence of the title through point-of sale and post-publication promotions.

Art director

This person is responsible for connecting the book with its potential audience and communicating its emotional promise, co-ordinating all visual information contained on its front, back, spine and inside folios. The art director works closely with the marketing department and co-ordinates a team of book designers and picture researchers who work on a number of publications.

Book designer

This person is responsible for the overall design of a particular book, working on all typographic elements and, where necessary, locating an image (or images) within the design.

Picture editor (or picture researcher)

Working with the art director and book designer, this person is responsible for the sourcing of images for both the outside and inside of a book. Their role is a creative one, and they also think laterally in sourcing potential imagery for a book cover. They will have an extensive knowledge of online commercial collections, museum and gallery collections and modern practice within the fine and applied arts. They will have considerable experience in terms of licensing agreements and charges for the use and reproduction of images.

5

Once the cover committee has agreed on the illustrator, they will be sent a contract (which will normally contain a 50 per cent cancellation fee), or, if the book has not yet been completed, they will be given a verbal or written briefing. At this stage the illustrator will secure a purchase order for the commission from the finance department of the publishing house.

6

The illustrator develops roughs and presents them to the art director and book designer for approval. The author rarely has any control over the design of the cover, though may be asked for their comments.

7

The illustrator acts on the amendments requested by the art director and presents the final artwork at correct size and resolution.

8

The art director approves the final artwork and requests payment. The size of the illustrator's fee will depend on whether the publisher has negotiated usage rights for national or international regions of the world. The fee will also relate to the usage of the image on advertising outlets including websites, posters and promotional leaflets.

Finish

Example of a commission for adult fiction

The example featured here is for a series of classic horror stories (the Gothic horror series of Red Classics) that Penguin Books reissued in 2008. Coralie Bickford-Smith, a senior designer at Penguin, created the covers herself, working with both image and type. Coralie started by searching for an overall feel for the covers.

'The aim was to create a look that worked for the genre, but that didn't fall into some of its more over-used conventions, such as lurid type and lots of red and black. I opted for the striking yellow and blue combination, and a restrained type treatment that didn't compete for attention with the graphic elements.

'I went through lots of different stages with the covers. I tried some woodcuts, I tried some type, then I hit on cyanotypes (a light blue, translucent paper) which I felt had a really spooky, ghostly quality. Once I'd hit on that, I started experimenting and playing. Then I brought in the yellow. I was trying to make it really striking and modern, so that when the books sat on a table in a bookshop they would really sing out and people would know it was a series.

'One of the inspirations that led me in this direction was Romek Marber's iconic Penguin crime series. His photograms combine graphic simplicity with a fantastic atmospheric quality, so using an earlier photographic process contemporary with some of the titles in the series was a really attractive prospect.'

Right
The Haunted Dolls' House by M.R. James
Coralie Bickford-Smith: *'This was the first one I really nailed; I was really chuffed. It conveys the whole idea of the sense of scale, this big man who collects dolls' houses looking in through the window. The book is like the window… it's his big eyeball looking in… wide-eyed horror.'*

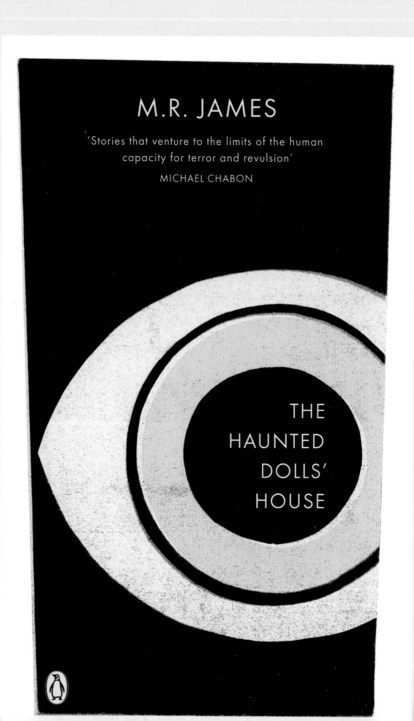

Above

The Spook House by Ambrose Bierce
Coralie Bickford-Smith: *'This was the first Saturday that I was really experimenting and the sun was really bright in the kitchen and I just put down two pieces of paper… I put two kitchen knives on and I really loved that cut. The Spook House is a good example of the benefits of the hands-on process. I wanted to try using knives to create an image, and the size of blueprint paper I had meant that I needed two sheets. I originally intended to join the two halves seamlessly in Photoshop, but I discovered that the bisected image was much stronger.'*

Right

The House On The Borderland by William Hope Hodgson
Coralie Bickford-Smith: *'My partner had made me a Valentine's card with the cyanotype and it had been sitting up there for ages. I found some off-cuts lying around in his study and that's what I scanned in to start making Borderland.'*

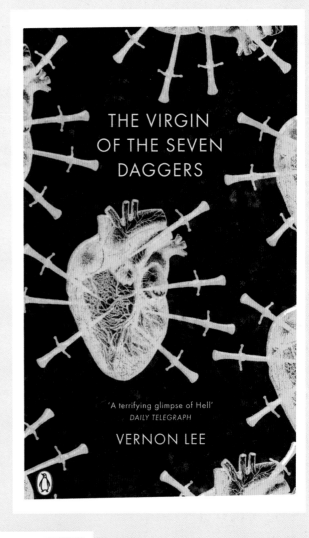

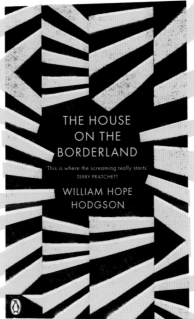

Above

The Virgin Of The Seven Daggers by Vernon Lee
Coralie Bickford-Smith: *'This was the last one I did in the series. I decided to use hearts, because it was all blood and lust. I looked at some anatomical hearts and I decided to do a collage and then photocopy it on to acetate. Then I put the acetate on to the cyanotype and it moved it to another level – it gave it some real depth with all the blues coming out. Using a more tonally complex image was really visually satisfying. The image references both the Madonna of the title, and the many hearts broken and the murders committed by the protagonist of the story.'*

Illustrating for the modern children's book brief

The children's book market is a dynamic forum that offers the illustrator work and recognition beyond the more ephemeral marketplace of editorial illustration. The children's book, often a large and attractive object, helps children to learn about language and life, contains visual jokes (e.g., connected to facial expression) and portrays key aspects of a child's emotional life. The illustrations in such a book serve to amplify words (as well as resonating with a child, they may also resonate with an adult reader) and to articulate aspects of life that cannot be communicated with words. The story functions in dealing with a child's anxieties within a safe environment (i.e., in the company of an adult) and teaches life skills and aspects of what it means to be human – in particular, a good children's book contains a recognition of what is the truth.

Though there are no hard and fast rules regarding illustrating for children's books, Guy Parker-Rees (illustrator of *Giraffes Can't Dance*) suggests particular consideration should be given to the following:

Above
Jorda rundt på 29 bokstaver ('Around the world in 29 letters'), written and illustrated by Kristin Roskifte. Magikon, 2007. The reader follows characters Alf and Beate on a vacation, in the process learning about the construction of language.

Left
Le Jacquot de Monsieur Hulot ('Mr Hulot's Parrot'), written and illustrated by David Merveille, after Jacques Tati. Éditions du Rouergue, 2006. Quirky subject matter and strong characters work well within the childrens' book genre.

Below left
Dragones desconocidos y dragones famosos ('Unknown Dragons, Famous Dragons'), written and illustrated by Istvansch. Ediciones del Plan de Lectura, Argentine Ministry of Education, 2009. This eye-catching book was given away free in Argentina to support the national reading programme for children.

Below right
'An Endangered Species', written and illustrated by Harriet Russell, from *Sorry, Out of Gas* exhibition catalogue. Canadian Centre for Architecture, 2007. Non-fiction projects provide an alternative focus for illustrators of children's books – these engaging illustrations explaining how oil is produced are from the children's component of an exhibition catalogue.

- A good children's book is reliant on a good story – though some illustrators do write and illustrate their own books, the majority of illustrators work with established children's authors.
- A story needs a strong and compelling central character (or characters) – in general, the cover will contain a dynamic depiction of the main character.
- Be aware of the age group that you are illustrating for – the book must be suitable for them, and must be an appropriate size to fit into the bookstore shelving unit for that age group.
- In general, there is no nudity (especially for more conservative markets).
- Attention should be paid to the book's flow (for picture books, the format is usually 32 pages) – scale change, composition, zooming in and out in a cinematic way and generating visual interest (and using the act of the reader turning the page) all help to create a dynamic reading experience.
- In general, the main character must be prominent and easily recognizable within each composition and should look out towards the reader.
- Animals are popular as characters because their use avoids issues around the depiction of specific people types. They are also powerful symbols that children can easily relate to (for example, a fox might represent slyness).
- As well as providing visualization of characters and backgrounds that exist within the story, illustrators can also add extra characters and sub-plots that can unravel visually over the course of the story.
- In general, the visual focus is primarily on the main characters, and including visually complex backgrounds may conflict with them.
- Carefully consider point of view – for instance, if we see the story through the eyes of a young child, then it may be appropriate to depict the action from a height that they would see the world from. Consistency within point of view should also be maintained; generally speaking, we see the story unfold through the eyes of the central character.

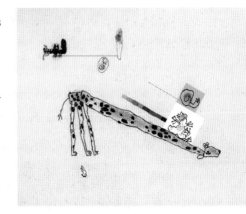

Above
Look, Look, Like This, written by Kambiz Kakvand; illustrated by Morteza Zahedi. Shabaviz, 2003. This book, which tells the story of a frog learning to eat, introduces children to important aspects of their daily routine in a creative manner.

Below
Het Circus van Dottore Fausto ('The Circus of Dottore Fausto'), written by Pieter van Oudheusden; illustrated by Isabelle Vandenabeele. De Eenhoorn, 2010. The circus world creates a richly entertaining storytelling environment for the young reader.

The creative roles within children's book publishing

Publishing director

This person has ultimate responsibility for the purchasing of content (often including illustrations as well as text). To this end, they co-ordinate a team of commissioning editors.

Commissioning editor

This person works closely with agents, authors and illustrators in the acquisition and shaping of new written material.

Author

This person writes the story, which is usually aimed at a specific section within the children's book market. The author will initially work closely with the book's editor, and will then be involved in discussions with the book designer and illustrator as the story moves through the design process from the roughs to the final layouts.

Editor

This person works closely with the author and illustrator in shaping the content of a particular book.

Progression of a typical commission for children's fiction

Start

1

A writer will send a text to the editor. When the editor considers it ready, they will set up a package for presentation at an acquisition meeting. Assuming that the writer is not the illustrator, the package will contain the complete text and could also include some character sketches and examples of the work of potential illustrators.

2

At an acquisitions meeting, the senior publishing team will decide which text to take on board as a future publication and which illustrator to commission.

3

The illustrator is approached by the art director about the project, and if agreeable, is sent an offer of contract. This is normally staged – a sum on signature as an advance on royalties (usually about five per cent for the illustrator), a sum on delivery of roughs, and a sum on delivery of final artwork. The book's format and size will also be stipulated in the contract – generally speaking, a children's picture book contains 32 pages (16 double-page spreads). This usually means 12 or 13 spreads for the actual story, plus endpapers, title page, half-title page and so on. The finance department of the publishing house should provide a purchase order for the commission.

4

Once the illustrator has accepted the commission, a discussion takes place between the illustrator, the art director and book designer. They will talk about the size of the type on the page, the breakdown of words across the pages, possible typefaces for the text and also layout ideas for each of the double-page spreads.

Sales director

This person has overall responsibility for the sales strategy of the publishing house including managing relationships with key sales accounts.

Marketing director

This person develops pre-sale marketing campaigns for each book and co-ordinates their implementation across a broad range of media, as well as ensuring the continued market presence of titles through point-of-sale and post-publication promotions.

Art director

This person is responsible for connecting the book with its potential audience. The art director works closely with the illustrator to ensure the whole package of text and illustrations works together and fits in with the brand identity of the publisher. They may also work with commissioning editors to match authors with illustrators.

Book designer

This person is responsible for the page layout of a particular book, working closely with the author and illustrator to refine the visual appearance of the book but also ensuring its commerciality and its fitness for print production.

5

The illustrator produces thumbnails/sketches. At this point the work is very fluid and can be easily changed. Being open to other people's ideas is crucial at this stage – a good book designer can substantially improve the visual appeal of a book and the way that the illustrations communicate. The suggested layouts will also be shown to the editor and author for approval.

7

The illustrator submits the final artwork, either as a digital file or as a physical entity. These will be given final approval by the art director and the senior publishing team.

6

The illustrator produces black-and-white roughs, with the text in place. These are laid out on a large table, in order to check that the pages work compositionally together and that there is sufficient visual variety from page to page. At this stage details begin to be tied down and amendments are suggested. If the roughs are accepted, the illustrator will submit an invoice for this segment of their fee, quoting the purchase order number and their terms of payment.

8

The illustrator receives the proofs (test printouts) of the pages and checks for colour saturation and balance. The publisher will request any corrections from the printer before giving final approval. After this, they will submit their invoice for the last segment of their advance, quoting the purchase order number and their terms of payment.

Finish

Example of a children's fiction commission

The example featured here is for a children's book written and illustrated by Marc Boutavant. Marc lives and works in Paris, France, and created *Around The World With Mouk* (originally called *Le Tour du Monde de Mouk: à Vélo et en Gommettes!*) in 2008. Having previously worked with traditional paints and brushes at art school, Marc abandoned these tools in favour of Photoshop and a Wacom tablet, which he now uses exclusively.

Marc describes the content of the book as follows:

'Around The World With Mouk is about a little bear who travels the world (Finland, Greece, Libya, Burkina Faso, Madagascar, India, China, Australia, Japan, Peru and America), meeting friends and friends-to-be, encountering new worlds and seeing the details in these new worlds.

These travels take place with the easiness of meeting, of encounters, an easiness that comes from [the act of] welcoming. The book is also about a bear (Mouk) deciphering a lot of things belonging to our world, but things that we have lost track of, and it's also a travel story that celebrates "welcoming".'

Marc describes his working process as follows:

'I work directly, by making forms until they please me, and then I get more and more precise.'

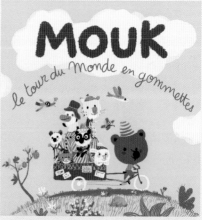

Alternative cover for *Le Tour du Monde de Mouk*.

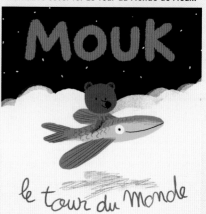

Alternative cover for *Le Tour du Monde de Mouk*.

Final cover for *Le Tour du Monde de Mouk*.

Work in progress on *Le Tour du Monde de Mouk*.

Initial shapes are blocked in.

Further shapes and details are added.

Text and final details are included to complete the spread.

Illustrating for the modern graphic novel brief

The graphic novel has risen to prominence over the last 25 years. Distinct areas within bookshops are now dedicated to this genre, which, although existing as a separate entity in its own right, has connections with the novel, the film, the comic and the cartoon. Graphic novels tell stories in pictures and words; the apparent simplicity of this formula has culminated in stories that have taken the reader into some very challenging situations (including concentration camps and war zones), with characters that we follow as they manoeuvre their way through obstacle after obstacle.

Whether you are both illustrating and writing a graphic novel yourself, or working on the images in conjunction with a writer, in general they are pitched to potential publishers as a fait accompli – that is to say, a graphic novel is written and drawn (and possibly even designed) before the illustrator/writer seeks out a publisher. This enterprise involves a huge risk in terms of the investment of your time and effort, with no guarantee of success, and it is best to view any involvement in this medium primarily as the pursuit of art, not money.

Below and opposite
Raj Comics For The Hard Headed, written and illustrated by Amitabh Kumar. Sarai, 2008. Originally published in Hindi, this graphic novel is unusual for the genre as it fuses drawing with photography.

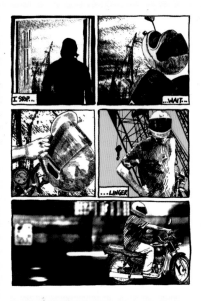

AS I MOVE ON, THE SENSE OF THE, **FAMILIAR STRANGENESS** BEGINS TO DEEPEN.

I TRY TO LOOK FOR CLUES TO THE SHIFT.

A PROOF.

A HINT.

Example of a graphic novel commission

The example featured here is *Fluffy* by illustrator and author Simone Lia. Simone first published *Fluffy* in four instalments, selling them in sole-trader bookstores. After successfully self-publishing these four editions, and achieving good responses from readers and salespeople alike, Simone approached the publisher Jonathan Cape for the book to be published in the mainstream. After a lengthy wait, and a letter to the publisher that coincided with several fortuitous events, Jonathan Cape agreed to publish. They offered Simone an up-front fee and further royalties on publication. After a period of negotiation, in which the publisher improved their offer, *Fluffy* was published in 2007.

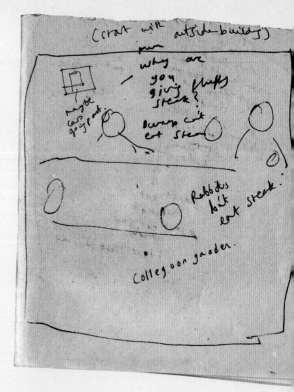

A dummy book chapter.

'My initial ideas for Fluffy *as a graphic novel were based on a drawing I did for my first comic –* First *with Tom Gauld. I drew a bunny in a dentist's waiting room – I quite liked the picture, and afterwards I started wondering about that bunny's character, who it was and who its "Daddy" might be and what their relationship could be. I developed the characters in strips for different publications, and when I had an opportunity to create a more substantial plot I knew the characters quite well. The bunny, Fluffy, is quite vulnerable and tiny and unable to accept that it's a bunny, and the father, Michael Pulcino, is a man who doesn't quite know how to deal with a bunny who can't accept that it's a bunny.*

Character sketches.

'I had an idea for a big story, but in my mind it was very vague. I knew that I wanted Michael and Fluffy to go on a long overland journey, and I had some ideas of characters – a slightly overbearing mother, an emotionally demanding nursery-school teacher and something to do with the mafia. It was so vague that I didn't plot it out too thoroughly, creating the story as I went along in a way that I would not recommend! I worked out roughs a chapter at a time and my roughs were very, very rough. The book was first published chapter by chapter, which was great because I got a lot of feedback from readers as I was writing, which was very helpful and encouraging.

'The main thing that I was interested in were the relationships between the characters and the whole being authentic, rather than a plot itself. I really enjoyed drawing the background scenery. For reference I made the overland journey to Sicily, and also took lots of pictures in my Grandpa's house in Malta as inspiration for the family's house in Sicily.'

After publication, Simone gave promotional talks on *Fluffy* at various literary festivals in the UK, where she found she could sell a good quantity of her books and also made valuable contacts with other writers of graphic novels.

Outside location sketch.

Cover of the Jonathan Cape edition of *Fluffy*.

A finished page.

Fluffy and Daddy at the dentist.

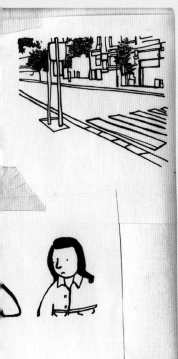

A panel from chapter 2.

Publishing illustration: summary of procedure

2
Prospecting for work

Find out who to make an initial approach to – usually you can find contact details for art directors on the publisher's website. This will normally include a CV and a cover letter, expressing your interest in working for the publisher and requesting a chance to show them your portfolio. You should also include some physical samples of your work – when tackling this, use your imagination and make something interesting, employing a creative approach to encourage people to look at your work. For example, an arresting image on your envelope may help your work stand out from the other stack of mail that the publisher no doubt receives on a daily basis.

The more that you can show of book-related projects the better – if you want to illustrate for children's books, you could even come up with an idea for a book yourself, and produce it as a one-off print run to promote your illustration skills. If the art director likes what they see, they will call you. At this point show willing – for instance, be prepared to do character sketches for a children's book to try to secure a commission. Sometimes large publishers have a portfolio drop-off system, a day when anyone can leave their illustration work to be considered for future projects by the publisher's design team. In this instance, make sure that you leave physical samples of your work for them to keep, complete with your contact details and your website address.

1
Initial research

If you are keen to work for publishers, the best way to start the research process is to visit a large bookshop, armed with pen and paper. Work out which age group and genre you are targeting, and find out which publishers formulate and merchandise those kind of books – make a note of their contact details and/or website addresses. Be realistic about your chances, carefully considering whether your illustration work is suitable for the work championed by that particular publisher.

3
Securing the commission

Once you have secured the commission, and received your offer of contract, with purchase order number and delivery deadlines for roughs and final artwork, you will be sent a copy of the book. If it is adult fiction, you will be invited to make interpretations of the text – it is unusual for you to be expected to read the whole text. You will be sent details of the exact size of the book and must bear in mind that in general an image for a book cover is in the 'portrait' format.

If your commission is for a children's book, for the roughs the art director might suggest the size of the type, a breakdown of the words over the double-page spreads of the book and possibly the typeface to be used and the general layout.

6

Producing the final artwork

Having responded to the discussion and made the requested amendments from the roughs stage, you will produce the final artwork, to the exact physical and technical specifications and on deadline.

5

Submitting the brief

For adult fiction, you will submit this work to the art director and design team. Be responsive to their comments and use the discussion to help you to produce the best artwork you possibly can to answer the brief. For a children's book, you will submit work to the art director and designer, who will also submit the work for approval to the editor and author – again, use their comments to improve the work.

4

Starting work

At this stage, the roughs will usually be pencil work, with the possible addition of some areas of colour. You will be working in a fluid, experimental way, exploring the brief and using your research to build in signifiers that point the reader to the contents of the book.

7

Securing payment

Quoting your purchase order number, you will submit your invoice, stipulating the time period by which the publisher must pay you.

Conclusion

As to the future of the book, we will have to wait and see. The book, as a physical object, has advanced technologically to a high level of production quality, while still retaining its affordability. As the world that we live in becomes ever faster, perhaps this object will offer people a sanctuary away from the bewildering array of choices that our digitized world provides.

On the other hand, perhaps the digital future of the book offers us new possibilities for it to become a multi-media experience that includes sound and moving image alongside the traditional format of the printed word and image. Ecological considerations, too, regarding industrial paper production and printing methods, are sure to dominate our thinking in the next few years.

But overall, the future of the book lies in the hands of the people responsible for its production – the publishers, and the people responsible for its purchase – the humble reader.

6.

L
T
E

The corporate identity and the advertising brief

'Painting is an end in itself. The poster is only a means to an end, a means of communication between the dealer and the public, something like a telegraph. The poster designer plays the part of a telegraph official; he does not initiate news; he merely dispenses it. No one asks him for his opinion, he is only required to bring about a clear, good and exact connection.'
A.M. Cassandre (a.k.a. Adolphe Jean-Marie Moreau), poster artist

Advertising, although it is complex in nature, works on a fairly straightforward premise: if we, the customers, purchase a particular product, then it will improve and enhance the quality of our lives. From this apparently simple 'interruptive' idea, inviting us to make a direct comparison between our product-less, unsatisfactory present and our brighter, product-owning future, a huge advertising industry has emerged through its symbiotic relationship with global enterprise.

This constructed graphic message (the advertisement) manifests itself in a myriad of creative formats, and is brought to mass audiences across the world in a combination of word and/or image via the channel of the poster, the pamphlet, the billboard, the shop front, the editorial advert, the film advert, the television advert, the website advert and the email advert. Since global commerce (the marketplace) has primarily allied itself with the advertising industry (as we have previously mentioned, this relationship originated shortly after the

Industrial Revolution), whether people are aware of it or not, every member of society is connected in some way to the creation and consumption of the commercial messages that companies pay advertising agencies to produce.

As well as representing the products that a particular company sells, advertising agencies (and graphic design companies) graphically represent the companies themselves. This is known as corporate identity work, and these word marks or image marks may also be accompanied by text and images in publications and outputs produced by that company. This area of creative design work also originates from the commercial successes of the Industrial Revolution, an era of mass mechanization that saw the birth of large manufacturing corporations that needed to represent themselves in a clear, coherent way. In essence, a corporate identity creates a recognizable image or interface that shows how a particular company wishes itself to be seen and remembered by its public. The final design for this kind of work is governed by various graphic and typographic rules (often included in a detailed design manual) that allow for the implementation of the new identity across all of the communication outputs that company personnel and advertising agencies produce concerning that particular company. This results in a consistent and disciplined application of the new identity.

Advertising and corporate identity work, although conjoined through their allegiance to commerce and industry (more often than not, they co-exist as elements within the same advert), differ in both strategy and execution. While the advertising of the products that a corporation makes can and will change with relative ease (and in many ways the general public expects them to do so), the role of a corporate identity is just that – a way for the public to identify and recognize a particular organization or body, in order to differentiate it from other, similar organizations. This process of identification is built up over many years, employing type and/or image. If changed too quickly or too radically, it has the potential to alienate a loyal client base and lose these clients to the market competitors.

For this reason, approaches to corporate identity work have remained fairly consistent over the years, while approaches to advertising have continued to change at a pace. From the 1990s onwards, a new term emerged in the communication design industry that in some ways saw the interweaving of advertising work and corporate identity work into one overall concept: branding. With its roots in the post-Second World War USA, branding represents a cohesive strategy in advertising, a strategy that seeks to create a synergy between a company, its corporate identity, its advertising outputs and its client base, thereby distancing itself from the specific products that it makes. The client base is now encouraged to emotionally identify with a particular company's brand (as opposed to forging an emotional connection to a particular product) and to view their relationship with that brand as an ongoing story. This in turn creates a network, a perceived community (music, too, has the ability to create large perceived communities), served by a brand that purports to represent the values and aspirations of that group. The brand,

however, is quick to emphasize that it is the audience who 'owns' the brand and not vice versa.

Digital advertising, now delivered with great economy to mass audiences via the internet, is also fast gaining in significance and influence; companies now spend considerably more money on commissioning digital adverts than they do on printed ones. Charges for these types of advert are partly based on hit rates (the number of people who have accessed the digital advert, a mathematically precise tally that is then reported to the client in detail by the provider of the media space). At present, this level of accuracy cannot be achieved in any other advertising outlet.

Advertising today can be categorized in three distinct forms:

- The *client-led* advert employs a low-risk strategy, operating in the client's belief that the general public needs to be served commercial messages in a relatively simple, straightforward way (i.e., they are not groundbreaking conceptually or visually, but still 'interruptive' as in 'stop, think again, maybe you need this?') that employs a recognizable format.

Below
Coca-Cola *Open Happiness* campaign in Dublin and Belfast, illustration by eBoy; art direction by Matt Whitby. Photoshop, 2008. Commissioned by Coca-Cola; advertising agency McCann Erickson Dublin; account manager Andrea Galligan. This poster shows the familiar style of the client-led advert, capturing the audience's eye with strong imagery that connects with the well-known product.

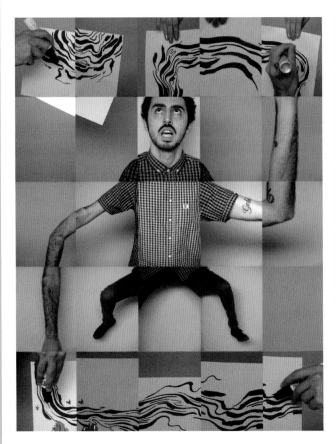

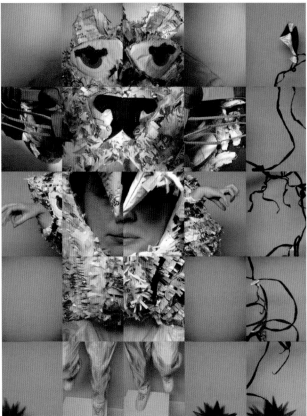

- The *creative school* advert employs a high-risk strategy that may potentially communicate to far fewer people (thereby selling less product) than a safer, client-led advert, but allows advertisers to search for new creative formats, and in the process potentially produce award-winning results (coincidentally, advertising has the highest number of industry awards of all the applied arts). These adverts are also 'interruptive' and are much closer to what the advertisers would ideally like advertising to be.

Above

The Replenishing Body, interactive video installation for Evian, illustrations by Shona Heath, Danny Sangra and Fred Butler; concept and interactive design Ross Phillips. Video installation, 2007. Commissioned by Evian. This interactive work consists of a 5 x 5 grid of squares that can each record a one-second film loop. Participants can create and orchestrate a giant composite moving creature or a collage of moving snapshots by recording a close-up section of a part of their body. The grid is empty at the start of the installation and becomes a constantly changing collaborative artwork.

Above and left
Giantkillers, directed by Intro. Commissioned by Nike; agency Wieden+Kennedy; production Intro. 2008. This animation shows how the viral advert can be roughly hewn and creatively risky, thereby encouraging the 'look at this, pass it on' phenomenon and in the process often gaining notoriety.

- The *viral* advert is a digitally delivered advert that is 'disruptive' rather than 'interruptive', relying on the 'I can't believe what I'm seeing!' shock value and originality of the advert to entice the viewer away from the high volume of other information that is available on the internet. These adverts rely on a word-of-mouth process, facilitated by the broadband capabilities of the internet, and they can achieve sizeable audiences. This type of advertising may gain further in influence, especially in communicating with a younger generation of technology-literate consumers.

Illustration and the evolution of advertising and corporate identity

Strategies and visual languages employed by advertisers to construct commercial messages have mutated and developed many times over the last 150 years. In its earliest and simplest form, during the latter half of the nineteenth century, an advertisement predominantly consisted of a small black-and-white image of a product (normally in the small-ads section of a newspaper or magazine) accompanied by the name of the manufacturer, claims about its unique properties and its price.

At the end of the nineteenth century, the advent of industrial lithography facilitated the colour reproduction of the printed image and a dramatic increase in its scale. This liberated advertising from purely editorial outlets and allowed it to blossom into the poster, a graphic advertising format that enjoyed an instantaneous and dominant street presence in cities and towns across the world. Paris, France, was a particularly noteworthy focus, serving up a plethora of rich, illustrative posters that advertised famous nightspots

and eateries within the capital, images that have since become as famous as
their creators.

Industrial lithography also facilitated a further development within the
'product and brand' archetype. A style of advert depicting a lush and colourful
graphic illustration of the product itself, simply endorsed by the name of the
company that made it, was termed *Sachplachat* ('the object poster'). This
simple and direct approach (very much alive today) gave way to more persua-
sive techniques, still using illustrative methods but employing symbolic and
metaphorical pictorial elements within the advert to suggest the positive and
unique properties of a particular product (such as a bull to advertise the fiery
taste of Coleman's mustard).

The early years of the twentieth century saw the language of advertising
harnessed with great effect by the now established commercial artist (often
responsible for both type and image). These early forerunners of the illustrator
went on to make a major contribution to the war effort, creating impressive
posters and pamphlets for the purposes of identification, information and
propaganda during the First World War.

The 1920s and 1930s were a rich period for illustration-led advertising.
This was a time when colour magazines emerged in the US (eventually
spreading across the Atlantic to Europe), allowing advertisers to communicate
with their audiences using imagery unprecedented in its lush appeal. This was
also a time when corporate identity work, driven by graphic design pioneers
in Europe and the US, achieved a high level of discipline and creativity and
became firmly established as a necessary and consistent aspect of the interface between a company and its customers.

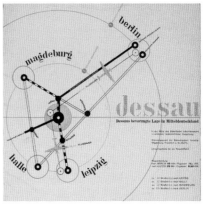

Above
Dessau, 1930 by Joost Schmidt. Letterpress print,
1930. This brochure for the city of Dessau shows
the influence of the Bauhaus school of art, notable
for its functional and rational modern approach
to design.

This period between the world wars also saw a 'purification' process in advertising, actively led by the Bauhaus art school in Germany, which sought to neutralize and objectify such material in its publicity department. Students and staff there employed clean typographic layouts (predominantly using sans serif typefaces) and incorporated the newly favoured visual medium of photography (illustration, in certain audience's minds, was connected with wartime propaganda, thus falling out of favour). Bauhaus-influenced work had a formal purity that delivered the interruptive message in a rational, clean and uncomplicated manner.

The Second World War saw the continued application of illustration in a time of war (it was often used in conjunction with photography), continuing to build on aspects of its employment as a powerful propaganda and communication tool in the First World War.

Above
Join the Royal Armoured Corps by Abram Games. Lithograph, 1941. Commissioned by the War Office. British graphic designer Abram Games was a master at transmitting war-related messages in a deceptively simple, dynamic and forceful way.

Left
Join the ATS by Abram Games. Lithograph, 1941. Commissioned by the War Office. During both world wars, the poster emerged as a powerful tool to promote civilian engagement in the war effort.

Below
Subway Posters Score by Paul Rand. Lithograph, 1947. Commissioned by New York City Subway. National corporations were great benefactors of postwar illustration and design.

The period after the Second World War seemed to deliver the people of developed nations a hard-won utopia that emerged from a bitter and dreadful conflict. Manufacturers, benefitting from the advances in technology that, ironically, the war had initiated, used illustration in their advertisements to offer well-designed, efficient appliances for the modern home. National corporations, too, such as rail companies, postal services and airlines, employed illustration to show people the bright new possibilities within their own lives, locating their product as part of a happy, fulfilled life – a life that was available to all. As well as commercial artists, many important fine artists worked within advertising during this period. Approaches to corporate design work continued to remain consistent, with the emergence of some corporate identities that allowed the image to dominate.

Design pioneers in the US drove advertising forwards in the latter half of twentieth century, exemplified by the 1950s advertising revolution that took place within the global communication design industry. Fuelled by the medium of television, the 'new American advertising' placed the art director's concept at centre stage. Now the visual vernacular was a movable feast, be it illustrative (ranging from a sketch to a fully rendered image), typographic or photographic in form. It was subjugated to the demands of the 'Unique Selling Point' (USP) of the product and flowed from the concept by which the public, again through a process of 'interruption', would be led towards a point of realization: that they needed the product in order to attain a happy, successful lifestyle, worthy of the envy of their fellow human beings. This approach to advertising functioned under the groundbreaking belief that an intelligent audience could and should interact with advertising; their reward would be the ability to decode the message of the advertisement, thus reaffirming their self-image as intelligent, affluent people worthy of owning the product itself.

This approach to advertising has dominated the work of agencies ever since. Where once illustrators enjoyed centre stage, even being invited to control the typography that accompanied their images, they now had to compete directly with photographers, as well as film directors, animators and typographers, for the attention of commissioning art directors.

There has been ebb and flow ever since. At times, the photographers have had the upper hand, since the medium of photography still has the power to represent 'truth' in the minds of an audience that no illustration is capable of doing and allows direct involvement from the art director. At other times, the illustrators have had the upper hand, delivering joyous and fantastical imagery during exuberant times, and delivering nostalgia-tinged memories of a romanticized past during times of hardship. In recent years, illustration has gained popularity within the advertising landscape once more because of its capacity to visualize our globalized world (a world where advertising must speak to everyone, everywhere); it can be used to represent characters and worlds that are not race-specific, location-specific, age-specific or gender-specific.

Top
UPS logo by Paul Rand. 1961. Commissioned by UPS. The corporate identity has become a well-established requirement for operating successfully within the national and international business sphere.

Above
Westinghouse logo by Paul Rand. 1960. Commissioned by Westinghouse. Rand used shape to great effect in communicating the identity of this company in an instantly recognizable and memorable way.

Illustrating for the modern advertising agency

There are two distinct types of advertising agency: 'above the line' and 'below the line'. This differentiation is connected directly with whether the agency purchases media space from specialist providers or whether the agency produces its own advertising material.

Above the line

These agencies originate advertising for the following channels:

- **Television** (film/video and animation)
- **Radio** (exclusively sound)
- **Newspapers** (photography and illustration)
- **Magazines** (photography and illustration)
- **Billboards** (photography and illustration)
- **Websites** (photography and illustration)
- **Corporate identity, literature, promotion**
  (typography, film, photography and illustration)

Below the line

These agencies originate advertising for the following channels:

- **Direct mail** (photography and illustration)
- **Promotional material such as leaflets or flyers**
  (photography and illustration)
- **Point-of-sale** (photography and illustration)
- **Shop displays** (photography and illustration)
- **Promotional events** (photography and illustration)

Above
Airmiles – Make Your Money ad campaign, illustrator and director Grant Orchard/Studio AKA. Agency Partners Andrews Aldridge; copywriter Dave Mance; art director Richard Worrow, 2009. Illustration is used in this TV advert to potentially communicate the client's message to everyone, everywhere.

Left
Toshiba multi-media ad campaign by McFaul Studio. Commissioned by Toshiba Corporation, 2007. This detailed illustration for a Japanese electronics company helps to create a three-dimensional environment within this website.

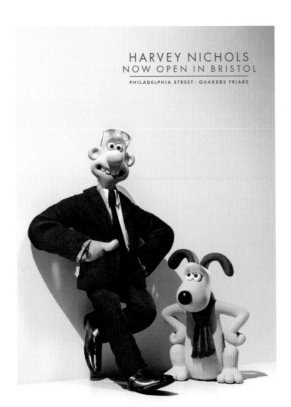

Above left

Harvey Nichols – Now Open In Bristol, illustration/model-making by Aardman. Commissioned by Harvey Nichols; agency DDB London; photography by Giles Revell, 2008. The two main characters from Nick Park and Aardman Animations' well-loved Wallace and Gromit animations were employed with great effect in this humorous and charming advert.

Above right

Selection of logos, design and illustration by McFaul Studio. These designs successfully combine illustration and type to communicate to a youth-oriented audience.

Far left

The Volkswagen Combi, art director Aurélie Scalabre; copywriter Patrice Dumas. Sixtieth anniversary print campaign for the Volkswagen Combi, 2008. The psychedelic visual language in this advert (which in turn had its influences in Art Nouveau) references the heyday of the VW camper van in the 1960s.

Left

Terrain: Stone, illustration by Claudia Schildt and Fabian Zell. Commissioned by Mercedes-Benz; creative directors Doerte Spengler-Ahrens (copy), Jan Rexhausen (art); advertising director Hisham Kharma, 2008. The choice of medium directly evokes the terrain capabilities of this off-road vehicle.

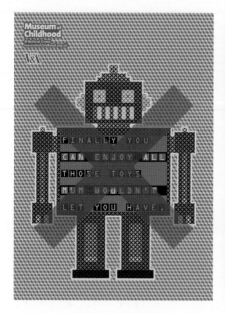

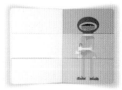

Above

Museum Of Childhood, art director Paul Pateman. Commissioned by the Museum Of Childhood (V&A); advertising agency Abbott Mead Vickers BBDO; executive creative director Paul Brazier; copywriter Mike Nicholson, 2008–09. The images in these posters cleverly visualize the idea that this museum is not just for children. The accompanying book encourages interactivity with a graphic 'take' on the traditional game of consequences.

Left

Greenbee Relaunch, illustrations by Andrew Bannecker. Commissioned by Greenbee (John Lewis Partnership); agency Partners Andrews Aldridge; copywriter Stephen Timms; art director Paul Walton, 2007. This direct-mail advert employs illustration to visualize a common accident in the home that would be covered by Greenbee's insurance product.

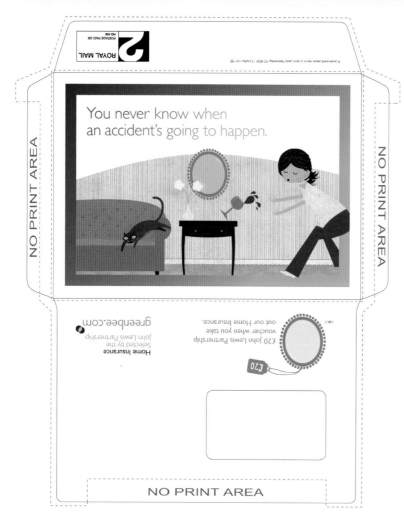

Left

In-store graphics for the Hugo Boss Orange Special Concept Store Shanghai, illustrations by Franz-Georg Stämmele. Silkscreen printing and rubber stamping, 2006. Commissioned by Hugo Boss; art direction Projekttriangle Design Studio. The in-store point-of-sale commission offers the illustrator the opportunity to work on a large scale to spectacular effect. Here, under the theme 'Good old Germany…', a six-metre-high (twenty-foot-high) fantasy tree was screenprinted. Wooden carvings and golden motifs decorate the changing rooms. A traditional rubber stamp set, consisting of ten life-size German songbirds and forest birds, has been used to cover walls and furniture by hand.

Centre

MyFaves Icon-Generator, illustration by Steffen Mackert. Commissioned by T-Mobile Deutschland GmBH, Bonn; design Mutabor Design GmBH, Hamburg; creative direction Axel Domke; graphic design Corinna Rödel; programming Patrick Decaix, Markus Lerner, Phi Mobile Media Services, 2008. Buyers could create personalized icons for their mobile phones using this point-of-sale software.

Below left

Zoot Allure window displays for Selfridges, illustration and design by Emily Forgot. Mixed media, 2009. Commissioned by Selfridges. The shop display commission offers the illustrator the chance to work on a large scale in three dimensions and to connect with a wide audience.

Below right

Stage graphics for 'Satanico' pop tour, illustrations by Jorge Alderete. Digital print on canvas, 2008. Commissioned by Los Fabulosos Cadillacs & Fa Sostenido. Illustrations for the stage are an important component of any live promotional event.

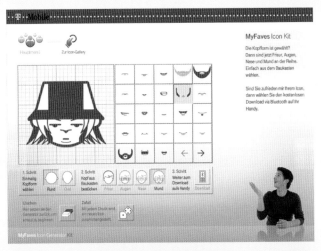

The creative roles within an advertising agency

The modern advertising agency has a mixture of creative personnel, who work in specifically designated areas.

Creative director

This person manages the work of the creative team (including approving the choice of an illustrator and the final artwork), ensuring that the advertising concept generated by the creative team tallies with the client's brief. In general, they are not available to view portfolios.

Creative team

This partnership usually consists of an art director and a copywriter – they generate ideas for adverts. The creative team is directly involved in choosing an illustrator and/or photographer to visualize their ideas. They are usually available to view portfolios.

Art buyers

These people assist the creative team in selecting a suitable illustrator for a particular job. The art buyers are also responsible for negotiating fees for commissioned work, overseeing production and viewing prospective portfolios. They are usually available to view portfolios.

Progression of a typical advertising commission

Start

1
The client (usually a company) approaches an agency with a view to commissioning a series of adverts.

2
An account handler (or 'planner') writes the brief with the client.

3
The account handler delivers the brief to the creative director and to the creative team.

4
The creative team, overseen by the creative director, produces a selection of ideas that are presented to the client. After dialogue, the client team (marketing strategists, company owners and so on) makes its choice.

5
The creative team/art buyers search for an illustrator (or photographer).

6
The 'book' (portfolio) of the suggested illustrator is submitted to the client for approval, including a quote for the commission from the illustrator. Particular attention must be paid to the formats in which the advert will be used.

7
Once the illustrator accepts the commission and secures a purchase order number, the creative director/creative team briefs the illustrator for the job.

Account handler

These people maintain close contact with the client and often present portfolios, estimates and final artwork. Their role is crucial in ensuring that any concerns voiced by the client are addressed during the life of a commission, that the client is properly represented throughout the job and that they are satisfied with the end result.

Traffic and production

These people are responsible for the correct technical production of the adverts, supplying them in a mixture of sizes and configurations (called 'adapts') specifically for editorial outlets, billboard hoardings and so on. Where an agency does not employ people in this area, the traffic and production people absorb the role of the art buyer.

8

A reproduction meeting is held.

9

The illustrator presents the roughs (also called 'pencils' or 'traces') to the agency for approval. Some minor adjustments may be requested.

11

The illustration work is incorporated into the graphic layout and supplied to magazines, newspapers and so on.

Finish

10

The agency presents the final artwork to the client for approval.

12

The illustrator submits an invoice for payment, quoting their purchase order number and terms of payment.

Example of an advertising commission

This example is a collaboration between London-based creative agency Neighbour, which specializes in art direction, design and brand identity advertising, and the artist Wilfrid Wood. The client, Levi's, asked Neighbour to devise a way to celebrate the tenth anniversary of Levi's Engineered Jeans.

Neighbour commissioned Wood 'to create three slightly twisted characters: Fingers, Hopper and Bernie. They each wear a different fit of Levi's Engineered Jeans "product", with the details sculpted and painted by Wilfrid.' Neighbour then designed an ATL communication platform to support the characters, which functioned in the same way as a collaborative art project, involving and showcasing 'twisted artists' on the blog site thetwistedoriginals.com.

The latest incarnation of the project is a photo shoot of the characters in the back streets of Las Vegas, directed by Neighbour in collaboration with photographer Leandro Farina.

Various characters sculpted in clay by Wood.

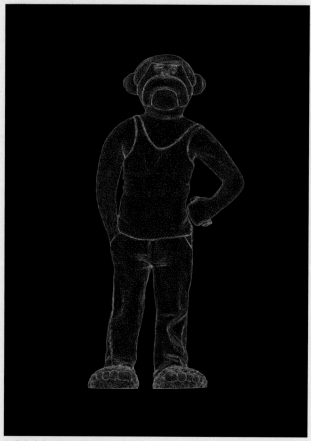

A digital drawing of Bernard.

The finished figure of Bernard.

What was the client's brief to Neighbour?

'There was no real brief as such, just a series of discussions. Levi's Engineered Jeans were celebrating their tenth anniversary in 2009 and wanted to do something to celebrate. We suggested the idea of creating a set of characters to represent the three different fits.'

How did Neighbour's ideas develop, and at what stage did you think that involving Wilfrid would be part of the solution?

'Levi's loved the idea but we knew our biggest challenge was finding the right person to create the characters for us. A friend of a friend suggested Wilfrid to us, and we loved the slightly sinister edge to his work. He popped in to meet us and we had a good chat about the project, after which we knew we'd found our man.'

What was Neighbour's brief to Wilfrid?

'We kept the briefing very simple. We asked Wilfrid to create three characters that represented the fits "Slim", "Regular" and "Loose". The only real stipulation was that the characters had to have two legs and therefore be capable to wear the jeans. Other than that, it was up to Wilfrid.'

A clay sculpture of Fingers.

Fingers, Hopper and Bernard.

Hopper.

Fingers.

How did Neighbour resolve the final ads?

'Wilfrid delivered pages and pages of ideas, all of them great. We had enough for a dozen characters but we managed to narrow it down to just three. Wilfrid took a few pictures during the sculpting phase but the first time we saw them in the flesh was about half an hour before the photo shoot. We asked Leandro, the photographer, to make them look dark and moody and we've just got back from Las Vegas where we've been shooting the characters for the new campaign images.'

How was the work received by client and public?

'The "Twisted Originals", as they are known, have been a big success. We've done two separate production runs of them to keep up with demand. They're not currently for general sale but we keep getting enquiries from collectors and the public so who knows in the future...?'

Illustrating for the graphic design brief

The contemporary graphic design landscape represents a very broad spectrum of activity, from traditional outputs within print-based media through to relatively new and evolving outputs within digital media. Some graphic design companies specialize within certain areas of communication design (web design, for example), while others are willing to take on a broad spectrum of work with a variety of media outputs. A graphic design company offering corporate identity work would expect to generate design outcomes for a company that would embrace both old and new media outlets, as well as extending into product-based outlets such as stationery and clothing.

Progression of a typical corporate identity commission

Start

1

The client approaches a graphic design company with a view to changing the corporate identity of the company or organization that they represent.

2

The creative director clarifies the brief with the client.

3

The creative director briefs the design team (which may or may not include an illustrator at this early stage).

4

The creative team, overseen by the creative director, produces a selection of ideas that are presented to the client. After dialogue, the client makes their choice and a design approach is agreed for development.

5

The creative team searches for an illustrator.

6

The 'book' (portfolio) of the suggested illustrator is submitted to the client for approval, including a quote for the commission from the illustrator.

6. The creative roles within a graphic design company

Creative director

This person manages all creative outputs of the company. They will prospect for work, quote for jobs and guide the creative direction of each commission taken on by the company, working closely with a team of designers. There can be a number of creative directors in any one graphic design company.

Designer

This person literally designs. They work closely with the creative director(s) in deciding specific approaches to finding design solutions to the client's brief, and will implement those solutions in an inspired and efficient way that pays close attention to visual detail.

Studio manager

This person ensures the efficient running of the creative studio. Though not in a creative role per se, the studio manager organizes the appointments of the creative director(s). As such, they may well be the first point of contact for an illustrator wishing to show their portfolio to the company.

7

Once the illustrator accepts the commission and secures a purchase order number, the creative director/creative team briefs the illustrator for the job.

8

The illustrator submits a final quote to the graphic design company for the work to be carried out.

9

The illustrator presents the roughs (also called 'pencils' or 'traces') to the graphic design company that in turn will employ them as part of the overall redesign of the corporate identity for client approval – some adjustments may be requested by the client.

10

The agency presents the final artwork to the client for approval.

11

The new corporate identity is implemented across the graphic outputs of the company.

12

The illustrator submits their invoice, quoting their purchase order number and payment terms.

Finish

Example of a graphic design commission

Sir Terence Conran established the Design Museum, London, some 25 years ago. Originally attached to the Victoria and Albert Museum in South Kensington under the guise of The Boilerhouse, it moved to its present location beside Tower Bridge in 1989. Its original corporate identity consisted of a simple, classic word mark that fused the 'n' of the word 'design' with the 'm' of 'museum'. However, in 2001, on the arrival of the museum's new director, Alice Rawsthorn, it was deemed an appropriate time to reconsider this word mark in light of the changing identity of the museum.

Alice Rawsthorn comments: *'I'd have liked to have changed the museum's identity as soon as I arrived, but waited to do so until we had changed the institution. However frustrating it is to have to work with an outdated identity, it's invariably a mistake to adopt a new one until the organization is on track. Otherwise the identity will have no integrity, however inspired its design. By 2002, a year after my arrival, the Design Museum had changed dramatically. Our exhibitions tackled a more eclectic definition of design, reflecting broader changes in design culture. More people were visiting, and our audience profile was much younger. We had also expanded our range of activities by introducing new programmes of talks and debates, adult learning, kids' creativity and community projects. We'd transformed the website, which was growing very rapidly and reaching many more people than were visiting the building. We needed a new identity to reflect all of that, and to convince those who didn't already know that the Design Museum had now changed to become much more engaging, dynamic and provocative.'*

The design company Graphic Thought Facility (GTF), run by creative directors Huw Morgan, Paul Neale and Andrew Stevens, came into the equation at this point. GTF had previously worked on a commission to redesign the signage system around the Design Museum. They had also worked on a collaborative project with the illustrator Kam Tang to design the new brochure for the Royal College of Art in South Kensington, London. In particular, they were very interested in Kam's sketchbooks, which expertly fused imagined worlds with representational worlds.

Alice Rawsthorn continues: *'We all loved GTF's work, and loved working with them. They have a rare combination of conceptual clarity and formal purity that produces intelligent, visually engaging design solutions that are absolutely fit for purpose. We had no doubt that they would do something great, and were longing to see what it would be. The brief was short. It was to produce an engaging, dynamic and provocative identity, which would reflect the breadth of activity at the Design Museum and work in many different media – website, print, signage, exhibitions, e-flyers, staff T-shirts, tickets and so on. It had to be instantly recognizable as belonging to the Design Museum, without becoming dull.'*

GTF set to work. They envisaged an identity and a word mark ('Design Museum'), supported by a large family of illustrations, from which they could use more or less, depending on the application. The drawings would serve to intimate aspects of the museum – design 'isms', styles and activities, in a way that they knew Kam could do. He employed a visual language that existed somewhere between the figurative and the abstract.

As Kam worked on the images, drawing on-site at the museum, GTF worked on the typography. The design that began to emerge was a monochrome identity that could function well across any medium. It had also been decided that the new corporate identity would last approximately four years, and remain low-profile in any new marketing campaigns for shows held at the museum. This allowed individual graphic designers to respond freely when reflecting the content and visual language of each new show, with the added advantage of protecting the new identity from over-exposure (and thus overkill).

As Alice explains, *'GTF's solution was to work with the digital illustrator, Kam Tang, on an identity that combined a customized typeface – DM Schulbuch – with monochrome silhouettes of things you could find in the Design Museum. Kam produced illustrations of hundreds of objects to be combined in different ways and at different scales, which gave us total versatility, while being completely distinctive. The museum staff suggested the things he could illustrate, thereby enabling them to contribute to the creation of the new identity.'*

A selection of Kam Tang's initial drawings and Graphic Thought Facility's ideas for joining the word mark with the imagery.

GTF submitted the final design. This consisted of a master set of logos in five different combinations. These were set units that could be used to cover all of the different applications of the new corporate identity. The huge amount of work that Kam did as part of the commission was kept on vector files at GTF and could be used in future design scenarios as necessary.

Alice sums up the experience: *'It was an inspired solution, which the staff loved, although a couple of conservative trustees hated it. They simply couldn't understand the rationale for a hybrid identity, and were wedded to the mid-twentieth-century notion of a homogenous identity that looked identical whenever and wherever it was used. The board asked Sir Christopher Frayling, who was a trustee at the time, to discuss the proposal with GTF on its behalf. Chris suggested a few very tiny tweaks, but GTF's proposal was implemented more or less intact.'*

A new Design Museum initiative, 'Young Designers of the Year', allowed the identity to be rolled out in a dynamic way – friezes, incorporating word mark and illustrations, were printed on to large display vinyls, and Californian mobile specialist Timothy Rose was commissioned to produce a giant mobile of the new identity. Products carrying the new identity, such as wrapping paper, phone books and notebooks, were also introduced in the Design Museum shop.

Alice Rawsthorn comments: *'The new identity was a huge success, and surpassed all of the objectives we'd set for it. As soon as the staff started wearing their new T-shirts, visitors wanted to buy them. We'd only ever intended to use the GTF identity for four or five years, before adopting a new one to reflect the ongoing development of the museum. It amazes me how often I see it being copied.'*

One of the simplified logos.

Additional colours in use at the cafe.

A mobile for the new identity by Timothy Rose.

The new identity rolled out for the Designer of the Year launch.

A wall frieze for the Designer of the Year launch.

Corporate identity and advertising illustration: summary of procedure

2

Prospecting for work

In general, it is the art directors and art buyers who make appointments to view illustration portfolios. The names of these people will be available from the agency website or by phoning the company receptionist. They are often very busy, working to tight deadlines, and will usually ask you to drop your portfolio (or 'book') into the agency rather than seeing you in person. They will then view your work over the next few days before asking you to pick it up. Having your own website is also invaluable in allowing art directors, art buyers and potential clients to view your work at any time, from anywhere in the world.

If you do secure an appointment to meet a particular art director or art buyer in person, you might want to check whether any other 'creatives' in the agency would like to view your work on the same day – this increases your chances of securing a commission from the agency in the future. During the interview, be polite, avoid confrontation, and don't be afraid to ask the person's opinion of the overall presentation and the selection of illustrations in your portfolio (especially any work that they particularly like or dislike); in general, people are very happy to give advice. Always leave some samples of your work (including website address and contact details), especially 'one-offs' or limited editions that will instantly appeal to people who have been to art school themselves.

Sometimes, agencies have exhibition spaces in their reception areas. If you can arrange to have your work exhibited in an agency foyer it will instantly promote your work to agency staff and potential clients alike. Again, always provide samples of your work with contact details and your website address and so on.

1

Initial research

If you are interested in working for a particular advertising agency, it is important to research their body of work – in most cases, this will be available on the website of the agency. Check whether it is an 'above the line' or 'below the line' agency and whether it employs illustration as an integral part of its creative outputs. Also check whether the general style of illustration work that the agency commissions is similar to yours – if it is, your chances of securing a commission may be improved.

3

Securing the commission

After the client has approved the ideas of the creative team, a number of illustrators will be considered for the job (this can amount to one or two people, but in extreme cases can amount to up to 30 people). If your work is being considered for the commission, the creative team may wish to talk to you in person to discuss with you how you might approach the commission. If you are then chosen, the approval of the creative director will be needed, followed by the client's.

The next part of the process is your quote for the job (unless there is a flat fee on offer). In general, illustrators cost work for advertising commissions according to the amount of public exposure that the advert will attain. The agency will already have details of what is called the 'media spend' – exactly where, and for how long, the advert will be placed.

You may also need to quote for 'adapts' – variations of the final artwork, including different sizes, different colourways (including black-and-white versions); all of this amounts to extra work and should be charged accordingly. In some cases, usually with a very large campaign, the client may choose to pay you for a licence for the usage of your illustration work to cover unlimited usage in a particular medium over a specific period of time (e.g., three months' national press and trade advertising in the UK). If the country you are working in has an 'Association of Illustrators', and you are not being represented by an agency, they may be able to offer you free costing advice.

Once your quote has been agreed, you will receive a written purchase order and number; this is crucial to receive before you start work, confirming that the agency has agreed to your quote and will pay you on delivery of approval of the final artwork. The written purchase order will outline the following:

- The quantity of work commissioned, including any adapts.

- The way in which the final artwork should be delivered (e.g., digitally, physical artwork on paper, transparencies and so on).

- The dimensions of all final artwork.

- Details of all agreed usages (if you are to be paid a licence).

- The price, stipulating payment currency.

4

Starting work

The creative team will normally arrange a meeting with you to discuss the brief. This is crucial in establishing a working rapport, to make sure everyone involved in a particular job is working along the same lines, and to clear up any uncertainties through face-to-face discussion. Establishing an open channel of communication will stand you in good stead as the job progresses.

On the agreed delivery date, you will submit your roughs to the creative team. These are rarely shown to the client. The art director will request any adjustments that need to be made.

Finally, you will submit your final artwork. Again, some revisions may be requested. Once any final alterations have been made, the work is submitted for approval by the creative director and by the client.

5

Securing payment

Once the advertising agency and the client have approved your final artwork, you will submit your invoice. This will include an invoice number, quoting the written purchase order number, outlining the commission and including your payment conditions – usually this is between 30 and 60 days.

If you have not received payment at the end of the stipulated payment period, then chase up the company. This is why it is so important to have a written purchase order at the beginning of the job – it is proof that the company agreed to pay you for the commission in the first place.

Conclusion

Although lucrative, working as an illustrator for an advertising agency can have its disadvantages. If the campaign you have been commissioned to work on is very high profile, it is inevitable that your work will become associated with that particular company. Ironically, although you may potentially reach the biggest audience in your career to date, this can deem your work unsuitable for other types of work, because other clients will not wish to remind their audience of the company you have previously worked for. You may also be offered fairly draconian client-driven terms, whereby you may not be allowed to produce similar illustrative work for other clients in the short term.

Clearly, people benefit from an advertising culture that subsidizes almost every form of media outlet. It also serves to inform us, to entertain us and to connect us to the world that we live in. Historically, however, strategies and cultures within advertising and corporate identity work (especially branding) have met with criticism, from academics, from practitioners within the communication design industry, and from governments, groups and individuals representing the public at large. These criticisms are predominantly of an ethical nature, citing issues around the age group, gender and treatment of the workforce of a company, its employment agreements, its attitude towards its competitors, its attitude towards the environment and, ultimately, its attitude towards its client base. Governments in many countries have the power to regulate advertising, aiming to safeguard truth, public taste and morality. This has culminated in some countries even banning advertising altogether from specific environments (for example, São Paulo in Brazil). As ethical and environmental issues continue to gather force in our societies, this level of criticism may continue to grow in both volume and influence.

7.

The light entertainment industry brief

'Without a doubt there has been a power shift in the industry. I used to work at EMI, and I worked at Virgin before that. I used to sit in planning meetings and be the very last person to speak – as everyone packed away their pens and were walking out I'd mumble my little bit about trying to put a video online. Today the internet is becoming the hub of the marketing campaign. Everything now hangs off what is happening online.' Dom Cook, marketing directing, MySpace

The term 'light entertainment' is a broad term for a collection of media channels that people choose to engage with outside of their busy working lives. They understand this commodity to be pleasurable, stimulating and life-enriching. It often involves watching, laughing, playing and thinking, listening, dancing and, perhaps most importantly of all, interacting with other people. It helps create human identity, forging unspoken allegiances between groups of individuals, and is a commodity that people spend their hard-earned money and hard-earned leisure time on.

The main components of light entertainment are popular music, television, film and gaming. Though there is cross-flow and dialogue between each and all of these media channels, we will discuss these four factors individually.

Contemporary (popular) music is an art form that is firmly connected to the young. Made *by* young people *for* young people, it is a form of expression that

Below

The Information by Beck, art direction Mat Maitland and Gerard Saint at Big Active, with Beck, 2006. Sticker images Jody Barton, Juliette Cezzar, Estelle & Simon, David Foldvari, Geneviève Gauckler, Michael Gillette, Jasper Goodall, Mercedes Helnwein, Han Lee, Mat Maitland, Ari Michelson, Parra, Melanie Pullen, Gay Ribisi, Aleksey Shirokov, Will Sweeney, Kam Tang, Adam Tullie, Kensei Yabuno and Vania Zouravliov. Commissioned by Beck/Interscope. This CD packaging is interactive by design, providing purchasers with a grid and an illustrated sticker sheet with contributions from numerous artists commissioned by Big Active, which can be arranged in any configuration as the purchaser sees fit.

fuses music and the sung or spoken word to communicate messages across a broad spectrum of content, from human relationships, politics and the environment to society at large. In order for this message to be packaged and distributed, a handful of large corporations (four at present), and a smattering of smaller independent ones, offer their services to musicians to promote, nurture and sustain their careers over the years. Since the lucrative heyday of the music industry, these companies have had to adapt to a marketplace that has changed almost beyond recognition.

Via the internet, a massive array of music can now be listened to before it is bought (or illegally copied for free). The audience picks and mixes the songs they like, assembling digital programmes of music in much the same way that a DJ arranges a sequence of tunes to entertain their club audience. Inevitably, this economic destabilization and fragmentation of core product has led to ever-shrinking budgets in the funding of the graphic, illustrative and filmic work created for the promotion and marketing of the musical product. However, the rise of the internet and broadband streaming has helped bands, with or without the backing of music companies, to promote and sell their wares over the web, reaching thousands (and sometimes millions) of potential fans, and at present these bands are still choosing to originate and develop a visual identity (including a music video) to accompany and personify their musical creations.

Contemporary television, both commercial and state-owned, serves as a conduit for editorial content such as news, arts, sport, science and drama, as well as facilitating the flow of comics and teenager's books into the medium through animations and live-action series. It also serves the younger generation by providing airtime for popular music and the stars that create it. Television, and in particular commercial television, has recently experienced stiff competition and fragmentation, losing a considerable amount of financial revenue to rival companies and to the internet, which in turn has led to reduced budgets for commissioned animation work and animated idents (lead-ins to programmes that illustrators can often be involved with, as we shall see later in this chapter). It has, however, also had some major commercial successes. In recent years, talent contests, provided by such franchises as *X Factor* and *Pop Idol*, have proven immensely popular, thus achieving hefty revenues from premium-rate telephone voting models, while continuing to make full use of traditional funding streams through advertisement breaks. The danger is that talent show pop stars may lack the skills to create their own material and formulate their own opinions (outside of those voiced by their management team), and rely exclusively on a television-generated fanbase that may prove short-lived.

Contemporary film continues to show its resilience in adapting to the demands and tastes of its younger audience, investing in cutting-edge technology that serves to amaze, move and thrill. At present, the future of the film industry seems secure; its heavy investment in CGI (computer-generated imagery) has facilitated the continued visual development of both animated

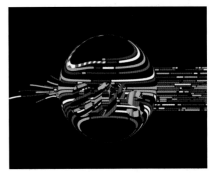

Above
Stills from *History of Dance* titles, designed by Universal Everything, 2006. This TV ident, for a programme about dance from the 1980s on, registers the forceful presence of popular music within the medium of television.

(*Wall-E*) and live-action features (the 'Harry Potter' series), allowing directors to tell stories to audiences in ways that their predecessors could only have dreamt of a decade ago. This technology has filtered down into short animations and also into music videos, where directors are constantly seeking fresh ways to reinvent the 'band performance' video. It has allowed for commissioned illustration and animation work to feature alongside live-action footage. The film industry has also invested heavily in protecting its core product. Constantly launching anti-piracy campaigns, it has anticipated the digital future by developing download accessibility across many platforms and creating business allegiances with key hardware providers. In recent years, some large film corporations have, encouragingly, refocused their priorities on the artistic talent employed within their companies, ensuring these individuals have a greater say in key creative decisions.

Above
Stills from *Grand Theft Auto IV* by Rockstar Games, 2008. The success of the 'Grand Theft Auto' series demonstrates the influence that film has had on gaming and vice versa.

Contemporary gaming, which reputedly has now achieved a higher annual revenue than film, is dominated by three companies: Nintendo, Microsoft and Sony. All of these develop hardware that dovetails with their software outputs, now in their seventh generation. Games generally slot into a cluster of genres that have evolved in the medium over the last 40 years. These genres have employed figurative or stylized representations of the worlds within which the games exist. Like the film industry, the gaming industry has consistently sought to improve and develop the experience of its gamers, in particular concentrating on building interactive capability and group gaming features. This has led to a new genre of filmic, interactive games that have been influenced by the graphic novel, some of which have attracted moral outrage, although their content is arguably no more contentious than that of many adult films. At present, there is still debate as to whether the recent Wii technology from Nintendo can be regarded as a new generation in gaming, though this motion-sensor technology is allowing gamers to physically compete with each other in ways unprecedented until now.

Illustration and the evolution of light entertainment

1950s

In the 1950s, the teenager (or younger generation) emerged in society as an economic and political force – a force that the relatively new music, television and film companies all sought to provide for. Teenagers immediately embraced popular music as their own, and the single bag and album cover quickly came to be recognized by music companies not only as a lucrative commodity but also as a marketing opportunity, a primary point of contact with its intended audience. Portraits (usually photographic) of the new rock and roll stars were placed on the covers of their creative outputs. Television companies, though cautious at first, soon recognized the power of these youthful personalities and their music, and consequently sought to facilitate their presence in programming. Film too, established as a live-action (photographic moving images) and animated (drawing-generated moving images) art form in the previous century, catering to adults and children alike, sought to reflect the new teenage experience. American stars such as Marlon Brando and James Dean provided a suitable degree of angst and rich visual subject matter for the commercial poster artists who were hired by the film studios to advertise their releases.

1960s

The 1960s, an era marked by social and political upheaval, allowed the established media outlets to give the newly politicized teenager and their opinions unprecedented coverage. As the Vietnam War raged on television (starting in 1959, it saw a rapid expansion between 1963 and 1969), pop stars became the spokespeople for their generation (as well as, sometimes, its scapegoats). They used their creative outputs to discuss youth-centric politics, travel and mind-altering substances, while continuing to uphold the staple themes of their musical genre, the 'loved-up' and 'loveless' emotional states. As the musicians reflected their new thoughts and experiences, illustrators were called in to chart this trip into the mind. They provided Asian-influenced and Art Nouveau-influenced psychedelic album cover art that, though still based around a portrait of the artist(s), reflected the internal teenage experience in a visual way that photography never could. As well as performing in clubs and at festivals, pop stars appeared on television chat shows and dedicated musical chart shows. They also began to act in feature-length films (Mick Jagger starred in *Performance*) and as characters in animations (such as The Beatles' film *Yellow Submarine*), as well as starring in shorter, live-action musical features that were the forerunners of the music video. This visual language, originated by illustrators, was to flow both into television and film. During this era, the first video game surfaced; called *Spacewar*, it entailed an interplanetary pursuit that relied on the as-yet undefined gamer having access to an enormous mainframe computer and an advanced understanding of computer programming code.

Above
French film poster of *East of Eden*, directed by Elia Kazan, 1955. This film captured the spirit of teenage rebellion, ably personified by the Hollywood star James Dean.

Above
Still from *The Jungle Book*, based on the novel by Rudyard Kipling, directed by Wolfgang Reitherman, 1967. © Disney Enterprises, Inc. This Walt Disney film, which is still popular with contemporary audiences, shows the artistic and financial phenomenon that the animated feature has become.

Above
Photograph of Otis Redding taken by Gilles Petard during the filming of *Ready Steady Go*, 1966. The medium of television gave talented soul stars, such as Otis Redding, the opportunity to communicate with mass audiences.

1970s

The 1970s saw the pop pioneers of the previous decade offer new experiences for their teenage and twenty-something audiences, while simultaneously cutting loose from the politics of their generation. The album became the double and triple album, the club became the theatre and sports hall, and the money went into the stratosphere. Themed shows, fantasy pop characters and concept albums all became established ingredients within the marketplace. Illustrators, and to some extent photographers, were prepared to abandon portraiture in favour of making album art that was redolent of the music within. This neo-Surrealist visual language was championed by the London-based design group Hipgnosis, whose design work dominated the outputs of the 'super groups'. Music-based television shows became more serious in both delivery and content, reflecting the deepening themes within the music and thus connecting with an audience base that had grown up alongside their heroes. In film, the emerging stable of American directors, who wished to entertain their audiences in spectacular new ways, dispensed with the painted poster in favour of the photographic advert or film still and sought to engage their teenage audience by reflecting the gritty and immigrant-centric stories emerging from the cities of America with films such as *Saturday Night Fever*. This turbulent era closed with the realignment of music to teenage youth and politics in the advent of the new musical art form of punk rock. Punk had a do-it-yourself, tell-it-straight initiative, giving illustrators and graphic artists new creative direction with the influence of the Situationists from France, although its time in the limelight proved brief. And in the home, the first video game, *Pong*, appeared, featuring a crude black-and-white interface.

1980s

In the 1980s, the stars of pop (the previous generation now jostling against the shoulders of the new) raised their game yet again, once more veering away from youth-oriented politics. Performances became stadium shows, produced on the back of albums (now in compact disc form), with steeply rising ticket prices and merchandise sales facilitating illustrators to design extravagant sets, costumes and, in the case of illustrator Gerald Scarfe, even creating animated sequences for shows and show-related feature films (such as *The Wall* by Pink Floyd). Pop videos were now firmly established as, at best, an art form, and in any case, a powerful marketing strategy, with their format dovetailed to the needs of commercial television (MTV, an American channel, based its entire business model around popular music).

Electronic instrumentation appeared in force, driving the popularity of dance clubs and extending the format of the 7-inch single into the 12-inch single. The visual language was dominated by a mixture of slick photography and hard, graphic illustration that again had its influences in Japan. This era saw the continued dominance of American film directors, who took audiences to new heights with their command of extensive post-production skills in films such as the comic book-based hero *Superman 2*. The animated feature film

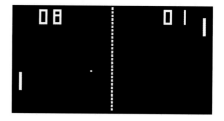

Top
Still from *Saturday Night Fever*, directed by John Badham, 1977. This film, which propelled its principal actor John Travolta to instant superstardom, set the tale of a young second-generation Italian immigrant to a vibrant disco soundtrack.

Centre
Still from *Pong* by Atari, 1972. Though very simple by the gaming standards of today, *Pong* became an instant must-have item on its release.

Bottom
'God Save The Queen' by The Sex Pistols, design and illustration by Jamie Reid, 1977. The immediacy and subversive nature of collage (sometimes used in ransom notes) was harnessed with great effect to package the single bags and album covers of the new punk bands of the 1970s. This visual language was successfully carried into the anarchy punk movement by bands such as Crass and Conflict.

Left
Still from *Akira*, directed by Katsuhiro Otomo, 1988. *Akira* was an innovative Japanese anime adapted from a Manga comic that helped bring the genre to a wider audience.

Below
Still from music video 'Take On Me' by A-Ha, directed by Steve Barron, 1985. This pop video for the Norwegian band A-Ha was groundbreaking in fusing live action with animated sequences.

also saw a Japanese anime influence begin to emerge in the West through films such as *Akira*. Home entertainment games, experiencing a dramatic crash mid-era because of poor product based on film franchises, re-emerged with a vastly improved commercial commodity (*Dragon Quest*) that dovetailed with the arrival of the internet and a new phenomenon in home computing hardware, the Apple Macintosh, and in software, Microsoft.

1990s

In the 1990s, the internet and internet-related technology democratized the creative marketplace: 'sampling', 'bedroom production' and 'burning' all became familiar terms within the private world of the teenager. Popular music was dominated by dance and hip-hop, and music videos were still a core part of every album marketing campaign. However, this new access to technology for teenagers also facilitated the arrival of Napster in 1999, the music file-sharing software that would change the fortunes of the music industry beyond all recognition, slashing budgets and damaging the revenues of graphic designers and illustrators alike (whose core business had also been damaged by programs such as Photoshop and Illustrator, allowing 'everyone' to make fashionable, traced imagery). For the while, commercial television continued to attract substantial advertising revenue, though big global players would aggressively compete for the audience's subscriptions in the evolving

Left

Goo by Sonic Youth, illustration by Raymond Pettibon. 1990. Commissioned by Universal Music Enterprises. This striking black-and-white album cover reinforces the rebellious stance that lies at the heart of this band's music.

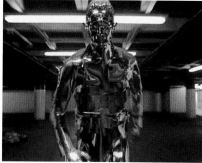

Above

Still from *Terminator 2: Judgement Day*, directed by James Cameron, 1991. The Terminator franchise constantly seeks to employ cutting-edge technology to thrill its audience.

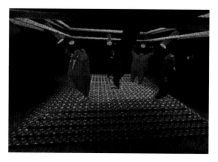

Above

Still from *Blahbalicious* by Avatar and Wendigo, Quake 1 Engine, 1997. *Quake* paved the way for interactive gaming over the web. *Blahbalicious* was a pioneering machinima movie that made use of the Quake 1 Engine.

international digital television marketplace. Film per se, however, maintained its dominant financial position through even more spectacular (largely animated) effects in films such as *Terminator 2: Judgement Day*. The gaming industry provided stiff competition by developing sophisticated interactive products (*Quake*), with the boundaries between games and films blurring significantly as games were turned into films and films turned into games.

2000s

In the 2000s, due to the significant shifts in the way that the teenager now purchased (or didn't purchase) popular music, musicians no longer sought the approval (and contracts) of the Artist and Repertoire employees of the major labels. Instead, they could communicate directly with their fanbase and sell their music over the internet. Though in time the most successful of these new marketeers did sign record contracts with major record labels, this has proved an empowering phenomenon for up-and-coming musicians and their fans alike. During this era, illustration sustained its momentum and popularity within the medium of popular music, as evidenced in releases by Thom Yorke (of Radiohead), Beck and The Arctic Monkeys, and continued to show a Japanese influence. Teenage-oriented film, too, maintained its pursuit of spectacle and the spectacular, with stories by J.R. Tolkein and J.K. Rowling being turned into popular films that amassed hundreds of millions of dollars in revenue. The full-length animation also continued to gain popularity, with *Spirited Away*, *Through A Scanner Darkly* and *Persepolis*. This era also saw the continued rise of the gaming industry, with internet-delivered interactivity built into the gamer experience (*Call of Duty*) alongside cutting-edge software and hardware game platforms – now games could truly be played with anyone, anywhere.

Above
St. Elsewhere by Gnarls Barkley, design and art direction by Tom Hingston Studio; illustration by Kam Tang, 2006. Commissioned by Warner Bros. Records. The paradoxical image on this album cover reflects the bittersweet nature of Gnarls Barkley's music.

Left
Still from *A Scanner Darkly*, directed by Richard Linklater, 2006. This animated film, made using the rotoscope technique, shows how the genre is connecting with a serious-minded adult audience.

Below left and right
Stills from E4 idents, concept, design and direction by Noah Harris, 2007. This animated ident for British television channel E4 is representative of the take-up of CGI from feature films and animations to television.

Illustrating for the modern music brief

The contemporary music industry is genre-led, and it continues to provide strong opportunities for the freelance illustrator. Each musical genre tends to have its own distinct identity, in as much as a hip-hop album cover has to look like a hip-hop album cover. It will be important for you to research these areas before you make any approaches to music labels and design companies for future employment.

Components of the modern music industry

- **Rock and pop** (illustration and photography)
- **Classical** (dominated by found imagery, usually painting)
- **Hip-hop** (dominated by photography and graffiti art)
- **Urban or R&B** (dominated by photography)
- **Dance** (typography and illustration)
- **Ambient** (illustration and photography)
- **Reggae** (illustration and photography)

Above
Funeral by Arcade Fire, illustration by Tracy Maurice, 2004. This album packaging, complete with gatefold and inner sleeve booklet, shows how popular illustration is with indie rockers.

Left
Life In Cartoon Motion by Mika, art direction by Airside, 2007. Commissioned by Universal/Mika. Upbeat and positive in feel, this illustration echoes the psychedelic feel of The Beatles' *Yellow Submarine*.

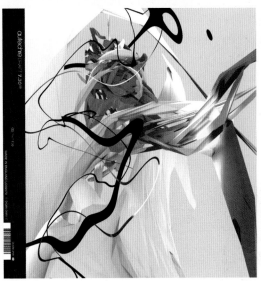

Top left

Horn EP by Spectac, art direction and design by
Non-Format with art print by Manuel Schibli, 2006.
Commissioned by LoAF / Lo Recordings. The cover
of this hip-hop album bucks the trend of rap stars
being photographed surrounded by scantily clad
women and their earthly possessions.

Top right

Born Dead With Life by Perfect, illustration by
Franke, 2008. This hand-illustrated cover reflects
the association of reggae with the Rastafarian
religion and the use of drawn imagery to promote
the musical genre.

Bottom left

The Warning by Hot Chip, design and illustration
by Darren Wall at Wallzo, 2009. This semi-abstract
illustration is redolent of a musical form that is
designed to get people dancing.

Bottom right

Draft 7.30 by Autechre, design and illustration by
Alex Rutterford, 2003. An abstract visual language
has proved popular in packaging the ambient
music genre.

The creative roles within the music industry

Label manager

This person is responsible for all of the artists represented by a particular label. They will have a strong notion of the brand identity of the label, and will be constantly seeking ways to nurture their existing cohort as well as searching for new talent that aligns with the vision and identity of the label. Depending on the size of the label, he or she may be available to view illustration work.

Product manager

This person manages all aspects of the public image and creative outputs of a particular musical act. He or she will liaise closely with a design team and with the marketing department of the record label in order to ensure that the creative outputs of the act are packaged and sold in an appropriate fashion. He or she will be available to view illustration work.

Artist and repertoire (A&R) manager

This person is responsible for signing new acts to a label. He or she will be constantly on the lookout for fresh talent, and will have a keen sense of how such talent could be represented and marketed by the label.

Progression of a typical music industry commission

Start

1

The label will decide which design studio the band should go with, depending on the style of music and the type of work the design studio is known for.

2

After a meeting with the product manager (and possibly the band), the design team will enter the research and development or early concepting phase. Working within a semiotic approach, they will develop 'look and feel' ideas, trying to find visual ways to express the identity of the music and the values of that particular group. They will also bear in mind the different formats within which the music will be packaged and advertised.

3

A further meeting between the marketing department, the band and the design team will take place. Agreement will be reached on the right visual identity for the release. Examples of an illustrator's work can be involved at this stage.

Creative director

This person will work closely with the product manager (and also possibly with the musical act), and is responsible both for co-ordinating the work and for the creative direction taken by the design team. He or she will also be responsible for commissioning any illustration that is required for the packaging of a new release.

The design team

Under the leadership of the creative director, the design team will develop the brief both conceptually and visually, designing all of the layouts (which will usually include both words and images) needed for each format in which the packaging will be realized.

4

The illustrator is contacted. Normally there is a set budget and contract for terms and conditions. Unfortunately this will exclude a royalty payment structure, even though the illustration on the music packaging will be integral to its success.

5

The design team prepares about four or five different ideas. The visuals are presented at actual size on foam core and the selection helps define the client's choice. Sometimes elements from a few ideas will be incorporated into the one finished design.

Finish

6

The final design is agreed and prepared by the design team for all of the different promotional outlets and product formats.

Example of a music industry commission

This example features a collaboration between the illustrator Jamie Hewlett and the musician Damon Albarn. After studying at art college in Sussex, England, Hewlett originated the popular comic-book character Tank Girl. Albarn, meanwhile, had gained considerable success with the British pop/rock group Blur. The two first collaborated on a musical project that Albarn originated, the virtual pop group Gorillaz. On Albarn's request, Hewlett created the characters within the group (which clearly had influences from Japan), as well as the world they inhabited. His artwork was applied to the Gorillaz musical products, and his animations featured in 'live' shows.

Hewlett and Albarn's collaboration on *Monkey – Journey To The West* originated in China. The theatre director Chen Shi-Zheng approached Alex Poots from the Manchester International Festival to consider developing a stage version of the classic Chinese myth *Journey To The West*. Alex Poots had previously collaborated with Hewlett and Albarn, and approached them to consider artistic and musical input into the project respectively. Once the two had met with other key personnel on *Monkey – Journey To The West*, the work began.

An early rendition of Monkey.

Jamie Hewlett comments: '*My first drawings of Monkey were completely wrong, and Chen Shi-Zheng really disliked them. Damon and I went to China in September 2005, and then did nothing on Monkey for six months while we finished the Gorillaz project. But when I started to draw the character, my head was still in Gorillaz world. I hadn't got fully around the Monkey character to do it right. And I was being asked to design a character for a real person who had to look like my designs but be able to move around on stage, to sing and dance and perform martial arts.*'

The resolved character design for Monkey.

(handwritten note in left margin) look at ecohurst/any magazine try and create an illustration

Slowly, however, the project began to gain focus.
Jamie explains: *'It took another two trips to China,
and lots more drawings, before I began to get
to a point where I was happy. By then, I had
met Fei Yang, who plays Monkey. After spending
time with him, eating meals, joking around and
getting drunk, I could take some of his character
– the cheekiness and playfulness – and put it
into Monkey. In fact, it all goes round in circles,
because he also began to take some of his character from my drawings, and eventually it all clicked
into place. But I am not completely satisfied with
them, even now.'*

Monkey's dynamic character emerges in this drawing.

Monkey in full costume.

A character design for Sandy, the Sand Monk.

Sandy, as translated to the stage.

Pigsy, as translated to the stage.

As work progressed, Hewlett developed visual identities for all of the characters in the cast. He says: *'My ideal would be to spend six months with the cast, really getting to know them in somewhere like Macau, before I put pen to paper and start to design the characters and costumes. Take Pigsy, who is played by Xu Kejia, a Mongolian martial arts expert who's a very powerfully built, muscular man. Although he looks so huge and strong, he's actually a real sweetheart who has become a good friend. To look at him you would not think he could sing so beautifully, but he has such a sweet voice. Damon persuaded him to sing in the studio, and it was so beautiful there were tears in our eyes. That influenced my drawings of his character. Similarly with Sandy, who's played by He Zijun, an actor who's a very cool man; when you see him in China, with his gang, he's the one who gets all the attention from the girls. All these things influence the drawings – and the more informed the artist, the better the characterization in the work.'*

A character design for Pigsy.

The popularity of *Monkey – Journey To The West* prompted the decision by Hewlett and Albarn to release an album of the songs included in the show. Hewlett comments: *'We never intended to do a Monkey album, but everyone was humming the tunes and asking for them. We talked about recording it in Beijing, but eventually did a studio album here. And this is truest to my vision of Monkey, a character unrestricted by cast require-ments or the demands of moving about and performing martial arts on stage. It is closest to Gorillaz – a Monkey as we really wanted him, produced by just Damon and me and our team. He became a lot darker, a lot bawdier. We focused far more on the sinister side and the sexier side – it is, ultimately, quite a dark tale full of sex and violence, although ending with enlightenment.'*

A darker side emerged for the album artwork.

As the show received critical acclaim, premiering at the Manchester International Festival, the BBC in the UK took notice. With the 2008 Beijing Olympics pending, they approached Hewlett and Albarn to work on an animated ident for the British coverage of the Chinese-hosted event. Hewlett explains: *'For the BBC's coverage, the characters became much more cartoony – they were more colourful and likeable. This was a big deal for the BBC, and we were taking Monkey to a big audi-ence of families in their living rooms. It is rather a vicious story: Sandy, for example, is a river demon who spends his days eating people and his evenings filled with angst over his cannibalism. We could not show him on the BBC with blood dripping from his mouth and eyeballs and entrails hanging off him. We also restrained Monkey's cockiness – he became more like the cheeky kid next door, not that horrible shit who wants to be a god but won't behave, which is really what the tale of Monkey is about. Then there were the changes forced on us by events. The ident began with Monkey exploding out of an egg, with rocks raining down everywhere, but this had to be changed after the Chengdu earthquake. But the BBC were cool, and in many ways it was this that crystallized the idea of Monkey as family entertainment, for chil-dren as well as adults.'*

Jamie Hewlett and Damon Albarn are now collab-orating on their third Gorillaz album.

A key scene with Monkey and the Snow Spider.

Illustrating for the music video industry

The contemporary landscape in music video generally works in two ways. The first method is facilitated by the significant advances in digital and web technologies, and involves a band making their own music video, which they will make available to their audience over the internet. In general, this is a much smaller way of producing a music video and will often be a lot less successful at reaching a large audience, mainly due to budget and talent.

The second method is facilitated by a commissioning system: this involves a commissioner from the music company approaching a number of directors. The commissioner will be interested in the director, rather than the company that represents him or her, although they must feel secure that this company can successfully produce the film. The director (one of a handful of directors from different companies) is asked to pitch for the job. The pitching director's treatment may include the use of illustration and/or animation and, if successful, he or she will be commissioned to make the music video that will form a key part of the music company's web-deliverable marketing strategy.

This pitching process, although viciously competitive, does make for creatively cutting-edge ideas to be constantly invested in the music video format. For instance, the film work of Michel Gondry for Björk's music videos is extraordinary; he and Björk have developed a professional working relationship as a visual artist and musician that has generated a greatly admired body of work.

Components of the modern music video industry

- **Pop** (film, animation and illustration)
- **Rock** (film, animation and illustration)
- **Hip-hop** (dominated by film)
- **Urban or R&B** (dominated by film)
- **Dance** (dominated by film)

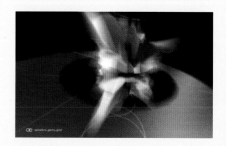

Above
Stills from music video 'Are You Ready For Love?' by Elton John, directed by Kate Dawkins/Intro, 2003. This pop video references the optimism of the 1960s Flower Power generation, as well as Elton John's impressive and lengthy track record in the music industry.

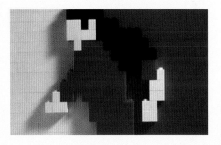

Above
Stills from music video 'Fell in Love with a Girl' by The White Stripes, directed by Michel Gondry, 2002. Gondry's work for The White Stripes has given him creative freedom to experiment with the pop video genre.

Above
Stills from music video 'I Changed My Mind' by Quannum, directed by Shynola, 1999. Animation has also found a niche in the hip-hop genre, for instance in this first video from the inventive Shynola collective.

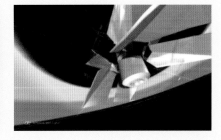

Above
Stills from music video 'Gantz Graf' by Autechre, directed by Alex Rutterford, 2002. The abstract language of Autechre's CD packaging flows effortlessly into their pop videos, where dynamic animated sequences are developed to accompany the music.

The creative roles within music video

Commissioner
Works for the record company liaising with representatives of production companies, on the lookout for new directors. They present the music video brief to the record company, and are instrumental in selecting the winning treatment.

Director
Pitches a treatment for the video, usually in written form but with picture references. To break with a standard performance video, he or she may stipulate the use of illustration and animation to complement live footage or to stand alone – commissioners want creative ways to film performances: they may want the band involved in an adventure or even not feature them at all. They are in charge of a creative team and the performers on the day of the shoot.

Artist and management
Both artist and music company management are involved in choosing the winning pitch, and the artist(s) will more often than not perform in the video.

Film cameraman and crew
The cameraman works closely with the director and is responsible for the cinematography of the video. He or she also manages the camera crew and the chief electrician (or gaffer), who in turn manages a team of electricians.

Progression of a typical music video commission

Start

1
The commissioner approaches the production company with a music video brief.

2
The film directors who the production company represents are asked to pitch a written treatment for the brief.

3
The production company presents the pitches to the commissioner.

4
The band, their manager and the music company decide which pitch to go for.

Assistant director

This person manages the timings and logistics of the film crew. They have a further second and third assistant director, who deal with the performers and a team of runners who generally help out.

Film crew

These people work closely with the cameraman and first assistant director, organizing lights, laying tracks for the camera to run on and facilitating the physical filming of the music video. They liaise with the art department, catering, wardrobe, and hair and make-up.

Art director

This person is responsible for the design of sets and props before and during the shooting of the video. They will lead a small creative team of assistants.

Choreographer and wardrobe and styling personnel

These people are responsible for any dance movements required in the video, and the clothing, make-up and hairstyling of those performing.

Illustrator and/or animator

If required, these people will work closely with the director in developing still or sequential imagery. Usually they are not present on the day of the shoot but are closely involved in post-production.

5

The chosen director briefs the creative teams. At this stage, if required, the director will brief the illustrator and/or animator, issuing a contract with a description of the work involved, delivery deadlines (usually two weeks) and a flat fee (generally, this will be paid in full, regardless of whether the illustration or animation work makes it to the final cut). At this stage, the illustrator should secure a purchase order from the production company.

7

The music video enters the post-production phase. At a post-production house, the rushes (film footage) are telecined, where the colour contrast and format will be adjusted. The film will then be digitized, before the director edits the film with an editor. He or she will liaise closely with the band, their management and the music company on the final cut. Any two-dimensional elements (illustration) or three-dimensional elements (animation) will be prepared elsewhere, before all of the different parts of the music video (including the final edit) are taken into a Flame suite. Large storage computers are used to assemble a high-quality version of the video, and the finished video is exported for the final colouring process.

Finish

6

The director shoots the music video with film crew and artist(s), usually over the course of a day.

8

The music company is presented with the finished music video and all parties submit their invoices and are paid in full.

Example of a music video commission

The example featured here is the stop-frame animation video for the song 'French Dog Blues' by Pete Doherty, from the album *Shotter's Nation* (2007) by Babyshambles. The video was a different take on a band performance, with animated illustrations by Neal Fox from the Le Gun illustration collective.

Pete Doherty.

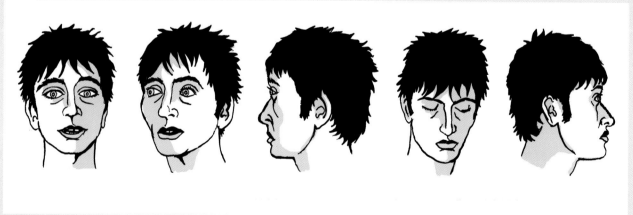

Drew McConnell.

The drunken dog.

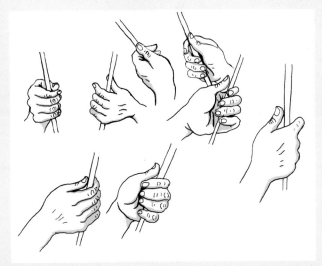

Adam Ficek's hands.

Fox explains: *'I had to draw each member of the band and their instruments from (I think) 12 different angles, going round 360 degrees. Then the animators in New York turned them into 3D characters, which could be further manipulated. Because Pete Doherty was in jail at the time, one of the animators had to get drunk and be filmed dancing around with 3D sensors on his limbs while watching videos of Pete so they could get his movements and mannerisms. I also had to draw a drunk French dog, based on a doodle that Pete does sometimes, mixed with a bit of Serge Gainsbourg and Snoopy. We wanted the figures in the band to have quite a raw cut-out look, a bit home-made. The setting for the video was the Le Gun Shoe Shop of Curiosities, which was a real shop we ran for a few months. An old cobbler in Hackney had recently died, and a friend of ours bought the shop and let us have it for a while to mess about with. We filled it with all kinds of weird stuff we found in the basement, like masonic coffin covers and stuffed animals, alongside our own artwork. So it was a ready-made film set that the director David Mullett animated with stop frame, and then integrated with my drawings.'*

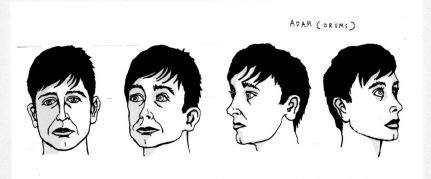

ADAM (DRUMS)

Adam Ficek.

Stills from the video.

Illustrating for the gaming industry

The game of today has moved on considerably from its earliest incarnations. Gaming companies are cloaked in secrecy, investment budgets are now akin to film budgets, time schedules run into years, and the end result is a highly polished entity, both technically and visually, that will keep the gamer(s) busy for weeks, if not months. Though existing genres have been established over many years and continue to please long-standing fans, new approaches to gaming – and in particular the 'Grand Theft Auto' series, in which adventures are set in the underworlds of large cities, such as the fictionalized 1980s Miami of *Grand Theft Auto Vice City* – have allowed gaming to reach out to new audiences with wider cultural reference points than the traditional gaming fan.

Components of the gaming industry

- Sport games
- Adventure games
- First-person combat games
- War games
- Civilization games
- Film franchise games
- Children-oriented games
- Filmic-genre films

Below left
Still from *Grand Theft Auto IV: The Ballad of Gay Tony* by Rockstar Games, 2009. The interactive filmic quality of the 'Grand Theft Auto' series has ensured its enduring popularity with gamers.

Below right
Still from *MotoGP 09/10* by Capcom, 2010. The sport genre has achieved an impressive level of realism that reflects the gaming industry's constant investment in cutting-edge technology.

Bottom left
Still from *Guitar Hero 5* by Activision Publishing Inc., 2009. This motion-sensor package puts the gamer at the heart of the action – on stage with the band.

Bottom right
Still from *Street Fighter IV* by Capcom, 2009. The long-running, multi-player 'Street Fighter' series of martial-arts games is centred on its hero, Ryu.

Left

Still from *Gears of War* by Epic Games, art direction by Chris Perna, 2006. Image property of Epic Games, Inc.; used with permission. War games make full use of the internet to capture the team element among soldiers in 'live combat' situations.

Centre

Still from *Sid Meier's Civilization IV: Colonization* by Firaxis Games, 2005. Civilization games have increased the cerebral content of gaming, rewarding strategy and wisdom with growth and development rather than destruction.

Below

Still from *Resident Evil 5* by Capcom, 2009. The relationship between the feature film and the gaming industries has proved economically beneficial for both, as in the case of the Resident Evil franchise, even if it can prove hard to maintain quality across all media.

The creative roles within the gaming industry

Artists

These people are responsible for the visual language and backgrounds of the game. Their work sits somewhere between the work of the pre-war commercial artist and the storyboard artist of the film world. This is potentially where today's illustrator will be involved.

Level designers

These people are responsible for the design and connection between the many different action levels or stages of the game.

Audio engineers

These people are responsible for the sound effects that accompany the action throughout the game.

Musicians

These people are responsible for developing any music that is featured during the unravelling of the game.

Progression of a typical gaming commission

1

Pre-production: A small team determines what the game will be, in terms of the genre that it will fit into, the way that the 'game play' will function and the visual style in which it will be created. In this phase the team (including artists/illustrators) will generate concept art, prototypes and design documentation. The team's aim is to ascertain what they will be working on over the next two years. The length of the pre-production phase depends on the company and the project, but typically it ranges from two to six months.

Start

2

Full production: This is the main production phase, lasting for two years or longer for a large project, and consists of a team of approximately 70 people. All of the art assets are created in this phase, including character design and modelling, animation, user-interface design, in-game movies and soundtracks.

Programmers

These people are responsible for generating the complex computing code
that underpins the functionality of the whole game.

Writers

These people are responsible for all of the various narrative elements within
the game, as well as the narrative arc, the backbone of the story that delivers
a beginning, a middle and an end.

Animators

These people are responsible for all of the character and object movement
(or animation) that takes place within the visual language of the game.

3

Bug fixing and polishing: The length of this phase depends on the project,
and is also reliant on the success of the previous phase. On modern console
games, the team gradually 'locks down' key features of the game, one by
one, until the game is finished in its entirety.

Finish

4

Submission: Modern console games are submitted to the platform holder
(Sony for 'PlayStation', Microsoft for 'Xbox' and Nintendo for 'Wii') to be
reviewed before they are released to the general public. Essentially this is
the end of the creative process for the developer – if the game passes submission, it is released to manufacture and will arrive on store shelves after a
two-week distribution period. If the game fails submission, the problems will
be fixed and a new version submitted for review as quickly as possible. For
this reason, a development team is typically on call during this review period.

Example of a gaming commission

Some gamers have described *The Sims*, designed by Will Wright and developed with the business acumen of Jeff Braun, as a 'digital doll's house'. Will Wright's inspiration for the game came from psychologist Abraham Maslow's 'hierarchy of human needs', and simulates the day-to-day activities of a group of virtual characters called 'The Sims'. They live in a suburban neighbourhood, within commuting distance of SimCity, and speak a unique language called Simlish (a mixture of Ukrainian and Tagalog, a language of The Philippines). Some of the characters are pre-made (there are the Newbie, Goth, Roomies and Pleasant families, as well as a solo character called Bachelor), while others can be created by the gamer, and they have to manoeuvre their way through the usual problems that every human being faces.

As Will Wright himself says of the psychology behind the game:

'I guess that, as a game designer, I've always assumed that people are – at some level, at least – very narcissistic. So, basically, the more it's about them, the more they're interested. The Sims "invited" people. I never said "Put yourself in the game," but the first thing almost everyone did when they first got The Sims *was craft representations of themselves. The Sims is really a juggling game: you juggle your time, money, opportunities, etc. So I think, for a lot of people, it captured that juggling aspect of their lives – in a whimsical, cartoon-like, caricature-like format. But it was still about them: they were really the core of the game.'*

When the original game, *The Sims*, entered the gaming marketplace, it defied the established categories of Combat, Adventure, Platform and Action, and still remains a one-off today. Just as in real life, the gamer has to make basic decisions about building and decorating their characters' home, choosing their career paths and having families (a typical Sims household comprises up to eight characters). The player can determine the age, gender and physical and psychological attributes of each of their characters. In this sense, *The Sims*' creators see the gamer as a 'designer' rather than a 'player', and invite them to interact creatively with the core materials that they supply.

The feedback for the game from the fanbase, which unusually comprises an equal amount of male and female gamers, has become an important element in the future development of *The Sims*; the gamers roughly fall into two categories. As psychologist Michael Stora says:

'There are mainly two types of Sims players: those who take pleasure in identifying with an avatar who has all of the qualities they themselves lack, and those who like to duplicate the person they actually are in real life, to experience relationships or situations that they wouldn't have the courage to attempt in real life.'

The Sims 3 identity.

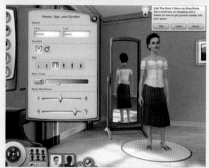

Creating a character in *The Sims 3*.

A good meal can alter the character's mood.

The end of the day.

Following on from the original game, *The Sims 2* took advantage of techno-logical developments in the industry. This led to the design of a more sophisti-cated product, with advanced animation content, the introduction of DNA so that the Sims could pass on genetic traits from one generation to another and more lifelike facial expressions and physical attributes. During the ongoing development of *The Sims* brand, concept artists and illustrators have always been an important component within the development team.

As Lyndsay Pearson (Producer – *The Sims 3*) says:

'We often rely on concept artists to help us visualize what the game could look like. Concept artists develop scenes of everything ranging from a full town square or house to a pair of shoes. Each of these images helps us to shape and direct the game and what it will look like in the end.'

The game is now in its third incarnation, *The Sims 3*, and is also available as an iPhone 'App'. This new version introduced an even greater choice in architectural possibilities, personality traits and municipal facilities in the characters' neighborhoods. Again, illustrators were a key component of the team in establishing a new perspective for *The Sims 3*.

As Grant Rodiek (Associate Producer – *The Sims 3*) says:

'Illustrators help define the look and feel of our worlds, the architectural styles, and the fashions our Sims wear. They also help us brainstorm exciting designs and moments we want to deliver in every game.'

As with each version, the game unravels indefinitely, with the player's main aim being to help the characters to achieve their own personal goals. There is no way to 'win' the game, and some gamers have gone so far as to compare *The Sims* to a toy, rather than a conventional computer game. With three ver-sions of the game, and seven additional expansion packs, *The Sims* brand has grown into a financial phenomenon, with sales of $2.5 billion; in 2007, 20th Century Fox bought the movie rights to the game, which is to be written by Brian Lynch and directed by John Davis.

Social interaction has a greater importance in *The Sims 3*.

Light entertainment illustration: summary of procedure

If you are interested in seeking employment within a gaming company, they will usually advertise vacancies on their website. For music videos, you will need to seek representation from a film company/agent.

2
Prospecting for work

You have two options when prospecting for illustration work for the music industry. First, you can make a direct approach to a major or independent label. Generally, you will need to arrange your portfolio to be viewed by the head product manager, the label manager or the artist and repertoire manager. On the major labels, you will probably find that each division within the record company has its own label manager. It will definitely be to your advantage to have some previous album illustration experience, but at the least it is a good idea to mock up some album covers that are relevant to the outputs of that label. Research the release history of the label, and choose work to show potential clients that is informed by this research. Try to keep your illustration content as broad as possible, and when you have developed your particular style or identity, produce a good quantity so that the person viewing your portfolio can see how it could be applied. Always have promotional material to leave behind.

3
Approaching a company

You can make a direct approach to a design company that is known for its work within the music industry. Research the work of the group before making an approach to show your portfolio to the creative director, and put together a body of work that bears some relevance to the type of illustration work that the group has commissioned in the past. Again, bring promotional examples of your work to leave with the company.

4
Securing the commission

Once you have been approached for a commission, you will need to take a close look at the contract and see if the terms and conditions are acceptable to you. Music-packaging budgets are not what they once were; generally you will be offered a fairly modest one-off fee without royalties.

1
Initial research

Spend some time researching the different genres within the music industry and the visual identities that those genres adopt. Visiting a large music store, where you can take time in looking at a vast collection of different types of music packaging, will prove advantageous.

6

Submitting the roughs

When you deliver the roughs to deadline, be flexible and allow input from the creative director, designers and the band. This practical discussion will ensure that the work is fit for purpose and will connect in an appropriate way with the fanbase of the band.

7

Producing the final artwork

Once the appropriate changes have been made, deliver the work to deadline and in the appropriate format. On acceptance, submit your final invoice, quoting a purchase order number and stipulating the time period within which you should be paid.

5

Starting work

The creative director will brief you, discussing the nature of the illustration work that the band requires and the overall concept and approach to the graphics.

8

Securing payment

Having kept a record of the date you submitted your invoice, check a week before the payment deadline to see if you have been paid. If not, call or email the finance department of the company to ensure that they will be making a payment to you to meet your terms and conditions.

Conclusion

It remains to be seen how the light entertainment industry will cope with the prospect of a purely digital future and the possible disappearance of physical product. Interactivity, too, increasingly seems an entity that companies cannot avoid, with the influence of gaming now established within the channels of television and music video, though not in any meaningful way as yet in feature films. While some light entertainment companies have prepared for the future over the years, others have been less prudent, experiencing enormous damage to their core business. Eventually this will probably separate out the companies who will continue to succeed in a very competitive marketplace from those who will not.

What is certain, however, is that the relationship between the provider and the consumer has changed beyond all recognition. The consumer, no longer passive and easily exploited, demands excellence in product, and has a myriad of options to choose from, with loyalty to none – the industry will ignore their increasing demands at their peril.

8.

Future pathways in illustration

Future pathways in illustration

'Jump fences. Disciplinary boundaries and regulatory regimes are attempts to control the wilding of creative life. They are often understandable efforts to order what are manifold, complex, evolutionary processes. Our job is to jump the fences and cross the fields.' Bruce Mau, art director

So far, we have looked at illustration in the context of commercial applications. These areas provide a mainstay of paid work for illustrators, but there are other areas that illustrators are involved with that, although still connected, are not driven by the stringent demands of the marketplace. These creative areas vary greatly, from collaborations with practitioners in other fields, to research-oriented, theoretical activities, to hybrid marketing situations involving new types of working relationships or new business models with potential partners.

Although peripheral to the main illustration marketplace, and unlikely to generate the same levels of income, these activities are important in allowing illustrators to explore new areas of application for their skills, and exposing them to unfamiliar subjects and fresh lines of enquiry without the constraints of the traditional client/illustrator brief. This freedom to experiment, to try out ideas and to follow personal trains of thought, serves to refresh the illustrator's approach to commercial commissions. If illustrators allow themselves to take risks, both artistically and intellectually, to explore concepts and image-making outside a comfort zone, to search with no firm end in sight, they will feel more confident about bringing these discoveries back to the marketplace.

College tutors will often encourage you to work outside your comfort zone. This serves as an invitation to enter a zone of open-mindedness, freeing your-self from old tricks – tricks of visual style, or over-familiar subject matter, or a medium you are inclined to use again and again when finding solutions to projects. At first, this level of openness may be difficult to embrace, but it is a healthy process with which to progress your work. Painting with colours that you never normally use, trying out new image-making processes with tools that you make yourself, or taking on 'live' subjects that you know little or nothing about, will encourage you to take your work into new creative territories.

As discussed in Chapter 1, Edward De Bono encourages creative thinkers to jack-knife themselves out of old patterns of thinking to find new patterns that are of value, before returning to the original cycle – the applied image in the marketplace. Some experiments will remain just that – experiments; others will have real potential and can be conjoined with the artistic and intellectual base skills that you have built around the core identity of your illustration work.

This chapter features illustrators whose work, with one exception, appears in one or more of the chapters on the commercial application of illustration. Through these projects, and descriptions written by the illustrators, you will discover how such activity has proved valuable, and, in turn, how it might prove valuable within the context of your own career as an illustrator.

Ryu Itadani

After graduating from art college in London, Ryu Itadani returned to his native Japan and established himself as an artist and illustrator in Tokyo. His work is featured in Chapter 4 (see pp. 86–87) and his clients include *Esquire* magazine (Japan), Starbucks and Portobello Books. In these examples, Ryu describes his experiences contributing to an exhibition in Tokyo and designing murals.

Omotesando from 'City, Things and Nature'.

Project Title: 'City, Things and Nature'
Date: April 2008
Location: Marunouchi Gallery, Tokyo

How did the project originate?

'I was asked to join a group exhibition in Paris in July 2005. The organizer knows the owner of Marunouchi Gallery, and I was introduced to the owner. The owner liked my artwork and asked me to do an exhibition. "City, Things and Nature" was my second exhibition at Marunouchi Gallery.'

How did the project evolve?

'I needed to set the theme for the exhibition first. I have many images about cityscapes, images of things and nature, so it was not difficult to set the theme.'

How was the project received?

'Quite a lot of people came to the exhibition and the gallery was able to sell many artworks as well. I also received quite good feedback about my paintings.'

How did the project benefit your main practice?

'After the exhibition, I got into doing my own projects rather than commissioned illustration work. Also, I got into making bigger artworks and doing more painting works. I have learned a lot about how to show my artwork in a gallery space.'

Project Title: Mural in Harbor City
Date: 2006
Location: Harbor City, Hong Kong

How did the project originate?

'I got the commission from a Hong Kong-based creative agency, ALLRIGHTSRESERVED. They wanted me to draw something on a wall in a shopping mall called Harbor City, Hong Kong. I suggested that I draw a picture of Hong Kong, as the city is one of the main themes in my artwork; they liked the idea.'

How did the project evolve?

'I asked ALLRIGHTSRESERVED's people to send me some photos of Hong Kong to use as reference for the artwork. I started drawing from those photos. I then sent them a sample print, which they used to paint the artwork onto the wall.'

How was the project received?

'I have not seen the mural yet, but some of my friends have visited it and told me there were quite a lot of people taking photos of it.'

The Harbor City mural, Hong Kong.

How did it benefit your main practice?

'I found it was quite difficult to draw from photos that were not taken by me, so I have decided to take my own photos for reference when making artwork.'

Roderick Mills

Since leaving art college, Roderick Mills has worked as a commercial illustrator in London. His work is featured in Chapter 5 (see p. 106) and his clients include Picador, *The Financial Times* and *New York Magazine*. In these two examples, Roderick outlines his experiences collaborating on an animation project, and working solo on a fine-art film project.

Project Title: *Immortal Stories*
Date: 2006

How did the project originate?

'Immortal Stories *was my first collaboration with the filmmaker Rosie Pedlow. Fragmented vignettes weave and divide in a film that plays with Hollywood's portrayal of cancer. Rosie approached me after seeing the work that I had done for the Folio Society Awards at the Royal College of Art, London.'*

How did the project evolve?

'After receiving the Sciart Award from the Wellcome Trust to research our project, we decided that we should use this research and make the short film. Rosie was gracious enough to work unscripted and make the animation intuitively as I do in my illustration work, letting the research develop the rhythm of the end result. This might have lengthened the production of the film, but it allowed me room to learn how to work in a filmic way.'

How was the project received?

'The film was received very well. It was selected by numerous international film festivals, including San Sebastián 2008, Clermont-Ferrand 2008, L'Alternativa Barcelona 2007, Cork 2007 and Edinburgh 2006, and the film was awarded the Special Jury Mention at Festival du Nouveau Cinéma Montreal 2006. Attending festivals with the film gave me greater insight into the work, and perspective on the process of making the film. The dialogue with an audience also illuminated how the film communicated, and gave me confidence to make further films.'

How did the project benefit your main practice?

'As an illustrator I find it essential to continue developing, and to explore other areas and media. It's good to be challenged and not to fall into the safety of commercial applications of the work. I see both commercial and non-commercial aspects of my work feeding one another. I enjoy the length of film projects as well. It allows for greater research and the development of new techniques.'

Opening credits of *Immortal Stories*.

Closing credits of *Immortal Stories*.

Project Title: *Beach Film*
Date: 2007–

How did the project originate?

'Beach Film *came about through my fascination with beaches, with the film being a documentation of a piece of shore over 12 months using a webcam.'*

How did the project evolve?

'The concept for the work came through the daily observation of a stretch of beach via a webcam. I slowly became fascinated by the subtle changes of light on tracks on the sand.'

How was the project received?

'Although the project is still in progress, it has had very encouraging feedback and I look forward to eventually exhibiting the piece.'

How did the project benefit your main practice?

'I'm not entirely sure how my film and photographic work relates to my drawn illustration, but I see both feeding me as a visual artist. At the RCA I was encouraged to be inquisitive and explore other media to express ideas beyond the drawn form.'

Stills from *Beach Film*.

Howard Read

After graduating from art college, Howard Read established himself as an illustrator in London. His work is featured in Chapters 2 and 4 (see pp. 22 and 90–93), and his clients include *The Financial Times*, *The Economist* and Benfield Industries. In this example, Howard outlines his experiences working on a project that involved documenting the dramatic changes taking place within a small community in London.

The estate.

Youths living on the estate.

Project Title: 'Elephant'
Date: January 2009
Location: The Barbican Library, London

How did the project originate?

'The regeneration of the Elephant and Castle – specifically the Heygate housing estate and its occupants – was something I wanted to document through drawing. Very swiftly an established community was about to disappear. The social demographics of the area were being reordered, and I felt ambivalent about this as I walked past the estate everyday.'

How did the project evolve?

'In practical terms, the project evolved through a series of sketchbooks. I then spent the summer working up these drawings and adding figures to the compositions. I wanted to give a sense of time and place; the estate is run down and in parts minatory, and I wanted the drawings to reflect this. The research department at Central Saint Martins College in London helped support the project. I then approached the Barbican Library exhibition space to show this work.'

How was the project received?

'The Barbican was happy to show this work and once the exhibition opened I was invited onto Robert Elms's show on BBC London Radio to discuss the project. The comments from the exhibition were positive. Even the less-than-positive ones made me laugh – for example: "Excellent – seeing shape and beauty in a shit-hole. Exemplary." Much of the work sold, and many people and future contacts asked to be emailed or contacted.'

How did the project feed back into your main practice?

'The exhibition has led on to new work, drawing on-site for the architects AHMM [Allford Hall Monaghan Morris] on long-term building projects. Showing line drawings has opened up new areas of work and commissions for me, often with more freedom and fewer restrictions than conventional platforms for illustration. I think it has really highlighted the importance of taking on self-initiated projects and being proactive about this.'

Local transport to and from the estate.

Neighbours chatting.

The broadsheet for the show's opening
at the Barbican Centre, London.

Russell Mills

Since graduating from art college, Russell Mills has worked as an illustrator and artist across a broad spectrum of media. He is based in Cumbria in the north-west of England. His work is featured in Chapters 3 and 5 (pp. 72 and 106), and his clients include Brian Eno, Peter Gabriel and Nine Inch Nails. In this example, Russell talks about the experience of communicating particular aspects of the socio-economic history of an area in Portugal through imagery.

Porto.

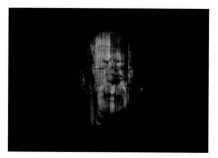

Project Title: *Blue Tears*
Date: 2005
Location: The Silo Espaço Cultural, Porto

How did the project originate?

'I was commissioned by the Fundação de Serralves (the Museum of Contemporary Art) in Porto, Portugal, to create a multi-media installation for the Silo Espaço Cultural as part of a trio of commissions entitled 'In Loco'. The Silo Espaço Cultural is a vast two-storey circular tower designed as a flexible and iconic exhibiting area by the award-winning architect Eduardo Souto de Moura.

'The installation was conceived by myself and my long-time friend and collaborator Ian Walton, with sound design and film production by myself and Michael Fearon. The installation took place from 24 March to 24 May 2005.'

How did the project evolve?

'On a site visit to Porto, while walking along the quays beside the River Douro, we noted that the majority of the small houses that are crammed onto the hill that rises from the sea are covered in sheets of rusted corrugated metal, corroded by exposure to the sea air thick with salt. This is the main part of the old town and has evidently grown organically, as the town's wealth built on the wine and port trade has grown.

'Quite quickly we were thinking about the symbio-sis between the town as place of human habita-tion, of human settlement, and its position and reli-ance on the River Douro and the routes out to sea. The location of most human settlements has been determined by proximity to water. Access to rivers and seas has enabled us to grow agriculturally, industrially, culturally and economically. Our occu-pations and our cultures have been shaped by our specific environments, and in this case Porto very definitely has been shaped by the sea.

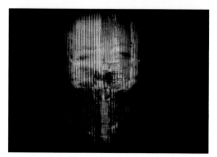

'Salt became the core theme that we felt could conceptually tie in ideas of environment with our emotional lives. Much research then followed into salt, its history, uses and properties, not just as a mineral but as a component of both the sea and tears. While much of our research was dedicated to making correspondences between salt, tears and the city of Porto, we were always taking tan-gential, conceptual walks in an effort to find a more universal way of creating an installation that, while having stemmed from ideas seeded in Porto, would be potentially relevant, especially emotionally, to any audience.

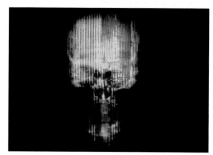

The face of a local man morphs into a skull.

A photograph of the installation.

A photograph of the installation.

'Research also involved looking into the history of Porto, its development of wines and port wines, shipping, the effects of sea routes on trade and cultural exchange, corrugated metal sheeting, tears (chemically as well as culturally), the symbology of hand gestures and the reciprocal relationship between people and the environment – among other subjects.'

How was the project received?

'Generally extremely well; many visitors related to us and to the organizers and curators that they had been profoundly moved by the experience. Many had made connections that related very closely to those that we ourselves had been striving to convey, while others found new, personally pertinent, familial themes emerging from their visit.'

How did the project benefit your main practice?

'This is part of my main practice. All of the areas I work in are equally important to me. I don't discriminate between areas or genres of work as I feel most are merely separated by differing tools, but even this state is under change as technological changes are encouraging (at last) a far more multi-disciplinarian approach to creativity. For me, all areas of work that I choose to pursue are equal and as such demand equal commitment, the same rigorous research, and the same attention to contextually anchored processes. The lessons I learn from creating multi-media installations inspire and inform my other works enormously and the converse is also true.

'I believe in, and try to practise, a lateral, cross-disciplinary approach to the creative process, whether working alone on a painting, collage or assemblage, or in collaboration on an installation, recording music or when involved in teaching/tutoring students, that may encourage a richer flow of ideas. Just as public spaces (such as cafés and restaurants) are not organized into specific areas of expertise and interest, the way most universities or corporations are, but are instead places where manifold professions can and do mix and where all kinds of people can and do exchange stories, ideas, knowledge and skills, I attempt to do the same in all areas of my work. I believe that with convergence, consilience and collaboration, in business, the sciences and in the so-called professions, as well as in the arts, we can learn more.

'In England we are naturally suspicious and cynical towards anyone who has the audacity to attempt to do more than one thing, especially in the arts. This seems oxymoronic to me. I constantly find myself being frowned upon as I don't easily fit into any known, recognizable taxonomy or genre. By the so-called fine-art world I'm considered as a fellow traveller but I'm driving in a different vehicle – in fact by those who are addicted to being discipline-bound I'm considered as such. I'm not particularly bothered by this attitude; in fact it confirms my suspicions and merely serves to spur me on to more variety, more collaboration and more cross-disciplinary thinking and practice. I believe that the cross-disciplinary approach is the only way we're going to achieve any meaningful (and hopefully exciting) progress.'

Neal Fox

Since graduating from art college, Neal Fox has worked as an illustrator in London. His work is featured in Chapter 7 (see pp. 170–71) and his clients include *The Guardian*, *The Independent* and Random House. In this example, Neal talks about a chance encounter with his own family history that became the creative starting point for a much larger project.

Project Title: 'Little Drop Of Poison'
Date: 2008
Location: Loft 19, Paris

How did the project originate?

'When I went to Camberwell College in London to do my foundation, no one there really drew so I started making weird films and taking photographs, and forgot about drawing for a while. But then I was travelling around Europe when I was about 21, and in an old junk shop right on the end of Crete I found a book by my grandfather, John Watson. It's a novel called Johnny Kinsman, *based on his time as a bomber pilot in the Second World War. I was reading it at the same age as my grandfather's character is in the book. I really identified with him. He died when I was four, but I've always heard stories about him. I started drawing images from the book and from his life, blurring fact and fiction, and that was when I got back into drawing. When I got to the RCA in London I started drinking in Soho, in my grandfather's old haunts, the French pub, the Colony Room. I started to imagine my grandfather's ghost on a crazy bender through time and space with the other ghosts of Soho.'*

A Little Drop of Poison.

How did the project evolve?

'The drawings have become a lot larger and more complex, more surreal. Since I got into doing the big pictures they've become much more layered. I think it makes your ideas bigger and makes you feel freer. As an illustrator you are tied to working in a certain size at your desk, but working on giant collaborative pictures with my friends at the design and illustration collective Le Gun has made me more ambitious with scale. The drawings take in everything I'm reading about and listening to; I bring in whatever characters from culture I become interested in and link them together. At the moment I'm working on a ten-metre-long drawing imagining Brian Jones from the Rolling Stones having an acid trip, travelling through Joseph Conrad's Heart of Darkness, *ancient Egypt, and Mikhail Bulgakov's* The Master and Margarita.*'*

How was the project received?

'I put on an exhibition in the French pub in Soho where my grandfather used to drink. By chance, a gallerist called Daniel Blau from Munich came into the pub and liked my work, so he asked me to put on a show at this gallery in Munich. Then he sorted it out for me to do a show at a new gallery called Loft 19 in Paris. The show sold out on the opening night, which was mad – I was drinking champagne for the next couple of weeks.'

How did the project benefit your main practice?

'It's pretty much become my main practice. I still do a drawing every week for The Guardian, and other bits and bobs if I'm asked, but I've been able to live just off doing my own drawings for the last couple of years, which is marvellous. The good thing is it means I only do illustration commissions if I find them interesting, like the video for Babyshambles, rather than for the money. It's not bad being able to live off drawing whatever comes into my head everyday; I hope I can keep doing it until I kick the bucket.'

Danse Macabre.

Josie Lynwode

After graduating from art college, Josie Lynwode has used her illustrations exclusively to promote musical events that she produces in collaboration with her husband and business partner, DJ Rob Da Bank. In this example, she describes developing the work for their latest musical venture, Bestival.

A page from the Bestival website.

Promotional material from the 2009 Bestival.

Project Title: Bestival
Date: 2008–09
Location: Isle of Wight

How did the project originate?

'Robby, my husband, and I had been running parties in London, Ibiza and various other parts of the world for about seven years. I would do the artwork, and decorate them as well as organize them. In 2003 we decided to try our hand at running a festival.'

How did the project evolve? How was the project received?

'The first Bestival was a great success; it got great press over the next year and by 2004 the show had increased in size and tickets sold well. We never set out for it to be so big; it's been a very organic process.'

How did the project benefit your main practice?

'Since starting the shows, I have had lots of offers for illustration jobs but I have decided to keep my style exclusive to the Bestival brand and anything else that's related. My husband and I own the shows, so it's the most important business right now. I am also the main organizer so I'm very busy. Hopefully this won't always be the case.'

Promotional material from the 2008 Bestival.

Andy Forshaw

After graduating from art college, Andy Forshaw has worked as an illustrator in London. His work is featured in Chapter 5 (see p. 101), and his clients include Graniph Japan, Faber and Faber and Virgin/EMI Records. In these two examples, Andy describes the experience of translating his illustration work on to a three-dimensional object, and collaborating with colleague Danny Sturgess on a typographic project.

The drawn logo and additional patterning appearing on Nike trainers.

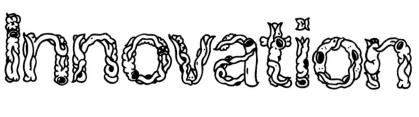

Drawing of the Nike Innovation logo.

Project Title: Nike's Innovation trainer range for Spring/Summer 2008
Date: 2008

How did the project originate?

'The commission came about following some logo work I did for David Johnston of the designers Accept & Proceed. He was approached by Nike to art direct a Spring/Summer trainer edition based on the theme of sweets and flies. David asked myself and several others if we'd be interested in pitching some ideas, and it all developed from there.'

How did the project evolve?

'I was given about half a day to come up with initial concepts and David fed them over to the design team at Nike Amsterdam. It was a commission not too far out of college, and in those days the time I spent on each piece was a long way from the few hours I had to finish this. It was pretty stressful, but by early afternoon, and five or so mini tiled illustrations later, I developed a route they liked.

'I was given the following day to tidy the ideas up. Then came the process of trying to tile the pattern, which proved tricky as I had never attempted this before. They wanted it as a repeat pattern roughly ten centimetres square so they could use it across any Nike medium, be it apparel or indeed shoes.

'I vectorized it for print and set about designing the type on the sockliner. This again took several attempts, each time simplifying the linework. My way of working involved quite detailed and tight pen work. The temptation was to over-detail the typography, which would ultimately be printed a quarter of the size inside the shoe.

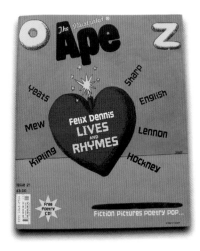

Cover of *The Illustrated Ape* magazine.

Inside spread for *The Illustrated Ape* magazine featuring drawn type.

'After about a week, everything I'd done was put to Nike and from there they chose four illustrators to be included in the Spring/Summer 2008 range. My work was laser-etched into the uppers of five different Nike trainers sold around Europe.'

How was the project received?

'The project got quite a bit of attention from the sneaker and design world and was featured in Creative Review. It circulated around all of the trainer blogs, which was quite a scary thing – they're pretty fierce critics when it comes to defacing their favourite pumps. The project definitely gave me a bit of kudos; it was a once-in-a-lifetime commission and something that I'm immensely proud of doing.'

How did the project benefit your main practice?

'It garnered a lot of attention and that for an illustrator is all-important – getting noticed when so many others are out there trying to do the same. I don't know if I've ever been directly commissioned from it, but no doubt people will have seen the shoes out there, be it on the web or in person, and that will have led them to my other work on my site.'

**Project Title: *The Illustrated Ape* typography spread with Danny Sturgess
Date: 2005**

How did the project originate?

'The Illustrated Ape commission was my first out of college. It was a magazine that I liked so I was pretty chuffed to be asked to contribute. A woman called Mai from Central Saint Martins College in London contacted me as she was art-directing the issue and liked my work from the graduation show. She briefed me on what she wanted – a double-page "MANIFESTO" typographic spread. I had a few days to complete it but was heading off to Argentina before the deadline. I therefore asked if I could get my colleague Danny Sturgess involved and make it a collaborative effort. I thought it would be an interesting mix of styles – pen vs. pencil – and obviously would help get the job completed in time.'

How did the project evolve?

'Danny and I had a look at the copy and decided on themes and ideas that would fit. We pretty much divided the work equally and chose words we each wanted to illustrate. We worked from our separate houses and conversed through email, looking at how each of us was progressing and trying to adapt our work around the other's. We worked through a few days and evenings; the final composition was left to Danny as I was in danger of missing my flight. Danny sent it through to me as I was sitting in an internet café in Buenos Aires – that was quite a strange way to end the project.'

How was the project received?

'I think people liked it; it's difficult to gauge as it's a magazine and you don't necessarily provoke an internet response from editorial work. I know future clients have referenced it in commissioning me for other typographic work so I guess it has been received well.'

How did the project benefit your main practice?

'I think it benefited me in that it was my first experience in dealing with a client – working to a deadline that could never change and the pressures that come with that. The work itself led me into more typographic projects, and resulted in typographic work for the publishers Bloomsbury and Faber & Faber and for The Guardian newspaper.'

Debbie Cook

Since graduating from art college, Debbie Cook has worked as an illustrator in London. Her illustrations are featured in Chapter 6 (p. 126), and her clients include Air India, *The Observer* and the Post Office. In these two examples, Debbie describes her experiences in contributing to a publication (and consequently a series) generated by staff and students at the Royal College of Art, London, and in applying her illustration work to the reinvention of an early form of product promotion.

Three of the Critical Forum publications.

Project Title: *The George Hanson Critical Forum: Self for Sale*
Date: 2004

How did the project originate?

'The illustrator Anne Howeson and I developed the thoughts around Self for Sale *while walking on Hampstead Heath. We were interested in how we could draw on our own private experiences to bring a sense of authenticity to the stories we are asked to tell in our role as commissioned artists.*

'The article documents a debate that was part of "The George Hanson Critical Forum", a series of student-led round-table discussions exploring the landscape of art and design practice in the department of Communication Art and Design at the Royal College of Art. The forum was established in response to a consensus of opinion among staff and students that a more effective critical discourse was needed in the department.'

How did it evolve?

'The Critical Forum programme has become a formal and influential part of the course. Two further books were published for the "Buryport" and "Woodhill Park" critical forums, and a college-wide "Interdisciplinary Critical Forum" was set up following a similar format. The discussions are now published on the web.

'Artist David Blamey and I edited the "Buryport" publication, and we work together to structure cross-disciplinary student-led learning in the department.'

How was the project received?

'These are some of the reviews we received:

'Julia Moszkowicz, in design magazine Eye, said: "This is a book that will appeal to those whose creative convictions put them in daily contact with the contradictions, and apparent borders, of their commercial practice."

'Rick Poynor said: "A quirky, absorbing and illuminating report from the frontline about what's preoccupying the current generation of communication art and design students and their teachers."'

How did the project feed back into your main practice?

'I have become interested in how dialogue feeds into practice, in the parallel roles of drawing and talking, and how knowledge and perception develop in a similar way through each. It has led me to reflect on my previously held opinion that voice was only used to articulate the real work, the work that happened by intuitively doing.

'It is rewarding to see students take responsibility for their own learning. I now aim to foster a climate in my teaching, described by Jill Tarule in her writing on collaborative learning, where "the role of authority and expert is lodged in the conversation just as the construction of knowledge is".'

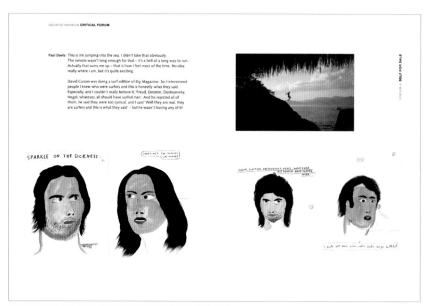

An inside spread from *The George Hanson Critical Forum*.

A selection of the drawings photographed in situ.

The French knickers photographed in situ.

Project Title: *Shelf Life*
Date: 2007

How did the project originate?

'Shelf Life (2007) explored ideas around English domestic interiors, and responded to the 606 Universal shelving system designed by Dieter Rams. The drawings were shown at design art gallery Vitsoe at 72 Wigmore Street, London. The space reflected the trend for gallery/retail spaces akin to Moss in New York.

'Dieter Rams said, "My goal is to omit everything superfluous so that the essential is shown to best possible advantage." Mark Adams at Vitsoe saw a parallel between the rigour by which I refine drawings through many iterations and Rams's approach to the design.'

How did it evolve?

'We wanted to find a way to weave traces of a life into the space, and in doing so open up new possibilities of how the shelves could be used. The drawings illustrate an everyday shelf life and depict a feminization of Vitsoe.'

'The drawings present themselves as showcards – a tool of the retail trade, particularly in the interwar years. They were used as visual prompts, promoting new and special lines of merchandise, or for suggesting goods in the absence of the real thing. The drawings suggest another way of living with the 606 shelving system.'

How was the project received?

'Very well.'

How did the project feed back into your main practice?

'The project reinforced the value of working collaboratively, and the importance of stretching your own vision to share another's. The 606 shelving system now brings calm into my life by ordering the chaos of my studio.'

Conclusion

In all of these examples, it is clear that working outside the comfort zone has benefited each of these illustrators. Their willingness and determination in taking on new creative challenges, sometimes alone, and sometimes in collaboration with others, has led to illustration work that contains a real sense of discovery, consequently offering them new directions within their careers.

This spirit of adventure is something that you can willingly embrace – a 'can do' rather than a 'can't do' attitude. Should you need any practical guidance, look no further than Bruce Mau's *An Incomplete Manifesto For Growth*, which contains Mau's humorous, challenging and controversial suggestions to escape from the constraints of one's own creative complacency.

9.

Working as an illustrator

'Making money is Art and working is Art and good business is the best Art.' Andy Warhol, artist

We have covered a great deal of territory in this book, territory that you should now have a firm grasp of. Without this knowledge, there is little chance of you bringing a product of quality to the marketplace. However, alongside the creative, intellectual and artistic skills that are required to succeed as an illustrator, practical business skills are also crucial in the successful marketing of your product.

Whereas the majority of graphic design graduates will gain employment within a design company, the illustration graduate is in general a sole trader or freelancer. This means that on leaving college the illustrator must establish their own business, which they will individually own and which will, at least in its initial phase, be their sole responsibility. This business must be established with great care and, once started, must be nurtured and sustained in all of its key operational areas. This requires skills that may differ from those needed to produce high-quality artwork. These skills are primarily connected with business, and will include organization, interpersonal communication, accounting and marketing.

In Chapter 1, we mentioned that Edward De Bono referred to the more business-related types of skills collectively as 'operacy' – in other words, the skill set that enables you to operate with success as a person among your fellow human beings. These skills are connected with self-discipline, getting people to like you, being dependable, working as part of a team, asserting yourself where necessary and working efficiently both with other people and alone. To some extent, these skills are acquired through 'peer learning' from primary school onwards, although they may also depend on your cultural background, your life experiences and, perhaps most obviously, your personality traits. Whether you are an introvert or an extrovert, a blue-sky thinker or a detailed thinker, a dreamer or a doer, will give you certain advantages and disadvantages within the area of operacy. It is important to recognize and understand your own strengths and weaknesses; you will naturally gravitate towards your areas of strength rather than your weaknesses, and while the former may give you little to worry about, you will ignore the latter at your peril. Often it is the more mundane tasks, so crucial in sustaining activity within creative tasks, that illustrators tend to ignore.

Operacy is about getting your work out into the public domain, thereby gaining recognition from your peers and the public and, perhaps most importantly, gaining adequate financial reward for the work that you carry out. To achieve a sustainable livelihood from your illustration work is no mean feat, and the completion of your first commission on leaving college will give you an enormous sense of satisfaction. This will involve a sequence of interconnected activities that will form a single cycle of work.

9. The single cycle of work

1

Prospecting for work.

2

Communicating your product to a potential client.

3

Receiving an offer of commission from that client.

4

Reading the offer of commission carefully, before quoting the client for the charges for your product, the exact amount of product involved, the legal rights over the product that you are granting to the client or retaining for yourself, and setting out and agreeing to delivery dates for roughs and final product.

5

Negotiating the counter-demands of the client where necessary, before finally securing the commission. This also involves ensuring that the client provides you with a job number and purchase order number for the commission.

6

Generating the roughs in a suitable location.

7

Delivering the roughs on deadline, listening to and addressing your client's concerns and agreeing to make amendments to the work wherever necessary.

8

Generating the final artwork in a suitable location.

9

Delivering the final artwork on deadline and in the correct technological and/or physical format(s).

10

Submitting your final invoice to the client, quoting the job number, purchase order number and your payment terms for the commission.

11

Tracking the payment in relation to the terms stipulated on your invoice and chasing up a late payment wherever necessary.

12

Receiving your final payment from the client, banking this (which should involve retaining a certain proportion of the sum for paying your tax bill at the end of the year) and entering the sum into your accounting system – this is essential for business and tax purposes.

As if this process was not demanding enough, there is the added challenge that the single work cycle does not necessarily happen in a neat and orderly fashion, where one cycle of work finishes before another begins. On the contrary, jobs will inevitably overlap, and/or run simultaneously, putting you under considerable pressure to meet your deadlines. At other times, you will have no new cycle of work pending, and could potentially have time on your hands. However, if this is the case, you will be able to spend time on less glamorous aspects of your job: compiling new promotional material, securing appointments to see art directors, reorganizing your work environment, researching new technology, meeting with your bank manager, chasing up new contacts, or even, as a reward, recharging your creative batteries by visiting a museum or art gallery. For this type of activity – the activity that surrounds, sustains and protects the single cycle of work – you will need a structure. And what better structure to choose for your purposes than a standard-issue business plan?

Your business plan

A business plan allows you to answer the most important questions regarding the type of business that you are about to establish; in turn, you can use it to raise funds, to provide a road map to guide you through your work-related activities and to serve as a benchmark to judge your progress by. As such, it should be approached with objectivity: generating a plan that is wildly optimistic serves little purpose. On the other hand, one that is cautious, well thought through, and perhaps even errs on the pessimistic side, will be a useful tool to guide you and chart your progress in the marketplace. It will also allow you to build up sustainability and momentum within your business, year in, year out.

A standard business plan can be found on the internet and will contain the following key elements:
- An executive summary
- A description of the business opportunity
- Your marketing and sales strategy
- Your management team and personnel
- Your operations
- Your financial forecasts

We will discuss each of these elements separately.

The executive summary
Although this appears first on the list, it should be tackled last. The executive summary is essentially a summary or outline of your entire business plan, and should include the most important material from each of the other sections of the plan. Its purpose is: *'To explain the basics of your business in a way that*

both informs and interests the reader. If, after reading the executive summary, an investor or manager understands what the business is about and is keen to know more, it has done its job.'

When writing your executive summary, it can be useful to imagine that you are explaining your business to someone who knows little or nothing about illustration. This will help you to avoid the trap of thinking that many aspects of your business are obvious and need not be stated or explained. This will also ensure that the document has the potential to communicate beyond an audience that has first-hand knowledge of the communication design industry. For this reason it will also serve its purpose when you approach funding organizations such as banks and grant authorities for financial backing.

Your business, its services and products

This section allows you to set out what your business actually does. This will include details about yourself, what you plan to do, what you have to offer and the marketplace that you want to operate within. This area of the business plan is divided into two main parts: an overview of your business, and a simple description of your products and services.

Overview of your business

This should include the elements listed below:

* The date you intend to start your business and your progress so far in preparing for the launch.
* The type of business (illustration) and the sector it is located within (the communication design industry).
* Your vision for the future. For instance, you may feel the future of commercial illustration lies in the digital field and this is therefore a growth market.
* The legal structure surrounding your business.

This legal structure generally involves demonstrating an understanding of the following 'rights' areas connected with your work.

Copyright This is a key right to retain. Although you may even sell a piece of artwork to a client, if you retain copyright it is you who has the right to reproduce that artwork, not them. In the unlikely event that you do wish to sell copyright to the client, the extent of the client's ownership over the image should be reflected in the fee paid.

Above
Stills from *How We're Helping* TV advert, magazine advert and in-branch poster for Lloyds TSB bank. Agency: Rainey Kelly; animation/production for TV and magazine advert by Studio AKA; poster by Billington Cartmell. Commissioned by Lloyds TSB, 2010. This bank has gained high exposure due to its commissioning of imaginative and distinctive animated TV adverts, and the style of illustration has subsequently been utilized across a wide range of media, including both above the line and below the line, as here.

Licence This grants a client the right to use your illustration for certain uses, within a specific timeframe, within certain formats and within certain global territories. Different types of media licences include:

- Press – your work used in newspapers.
- Web – your work used on the web.
- Consumer magazines – your work used in mainstream magazines.
- Trade press – your work used in trade-specific magazines.
- Outdoor – your work used in the external visual environment, such as advertising hoardings.
- Direct mail – your work used in promotional material delivered straight to people's houses.
- Point-of-sale – your work used in promotional material in situ in shops.
- Collateral – your work used, for instance, in direct mail and point-of-sale. Essentially this term bundles up several or more media outlets, alongside bigger, defined ones (such as press and outdoor). Be wary of agreeing to this, since you may lose money this way rather than granting individual licences for each defined media outlet for your work.
- Buyout – your work used in a number of media outlets for a certain amount of time and in certain territories. Generally the type of advertising is defined, for example: above the line (booked media channels such as television); below the line (self-generated media channels such as leaflets); and through the line (both above and below the line).

Moral rights This refers to your right to be identified as the originator of the illustration, and your right to not have it tampered with.

Key provisos In addition to this, an important paragraph to include at the bottom of your invoices (as recommended by agent and illustrator Darrel Rees in his book *How To Be An Illustrator*), is the following:

'Copyright and artwork remain the property of the artist unless otherwise stated. This fee is for the above stated uses only. Any additional usage would need to be negotiated and agreed. All work undertaken is subject to our (or "my") standard terms and conditions, a copy of which is printed on the reverse. Grant of rights is conditioned on payment in full.'

This phrase reiterates the extent of your ownership over the copyright and the physical artwork, the ways in which you have agreed for it to be used, and the fact that the client cannot use your work until they have paid you.

Your products and services

In the description of your products and services, consider the following points:
- What differentiates your product from your competitors?
  Within advertising, this is referred to as the 'USP' or 'Unique Selling Point'. Essentially, the answer to this is that your work will stand out because of the unique visual language, content and intelligence with which it is produced.

- What benefits does it offer?
  Your product will communicate visual messages in dynamic and engaging ways.
- Why would people pay you money for it?
  Your product will provide visual solutions to client-led problems, thereby enabling them to sell their own products and services.
- How do you plan to develop your product or services?
  Although this is a tough question to address when you have just invested heavily in four or five years of specialist training, it is worth considering how your product could change over the years to adapt to potential changes in the marketplace (remember 'PESTLE', the forces of change; see p. 70).
- Whether you hold any rights to your work.
  You should intimate an understanding of retaining copyright ownership of your work and being able to grant usage licences.
- The key features of your industry or sector.
  Using this book, you can cite an overview of the different areas of the communication design industry in which illustration is used. You may also wish to carry out some of your own research through your national design and advertising press.

Your marketing and sales strategy

Competing against established practitioners, as well as potentially hundreds of illustration graduates who are leaving college at the same time as you, can be a sobering thought. However, it needs to be addressed. This area is usually divided into two sections: your markets and competitors, and your marketing and sales.

Your markets and competitors

This involves conveying an understanding of how your chosen market operates and the people who you will be competing against for work. This section will usually contain the following:

Your market It would be useful here to convey an understanding of the size and annual turnover of your national communication design industry, quoting the 'monetary investment in design to increased business' ratio. This is a general indicator that if a firm invests in professional communication design, which could include illustration, then they will see an immediate and, hopefully, increased return on their investment.

Your target customer This relates very much to the type of illustration work that you want to do. Helping the client connect instantly with their client base is a very important aspect of illustration work. At the same time, it would be pragmatic to consider how many different types of audiences your work has the potential to reach, thereby dramatically increasing your chances of winning commissions from a wider variety of clients.

Above
Spock; *Bob Dylan*; *John Cleese* by Noma Bar. Commissioned by *Esquire* magazine, 2009; *Time Out* magazine, 2005; *Time Out* magazine, 2009. These striking and inventive portraits are immediately recognizable as the work of Israeli illustrator Noma Bar, yet his work has been commissioned by a wide range of publications.

Profile: James Joyce

James Joyce is a London-based illustrator. He set up his studio, One Fine Day, in 2006, and from these premises he makes limited-edition prints and carries out commissioned work. His clients include *The New York Times*, Faber and Faber and EMI Music Publishing. View the studio's website at www.one-fine-day.co.uk.

Above left
The One Fine Day studio, shared with other designers and illustrators – a functional and inspirational work environment will contribute greatly to the success of your business.

Above right
'Drawings and Other Objects', a solo exhibition of James Joyce's works held at Kemistry Gallery in Shoreditch, London, 2008. Exhibiting your work, either in a solo or a group show, will create useful exposure for your work, as well as allowing you to gain a sense of objectivity about the body of work that you have produced.

Left
Window graphic by James Joyce for the opening of Howie's first store in Carnaby Street, London, 2008. This commission allowed the illustrator to voice environmental concerns as well as creating an eye-catching window graphic for this ethical and eco-conscious clothing retailer.

Above

Cover for *Creative Review* magazine by James Joyce. Commissioned by *Creative Review*, 2008. Joyce's design for the cover of a special edition of *Creative Review* aimed at new graduates.

Left

Clown by James Joyce. Limited-edition giclée print, edition of 10, 2006. Any additional strings to your bow, such as selling limited-edition prints online, can greatly enhance your earning potential while also ensuring a degree of diversity in your income-generating activities.

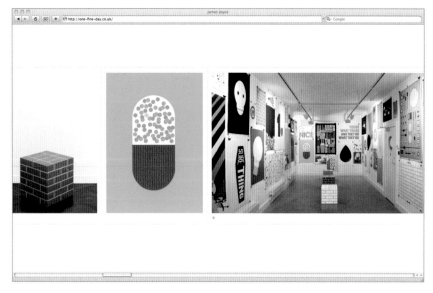

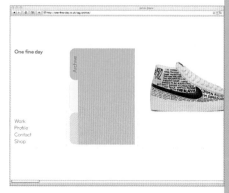

Your competitors Essentially, this concerns who they are, how they work and the market share that they hold. Though no one is that keen to talk about competition within the art school environment, it is a driving force within the marketplace that you must engage with. Rather than feeling threatened by this, observe and learn from your competitors. What are they doing that is better than you? What kind of clients are they working for? How are they being innovative within the marketplace? How are they promoting their product?

Anticipated changes in the market Consider how you expect your business and its competitors to react to these. Again, remember PESTLE, the forces of change. For instance, the introduction of the Apple Macintosh in the mid-1980s democratized certain types of image-making and made it very tough for illustrators to secure work for quite a while. Ask yourself how you can stay ahead of the pack and be as well informed as possible of any changes that are likely to take place within the industry.

Marketing and sales

This involves conveying the practical ways in which you will promote and market your product. This section will usually contain the following:

- How do you plan to position your product or service in the marketplace? This involves creating a simple marketing strategy.
- Who are your customers? Glance back through this book and pick out customers you would like to work with from the 'key personnel' sections.
- What is your pricing policy? This involves research on the website of your national illustrators' association website, and will usually break down into the category of the brief (for example, editorial), whether the image is black and white or colour, the size of the artwork and its context.
- And finally how will you do your promoting and selling...

Above
One Fine Day website. Joyce's website is a cleanly designed web presence that showcases his work to its best advantage. It is divided into four straightforward categories: Work, Profile, Contact and Shop.

How will you do your promoting?

There are many ways in which you can promote yourself:

A website Make sure that you learn to construct a website while still at college. A standard web construction program is Adobe Dreamweaver. This allows you to construct webpages with words, pictures, sound and image, without needing to learn programming. If you're feeling more ambitious, then Flash is a good alternative. The key elements of a good website are speed and ease of use. Although an idiosyncratic website can stand out against your competitors, if the site does not function well, any potential client will quickly tire of those idiosyncrasies. Research the websites of illustration agencies and individual illustrators to gain a feel of how successful operators within the marketplace present their work. Once you have set up your website, remember to constantly update it – that way, you give your clients a reason to keep coming back.

A physical portfolio Although websites are now industry standard for 'first filter' viewing of illustration material, a physical portfolio of work will still usually be requested by potential clients at the 'second filter' stage. This allows the client to view your work as a physical entity, at the correct size, and in its correct 'primary, intended form', which will no doubt help contextualize your work in the client's mind.

A portfolio should be A4 or A3 size, should contain about 12 pieces of work (with as much commissioned work as possible), and should be carefully geared towards the type of work that you are trying to gain a commission in. Generally speaking, you're creating an argument for the client to give you some work. Start with some very strong pieces, maybe diversify a little in the middle, and finish on some more strong pieces, thus creating an argument that goes something like this: 'I'm very good, and, as you can see, I'm prepared to take a few risks, but, by the way, I'm still very good.'

Promotional material This is an established method of advertising your product to new customers and keeping your existing customers updated on your activities. It's best to include a selection of your recent work; this creates better odds that they will react positively to at least some of the images that you send to them. This material can be printed or delivered by email (see 'How will you do your sellling', below).

Illustration annuals Though it can be an expensive method of marketing, paying to have your work featured in an illustration annual published by your national illustration association can also be effective. Advertising agencies in particular tend to use annuals to hunt for suitable illustrators for commissions.

Top
Monday Morning Says. Illustration zine set up in 2009 by Minho Kwon, Mayumi Mori, Jung Eun Park and Gwen Lee. Self-publishing a monthly zine has proved a useful publicity tool for this London-based Korean illustration collective, which also participates in live cultural events. View the website at mondaymorningsayszine.blogspot.com.

Above
Le Book annual. *Le Book* (also accessible online as www.lebook.com) is a cutting-edge directory of international creative talent.

How will you do your selling?

There are various ways in which you can sell your product:

Telephone call This type of marketing can seem daunting and potentially intrusive, especially when most art directors are extremely busy people. However, if you make an effort to send a pack of printed material beforehand, giving you the opportunity to ask politely whether they have had time to look through the material that you sent them, then the call can serve as a useful prompt to encourage them to agree to a meeting with you to discuss your work. However, be prepared for rejection, and accept a 'no' with good grace. If you get a 'yes', thank them, arrange a date to see them and the amount of time you will be allocated, and start preparing your portfolio for the meeting.

Email This marketing method can be very hit and miss. Often potential clients don't like to be approached in such an impersonal way, and, even worse, with a huge list of others emailed at the top of the email. You should also take particular care with wording – a 'madam' will not take kindly to being addressed as a 'sir', and vice versa. However, on the plus side, an email is more carbon-friendly than printed material and is supremely economical in communicating to a large audience.

Above
Big Active postcard pack, with illustration by Matt Furie. The illustration agency Big Active promotes its impressive stable of illustrators with a comprehensive website (www.bigactive.com) and printed postcard promotions.

Left
Shoboshobo business cards and badge, 2009. The Shoboshobo illustration collective (www.shoboshobo.com) provided this physical promotional material at an art fair in Copenhagen.

Post Though people now live and breathe a digital existence, for some reason they still like receiving, handling and looking at printed material. At best, your leaflet or postcard will be put up on the pinboard of a busy advertising agency, for art directors and visiting clients alike to view; at worst, it will end up in the bin. While it is best to be realistic about the relatively low hit rate of mail shots, those clients who already like your work will use the promotional material that you send them as an aide memoire and will bear you in mind for future commissions. Sending Christmas cards to your clients can also be a good add-on to this type of approach.

Face-to-face meeting Though more and more elusive, this type of encounter allows you to have the undivided attention of your potential client. Be well prepared for the meeting, having thought carefully about what you can realistically achieve within a limited timeframe, arrive in good time, talk positively and articulately about your work, listen to their reactions with good grace, give them some of your publicity material and, most importantly, ask them if they think that your work is suitable for their needs and whether any commissions are coming up in the near future.

Exhibitions Either group or solo, the exhibition is an excellent way to promote your work to new and existing clients in a way that is both pleasurable and relaxed – you may even sell some original pieces of artwork.

The skills of your team

As we have already discussed, the illustrator operates as a sole trader or freelancer, so you may not think this section of the business plan is relevant to you. However, there is at least one established option at your disposal that means that you do not necessarily have to work alone. This option involves engaging with an illustration agent and should culminate in a 'respectful and mutually beneficial relationship'.

After leaving college, it is unlikely that you will immediately secure representation from an agent. You need time to find your feet in the working world first, and to carry out some commissioned work (editorial is your most realistic option) to add to your graduation portfolio, a portfolio that you have created within a very specific environment. However, a visit to an agent for some free advice, followed by a catch-up meeting six months later, can be most beneficial. This in turn may lead to representation in the future.

As cited by Abbey Glassfield at agents Eastwing Illustration, having an agent has its advantages, as well as its disadvantages:

Pros of having an agent
- An agent will have an established client base.
- An agent will have an up-to-date mailing list.
- An agent will secure you a contract for each commission, dealing with selling rights usage licences for your work.

Above
Ryu Itadani's travelling exhibition, 'City, Things and Nature', in Dalian, China.

Profile: Sergei Sviatchenko

Sergei Sviatchenko is a Ukrainian artist who has been based in Denmark since 1990. In 2002 he co-founded Senko Studio, an exhibition space for his own work as well as the work of others. His clients include Price Waterhouse Coopers, Nokia and Danske Bank. View his websites at www.sviatchenko.dk and www.closeupandprivate.com.

Above
Sergei's creative environment (an attic studio in Viborg, Denmark) gives us clues as to his creative activity and sources of inspiration.

Left
Dreamt Constellations Sang by Motohiro Nakashima; art direction and design by Non-Format with art print by Sergei Sviatchenko, 2006–07. Commissioned by LoAF / Lo Recordings. 3-inch CDs, 5-inch CDs or 7-inch vinyl are accompanied by prints by various artists. These are enclosed in a sealed plastic document envelope attached to a greyboard cut to 12-inch or 16.5-inch formats, and then silkscreen-printed. This packaging provided a rich graphic environment for the enclosed photomontage work by Sviatchenko.

Above
Poster from *Mirror By Mirror, Homage To Andrei Tarkovsky* by Sergei Sviatchenko, 2008. Sviatchenko uses direct montage techniques to reflect themes in the film *The Mirror* by Russian filmmaker Andrei Tarkovsky.

Left
Mirror By Mirror, Homage To Andrei Tarkovsky by Sergei Sviatchenko, 2008. This collection of fold-out posters, created following a visit to Moscow, incorporates photomontages of original film by Russian filmmaker Andrei Tarkovsky that were given to Sviatchenko while studying in Kiev in the 1980s.

Left

The Heart Diary, 2010. Designed by Jason Godfrey; illustrations pictured here by Michael Gillette (cover and bottom), Ben Kirchner and Phil Hankinson (below left and right). The annual diary issued by Heart Agency includes work by each of the artists it represents, combining functionality with effective promotion.

- An agent will actively promote your work.
- An agent will provide a buffer zone between the client and illustrator.
- An agent will often demand higher fees for commissioned work.
- An agent will represent a stable of illustrators and generate a strong group identity for the agency, which in turn benefits a recent recruit by association.
- An agent will provide additional promotional opportunities via group mail-outs, annuals, postcards and emails.
- An agent will handle all of the paperwork associated with each commission you undertake – from specifying and agreeing the contract through to chasing unpaid invoices. They will submit a monthly statement to you of what is still owed.
- An agent will have experience in covering national and even international markets.

Cons of having an agent

- An agent's services will come at a price; usually they take 25 per cent on jobs with small fees; on larger ones they will take 30 per cent.
- An agent will expect you to sign a contractual agreement. Some may even demand a percentage for all illustration work that you undertake, regardless of whether the agent secured you the commission or not. Check with The Society of Artist's Agents in the UK or The Society of Illustrators in the USA for information on a reasonable contract to agree to with an agent.
- An agent will not be the answer to all of your problems. Although you should expect them to secure you a certain amount of work, you will still need to actively seek work yourself. Remember, they make their living from securing work for a whole group of illustrators, not just you.

Your operations

This section is a chance for you to consider the whole environment within which you will work.

Location

Most illustrators either work from home or they hire a space in a shared studio. Both have their advantages and disadvantages.

Pros of a home studio

- No added expenses.
- No commute to work.
- No limitations on when and how you work.
- No unwanted interruptions.
- No studio politics.

Cons of a home studio

- Lack of separation between work and home.
- Lack of variety to the working day.

- Lack of motivation and self-discipline may be an issue.
- Lack of company.

Pros of a shared studio
- Provides 'up' and focused working environment.
- Provides on-tap peer advice.
- Provides networking opportunities.
- Provides after-work social life with like-minded people.

Cons of a shared studio
- Involves considerable additional expenses.
- Involves potential distractions around you.
- Involves a commute.
- Involves limitations to when and how you work.

As you can see, both the home studio and the shared studio options have their plus and minus points. If you choose the home studio option, be sure that you have the self-discipline to get on with your work without being observed by anybody else. If you go for the shared studio option, be sure that you like and respect the people that you will be working alongside. You will also have to consider the location of a shared studio carefully – since you may be leaving late at night, is it in a safe area? Are there facilities surrounding the studio? Of course, these factors will be balanced by cost. You might even want to use the problem-solving process featured in Chapter 1 to generate options for yourself, before setting out your criteria to judge which of the possibilities you have generated is the best option.

Illustration collectives
A third option available to you (which can dovetail with either the home studio or shared studio option) is to become part of an illustration collective. This will involve getting together with a group of like-minded creatives and forming a collective that shares certain philosophies and operacy values. This model will provide both friendship and collaboration, allowing your collective to create a website, mount group exhibitions, co-publish collective-related magazines, and arrange meetings where projects can be planned and good practice shared – in other words, a mutually supportive group of people who can provide each other with encouragement and networking opportunities, all especially important in the first two years or so after leaving college.

Although some collectives share premises, others don't, simply relying on the internet and telephone for communication. They may physically meet up every now and then in a local café or bar. The illustration collective, now established as a viable alternative to being a sole trader, has proved particularly interesting to the design press, who have been very supportive in reflecting and promoting the work of such contemporary collectives as Monsters, Peepshow, Le Gun, INK illustration and Nobrow.

Above
Chôjin Club poster by Akira Nishitake, 2007.
This poster by the Tokyo-based illustrator Akira Nishitake for the Chôjin Club collective showcases his drawing and typographic skills.

Information technology

Nowadays, as well as having the office standards of a telephone and a fax machine, no illustrator can afford to work without the following services and equipment:

- Access to internet broadband, with an email account that can handle large files.
- A computer, laptop or stand-alone.
- A scanner.
- A colour printer.

You will also need to invest in some, if not all, of this computer software:

- Microsoft Office
- Adobe Photoshop
- Adobe Illustrator
- Adobe Flash
- Adobe Dreamweaver
- Adobe InDesign

All of this equipment needs to be housed on a good-sized table or desk with additional space for you to produce physical roughs and artwork. You should also have plenty of storage space nearby.

Financial forecasts

You should ideally generate financial forecasts that run from three to five years. Although this can be very difficult to ascertain, if not impossible, when you are starting up in business, it will at least allow you to set yourself some targets. It gives you a realistic understanding of the amount of work you need to take on to cover your own expenses and hopefully break even. You may

Below
Though in this case your cumulative cash balance reflects a profit, remember that you invested £500 per month of your own savings into your business and £1000 per month from a small business start-up loan. So in actual fact, you're operating at a small loss, which is the norm in the first three years of trading.

Month	April	May	June	July	August	September
RECEIPTS						
Sales	1,500	2,000	4,000	3,000	1,000	3,500
Owner's investment in business	500	500	500	500	500	500
Small business start-up grant	1,000	1,000	1,000	1,000	1,000	1,000
TOTAL CASH IN	**3,000**	**3,500**	**5,500**	**4,500**	**2,500**	**5,000**
PAYMENTS						
Electricity, gas, telephone	100	100	100	100	100	100
Wage	1,500	1,500	1,500	1,500	1,500	1,500
Advertising/web-hosting	50	50	50	50	50	50
Computing equipment	0	2,000	0	0	1,000	0
Premises rental	300	300	300	300	300	300
Travel	80	80	80	80	80	80
Student-loan repayment	50	50	50	50	50	50
TOTAL CASH OUT	**2,080**	**4,080**	**2,080**	**2,080**	**3,080**	**2,080**
Monthly cash surplus/(deficit)	920	(580)	2,520	1,520	580	2,020
CUMULATIVE CASH BALANCE	**920**	**340**	**2,860**	**4,380**	**4,960**	**6,980**

Profile: Nobrow

Sam Arthur, Eda Akaltun and Alex Spiro established Nobrow, a London-based illustration, book press and print studio in 2008. As well as producing commissioned illustration work individually, they work collectively with artists, illustrators and designers, publishing a themed magazine twice a year and a rolling programme of limited-edition books and posters. View their website at www.nobrow.net.

Below
The Bento Bestiary illustrated by Ben Newman with Scott James Donaldson. Published by Nobrow, 2009. The screen-printed bestiary explores the facets of the Japanese Yokai pantheon.

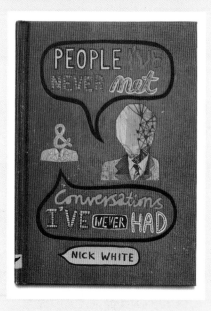

Above and right
People I've Never Met by Nick White. 36-page hardback monograph of Nick White's most recent collection of works, published by Nobrow, 2009. Nobrow's set-up is highly flexible in terms of the inception and realization of limited-edition book projects.

Left and below left

Gods & Monsters by assorted illustrators. Numbered edition of 3000 published by Nobrow, 2009. Nobrow release a bi-annual textless publication in May and November each year. The artists and illustrators featured in each issue are carefully selected and invited to contribute work based on a theme. The work is printed in two spot colours on heavy paper in an oversized format. Printing this magazine in two colours, governed by a tight budget, contributes greatly to its distinctive identity.

Above

The upstairs of Nobrow's studio gives the collective a suitable base to generate and develop their creative projects.

Left

The downstairs of Nobrow's studio allows the collective to produce their limited-edition screenprint runs.

also want to include financial information that relates to other ways in which you go about generating income in order to sustain your illustration career in its early stages. A financial forecast will usually include the following:

- **Cash-flow statements**
  These show your cash balance and monthly cash-flow patterns for 12 to 18 months. You may want to consider carefully any particular financial pressure points in the pattern – for instance, when your studio rent is due in each month.
- **Profit and loss forecast**
  This predicts any profit or loss that you will make once you have compared your incomings against your outgoings.
- **Sales forecast**
  This relates to the amount of money that you expect to raise from selling your product.

As with the overall business plan, it is best to err towards pessimism rather than optimism for your financial forecast. A wildly optimistic forecast will only create targets that you have no hope of achieving, whereas a pessimistic forecast may be highly achievable, with the possibility that you could do better than you predicted. You must also think carefully before borrowing additional funding to start up your business – any loan repayments will have to be included in your financial forecasts.

A financial forecast should also include risk analysis: this shows that you have reviewed the risks that you may be exposed to when operating your business. Essentially this could include loss of earnings due to illness or injury, fire or flood damage to your premises and equipment, costly repairs to computing equipment and so on. Though paying for insurance cover for these potential risks to your business may not be an attractive option in the short term, in the long term it may determine whether your business flourishes or falters.

Some final advice

A business plan takes time and care to get right. As it develops, you should ask others to read it and give you any objective advice that they can offer. You should also seek specialist advice (which is usually free in its initial phase) from accountants (who also have detailed knowledge of your national tax requirements), bank managers and small business advisors. Once your business plan is complete, you should refer to it constantly as an important guide and overriding structure to guide your business activities. It should also be well designed and well presented, and be available in both digital and physical formats.

If you go through your business plan methodically, you will create a document that is fundamental to your progress. In addition to this, here are some useful tips:

- **Don't work for free**

  This is called 'free pitching', where the client wants to see your initial ideas before discussing a fee. Generally these pitches involve little or no money, while the client dangles the hope of more work with higher fees to follow, which of course rarely materializes. This phenomenon is damaging to the industry, and illustration associations will strongly advise against this type of practice.

- **Don't be afraid to negotiate**

  Negotiation generally involves generating an ideal outcome and a fallback position or 'bottom line'. Your willingness to negotiate can generate respect from your client. Bear in mind that some clients (particularly in editorial) will have set fees for the types of work that they commission and are not in a position to negotiate.

- **Conduct yourself professionally at your graduation show**

  Clients and agents will be in attendance, so save the celebrations for another night. Be prepared to talk articulately about your work to these people, in the hope that you may secure a meeting with them in the near future.

- **Be tenacious**

  Keep promoting yourself, keep bothering people and keep moving forwards. You will have good years and bad years, but the most important thing is to keep projecting into the future. Remember, it's dangerous to assume that you can do exactly the same thing for the rest of your life and still make a good living.

- **Be prepared to stick up for yourself**

  If a client is demanding the world, set out your own demands – often they will acquiesce.

- **Be wary of clients changing your work**

  Generally speaking, any changes to your work should be made by you. Avoid this phenomenon by not sending the client layered files.

- **Be efficient**

  Get jobs done quickly – the last thing you want is a backlog of work, with clients pounding at your door demanding their artwork.

- **Be positive**

  Don't let yourself get knocked back by a few rejections – as the saying goes, when one door closes, another door opens.

- **Be versatile**

  If you have the talent, diversify into other creative areas as and when the opportunity arises, thereby broadening your income base.

Conclusion

Although running your own business can appear daunting at first, it will give you immense personal satisfaction as it successfully unfolds. Though sometimes it will prove difficult, it will also facilitate you living a rich and varied existence and underpin your ambition to make your livelihood from your artistic and intellectual talents. All that remains to be said is this: as that famous advertising campaign for a well-known brand of trainers once stated: 'Just Do It.'

Further reading

Chapter 1

John Berger, *Ways of Seeing*, London: Penguin, 2008

Edward De Bono, *Six Thinking Hats,* London: Penguin, 2009

Edward De Bono, *Lateral Thinking: A Textbook of Creativity,* London: Penguin, 2009

Edward De Bono, *How to Have Creative Ideas: 62 Exercises to Develop the Mind,* London: Vermillion, 2007

Steven Heller and Marshall Arisman (eds.), *The Education of an Illustrator,* New York: Allworth Press, 2000

Steven Heller and Seymour Chwast, *Illustration: A Visual History,* London and New York: Abrams, 2008

Richard Hollis, *Graphic Design: A Concise History,* London: Thames & Hudson, 2001

John Montague, *Basic Perspective Drawing: A Visual Approach,* Chichester and Hoboken, New Jersey: Wiley, 2010

Herbert Read, *A Concise History of Modern Painting,* London: Thames & Hudson, 1975

Chapter 2

Banksy, *Wall And Piece,* London: Century, 2006

John Barnicoat, *A Concise History of Posters,* London: Thames & Hudson, 1972

Rebecca M. Brown and Deborah S. Hutton (eds.), *Asian Art (Blackwell Anthologies in Art History),* Malden, Massachussets and Oxford: Blackwell, 2006

Owkui Enwezor and Chika Okeke-Agulu, *Contemporary African Artists Since 1980*, Bologna: Damiani, 2009

John Fleming and Hugh Honour, *A World History of Art,* London: Laurence King Publishing, 2009

Ernst Hans Josef Gombrich, *The Story of Art,* London and New York: Phaidon Press, 2003

Danny Gregory, *An Illustrated Life: Drawing Inspiration from the Private Sketchbooks of Artists, Illustrators and Designers,* Cincinnati, Ohio: How Books, 2008

Robert Hughes, *The Shock of the New: Art and the Century of Change,* London: Thames & Hudson, 1991

Angus Hyland (ed.), *The Picture Book: Contemporary Illustration*, London: Laurence King Publishing, 2006

Garth Lewis, *2000 Colour Combinations: For Graphic, Textile and Craft Designers,* London: Batsford, 2009

Cedar Lewisohn, *Street Art: The Graffiti Revolution*, New York: Abrams, 2008

Alan and Isabella Livingston, *The Thames & Hudson Dictionary of Graphic Design and Designers,* London: Thames & Hudson, 2003

Alan Male, *Illustration: A Theoretical and Contextual Perspective,* Lausanne: AVA Publishing, 2007

Bruno Munari, *Design as Art,* London: Penguin, 2008

Alan Powers, *Art and Print: The Curwen Story,* London: Tate Publishing, 2008

Annemarie Schimmel, *The Empire of the Great Mughals: History, Art and Culture,* London: Reaktion Books, 2004

Chris Spring, *Angaza Afrika: African Art Now,* London: Laurence King Publishing, 2008

David Sylvester, *Brutality of Fact: Interviews with Francis Bacon,* London: Thames & Hudson, 1987

Julius Wiedemann (ed.), *Illustration Now!,* Cologne and London: Taschen, 2008

Frank Willett, *African Art,* London: Thames & Hudson, 2002

Chapter 3

Dawn Ades (ed.), *The Dada Reader: A Critical Anthology,* London: Tate Publishing, 2006

Umbro Apollonio (ed.), *Futurist Manifestos,* London: Tate Publishing, 2009

Roland Barthes, *Image, Music, Text,* London: Fontana, 1990

Roland Barthes, *The Semiotic Challenge,* Berkeley: University of California Press, 1994

Roland Barthes, *Mythologies*, London: Vintage, 2009

Paul Cobley and Litza Jansz, *Introducing Semiotics: A Graphic Guide*, Cambridge: Icon Books, 2010

John Fiske, *Introduction to Communication Studies,* Abingdon and London: Routledge, 1990

Sean Hall, *This Means This, This Means That: A User's Guide to Semiotics,* London: Laurence King Publishing, 2007

Charles Harrison and Paul Wood (eds.), *Art In Theory 1900–2000: An Anthology of Changing Ideas,* Malden, Massachussets and Oxford: Blackwell, 2003

Claude Lévi-Strauss, *Myth and Meaning,* Abingdon and London: Routledge, 2001

Robert McKee, *Story: Substance, Structure, Style and the Principles of Screenwriting,* London: Methuen, 1999

Marshall McLuhan and Quentin Fiore, *The Medium is the Massage,* London: Penguin, 2008

Jonathan Rabagliati (ed.), *George Hanson Critical Forum: Eight Round-Table Discussions from the Department of Communication Art and Design at the Royal College of Art, London,* London: Department of Communication Art and Design, Royal College of Art, 2004

Ferdinand de Saussure, *Course in General Linguistics,* London: Duckworth, 1995

Sven Windahl and Benno H. Signitzer with Jean T. Olson, *Using Communication Theory: An Introduction to Planned Communication,* Los Angeles, California and London: Sage, 2008

Chapter 4

John D. Berry (ed.), *Contemporary Newspaper Design: Shaping the News in the Digital Age: Typography and Image on Modern Newsprint,* West New York, New Jersey: Mark Batty, 2004

Robin Derrick and Robin Muir (eds.), *Vogue Covers: On Fashion's Front Page,* London: Little, Brown, 2009

Steven Heller, *Merz To Emigre And Beyond: Progressive Magazine Design of the Twentieth Century,* London: Phaidon Press, 2002

Steven Heller and Véronique Vienne, *Art Direction Explained, At Last!,* London: Laurence King Publishing, 2009

Horst Moser, *The Art Directors' Handbook of Professional Magazine Design: Classic Techniques and Inspirational Approaches,* London: Thames & Hudson, 2007

Chapter 5

Phil Baines, *Penguin by Design: A Cover Story, 1935–2005,* London: Allen Lane, 2005

Phil Baines, *Puffin by Design: 2010, 70 Years of Imagination 1940–2010,* London: Allen Lane, 2010

Joseph Connolly, *Faber & Faber: Eighty Years of Book Cover Design,* London: Faber & Faber, 2009

Will Eisner, *Comics and Sequential Art,* London: W.W. Norton, 2008

Nancy Lamb, *The Writer's Guide to Crafting Stories for Children,* Cincinnati, Ohio: Writer's Digest Books, 2001

Scott McCloud, *Understanding Comics: Invisible Art,* New York: HarperCollins, 1994

Scott McCloud, *Making Comics: Storytelling Secrets of Comics, Manga and Graphic Novels,* New York: HarperCollins, 2006

Martin Salisbury, *Illustrating Children's Books: Creating Pictures for Publication,* London: A&C Black, 2004

Martin Salisbury, *Play Pen: New Children's Book Illustration,* London: Laurence King Publishing, 2007

Chapter 6

James Aulich, *War Posters: Weapons of Mass Communication*, London: Thames & Hudson, 2007

David Bownes and Oliver Green (eds.), *London Transport Posters: A Century of Art and Design,*

Resources

Aldershot: Lund Humphries, 2008

Clive Challis, *Helmut Krone. The Book: Graphic Design and Art Direction (Concept, Form and Meaning) after Advertising's Creative Revolution,* Cambridge: Cambridge Enchorial Press, 2005

Tom Eckersley, *Poster Design,* London and New York: Studio Publications, 1954

Naomi Games, Catherine Moriarty and June Rose, *Abram Games, Graphic Designer: Maximum Meaning, Minimum Means,* Aldershot: Lund Humphries, 2003

Steven Heller, *Paul Rand,* London: Phaidon Press, 1999

Naomi Klein, *No Logo: No Space, No Choice, No Jobs,* London: Fourth Estate, 2010

Beryl McAlhone and David Stuart, *A Smile in the Mind,* London: Phaidon Press, 1998

Margaret Timmers, *A Century of Olympic Posters,* London: V&A Publishing, 2008

Eliza Williams, *This Is Advertising,* London: Laurence King Publishing, 2010

Chapter 7

Lawrence Bassoff and Robert Wise, *Crime Scenes: Movie Poster Art of the Film Noir,* Beverley Hills, California: Lawrence Bassoff Collection, 1998

Roger Dean, Peter Gabriel and Storm Thorgerson, *Album Cover Album,* Lewes: Ilex, 2008

Steven L. Kent, *The Ultimate History of Video Games: From Pong to Pokemon and Beyond: The Story Behind the Craze that Touched Our Lives and Changed the World,* Roseville, California: Prima, 2001

Emily King and Peter Saville, *Designed by Peter Saville,* London: Frieze, 2003

Matthew Robertson, *Factory Records: The Complete Graphic Album,* London: Thames & Hudson, 2006

Adrian Shaugnessy (ed.), *Sampler: Contemporary Music Graphics,* London: Laurence King Publishing, 1999

Iain Simons, *Inside Game Design,* London: Laurence King, 2007

Walt Disney Animation Studios, *Story (The Archive Series),* New York: Disney Editions, 2008

Richard E. Williams, *The Animator's Survival Kit,* London: Faber & Faber, 2009

Chapter 8

Steven Heller and Gail Anderson, *New Ornamental Type: Decorative Lettering in the Digital Age,* London: Thames & Hudson, 2010

Martin Manser and Stephen Curtis, *The Penguin Writer's Manual,* London: Penguin, 2002

Ian Noble and Russell Bestly, *Visual Research: An Introduction to Research Methodologies in*

Graphic Design, Lausanne: AVA Publishing, 2005

Susan Sontag, *On Photography,* London: Penguin, 1979

Chapter 9

Writers' And Artists' Yearbook 2011, London: A&C Black, 2010

Marshall Arisman and Steven Heller, *Inside the Business of Illustration,* New York: Allworth Press, 2004

Holly DeWolf, *Breaking Into Freelance Illustration: The Guide for Artists, Designers and Illustrators,* Cincinnati, Ohio: How Books, 2009

Steven Heller and Teresa Fernandes, *The Business of Illustration,* New York: Watson-Guptill, 1995

Liz Jackson and Michael Spain, *Start Up!: How to Start Up a Successful Business from Absolutely Nothing,* New York: Prentice Hall, 2006

J. Randall Stott and Mike Truman, *Teach Yourself Basic Accounting,* London: Hodder & Stoughton, 2003

Darrel Rees, *How to be an Illustrator,* London: Laurence King Publishing, 2008

Brian Sheehan, *Basic Marketing: Online Marketing,* Lausanne: AVA Publishing, 2010

Max Scratchmann, *Illustration 101: Streetwise Tactics for Surviving as a Freelance Illustrator,* Aberdeen: Poison Pixie, 2009

Francesca Simon, *Children's Writers' and Artists' Yearbook 2011,* London: A&C Black, 2010

Donald Trump, *Think like a Champion: An Informal Education in Business and Life,* New York: Vanguard Press, 2010

Magazines & Periodicals

a-n Magazine
Afterall
Art Monthly
Art Review
Blueprint
Contagious
Crafts Magazine
Creative Review
Dazed & Confused
Design Week
Eye
Fantastic Man
Frieze
Grafik
i-D
The Illustrated Ape
Illustration Magazine
Le Gun
Okido
Printmaking Today
Professional Photographer
Sight & Sound
Source Photographic Review
Varoom
Wallpaper*

Promotional Illustration Websites

Contact
www.contactebooks.com
Creative Handbook
www.chb.com
Creative Review Illustration Annual
www.creativereview.co.uk
Images
www.theaoi.com

Useful addresses

Index

Professional Bodies

Association of Illustrators
2nd Floor
Back Building
150 Curtain Road
London EC2A 3AT
Tel: +44 (0)20 7613 4328
www.theaoi.com

European Illustration Forum
Promotes illustration through member associations in: Belgium, France, Germany, Greece, Holland, Hungary, Italy, Norway, Portugal, Spain, Switzerland and the United Kingdom
www.illu.org/eif

Agencies & Representation

Beehive Illustration Agency
www.beehiveillustration.co.uk
Big Active
www.bigactive.com
Central Illustration Agency
www.centralillustration.com
Eye Candy Illustration Agency
www.eyecandy.co.uk
Folio Illustration Agency
www.folioart.co.uk
Heart Agency
www.heartagency.com
Lemonade Illustration Agency
www.lemonadeillustration.com
NB Illustration Agency
www.nbillustration.co.uk
SAA Illustration Hub
Access to Arena, Art Market, Artist Partners Ltd, Debut Art, Melkejohn Illustration, New Division, Phosphor Art, The Artworks, The Bright Agency, The Organisation and Eastwing
www.saahub.com

Competitions & Awards

Communication Arts
www.commarts.com
D&AD Student Awards
www.dandad.org
Images
www.theaoi.com
RSA Projects: Design Directions
www.rsadesigndirections.org
The SAA Illustration Awards
www.saahub.com
The Victoria and Albert Museum Illustration Awards
www.vam.ac.uk
YCN Student Awards
www.ycnonline.com

Credits and acknowledgements

The author and publisher would like to thank all the illustrators, agencies, publishers and other companies who have provided material for use in this book. Credits are given in full in the captions alongside the images, unless additional credits have been requested, as listed below. In all cases, every effort has been made to credit the copyright holders, but should there be any omissions or errors the publisher would be pleased to insert the appropriate acknowledgment in subsequent editions of this book. Particular thanks to Bill Wright for his images on pages 42–45 and on page 47.

p.6t Shutterstock / **p.7** Shutterstock / **p.8l** Advertising Archives / **p.8r** © Estate of Saul Bass / **p.9l** By permission of *Esquire* magazine. The Hearst Corporation. *Esquire* is a trademark of The Hearst Corporation. All rights reserved. Thanks to Lise Valeur-Jaques / **p.9bl** Advertising Archives / **p.9b** Getty Images/John Kobal Foundation / **p.10r** www.anthonyburrill.com/archive/woodblock-posters.html / **p.11** Library of Congress Photoduplication Service / **p.25** Nick White is represented by Heart Agency – www.heartagency.com / **p.29** Jim Stoten is represented by Heart Agency – www.heartagency.com / **pp.31br** www.owain-thomas.co.uk / **p.42–45** All images by Bill Wright / **p.46m** iStock / **p.47t** Images by Bill Wright / **p.47bl** De Laurentiis. Source: BFI Stills / **p.51b** Nick White is represented by Heart Agency – www.heartagency.com / **pp.52–54** With thanks to Garth Lewis / **p.55bl** Commissioned by Jeannine Saba / **p.62b** © 2009. The National Gallery, London/Scala, Florence / **pp.63b + 65b** iStock / **p.66** © Antony Gormley / **p.67** © 2007 Warner Independent Pictures / **p.70m** Source: BFI Stills / **p.71m** Rhino Records / **p.71b** Photo: Prudence Cuming Associates/© Damien Hirst. All rights reserved, DACS 2010 / **p.73** iStock / **p.78** Luke Best is represented by Heart Agency – www.heartagency.com / **p.79t + m** Mary Evans Picture Library / **p.79b** John Frost Newspaper Archive Service / **pp.80t + 81b** Jimmy Turrell is represented by Heart Agency – www.heartagency.com / **p.83tr** Tom Gauld is represented by Heart Agency – www.heartagency.com / **pp.86–87** All images courtesy Ryu Itadani / **pp.90–93** All images courtesy Howard Read / **p.95** All images courtesy Gorilla / **p.88t** Jim Stoten is represented by Heart Agency – www.heartagency.com / **p.102t** © 2008. Photo Scala, Florence/FMAE, Torino / **p.103b** British Library. © 2003. Photo Scala Florence/HIP / **p.103** Photo: Ruth Schacht. © 2005. Photo Scala, Florence/BPK, Bildagentur für Kunst, Kultur und Geschichte, Berlin / **p.106bl** roderick@roderickmills.com; Roderick Mills is represented by Heart Agency – www.heartagency.com / **p.106mr** Jimmy Turrell is represented by Heart Agency – www.heartagency.com / **p.106br** Copyright © Dorling Kindersley Limited / **p.110–111** All images by Coralie Bickford-Smith, courtesy of Penguin Group (UK) / **p.112l** *Le Jacquot de Monsieur Hulot* by David Merveille © Éditions du Rouergue, 2005 / **p.112br** © Canadian Centre for Architecture,

Montréal / **p.113t** © Morteza Sahedi 2011. All rights reserved / **pp.116–117** All images courtesy Marc Boutavant. Marc Boutavant is represented by Heart Agency – www.heartagency.com / **p.120** All images courtesy Simone Lia / **p.131t** Digital image © 2009, The Museum of Modern Art, New York/Scala, Florence. © DACS 2010 / **p.131b** Digital image © 2009, The Museum of Modern Art, New York/Scala, Florence / **p.132t + br** © Estate of Abram Games / **p.133br** Digital image © 2011, The Museum of Modern Art/Scala, Florence / **p.133t + b** Courtesy Manuscripts and Archives, Yale University Library / **pp.140–141** All images courtesy Wilfrid Wood / **pp.144–145** All images courtesy Kam Tang and Graphic Thought Facility / **p.150** © Big Active Ltd / **p152m + b** © Rockstar Games / **p.153t** Photofest/Warner Independent Pictures. © Warner Independent Pictures / **p.153m** © Disney Enterprises, Inc./Photofest. Disney images are copyrighted and may not be repurposed for any use. / **p.153b** Photofest/Fantasy Inc. © Fantasy Inc. / **p.154t** Photofest/Paramount Pictures. © Paramount Pictures / **p.154m** *Pong*® courtesy of Atari Interactive, Inc. © 1972 Atari Interactive, Inc, All rights reserved. Used with permission / **p.155t** Photofest/Streamline Pictures. © Streamline Pictures / **p.155b** Concept, design,direction: Noah Harris; E4 creative director: Neil Gorringe; Production: Hothead Films; Animation director: Olly Reid; Post-Production: Busty Kelp; Music: Si Begg / **p.156tl** © Universal Music Enterprises / **p.156tr** Photofest/TriStar Pictures. Photographer: Zade Rosenthal. © TriStar Pictures / **p.157m** © 2007 Warner Independent Pictures / **pp.162–165** All images courtesy CMO Management International Ltd / **pp.166–167t** Record company: Mercury Records; Production company: Intro / **pp.170–171** Illustrations courtesy Neal Fox; Stills: Neal Fox/David Mullett/EMI Music / **p.172tl** © 2011 Rockstar Games / **p.173t** © 2011 Epic Games, Inc. / **pp.176–177** © 2011 Electronic Arts, Inc. / **p.183** Images courtesy Ryu Itadani / **pp.184–185** Images courtesy Roderick Mills and www.folk-projects.co.uk. Roderick Mills is represented by Heart Agency – www.heartagency.com / **pp.186–187** Images courtesy Howard Read / **pp.188–189** Images courtesy Russell Mills. *Blue Tears* is a multi-media installation for the Silo, Fundação de Serralves Centre for Contemporary Art, Porto, by Russell Mills and Ian Walton with Michael Fearon / **p.190** Images courtesy Neal Fox / **p.191** Images courtesy Josie Lynwode / **pp.192–193** Images courtesy Andy Forshaw / **p.194** Images courtesy Debbie Cook. Critical Forum Programme Director: David Blarney. Associate Director: Debbie Cook. Published by The Department of Communication Art & Design, Royal College of Art. www.communications-rca.com / **p.195** Images courtesy Debbie Cook. Client/creative director: Mark Adams at Vitsoe; Curator: Jane Audas; Designer: Brian Webb / **p.201** Courtesy Lloyds TSB / **pp.204–206** All images courtesy James Joyce. Studio photography by Michael Bodiam / **p.209** Courtesy Ryu Itadani / **pp.210–211** Images courtesy Sergei Sviatchenko / **p.212** Courtesy of Heart Agency

– www.heartagency.com / **p.216l + bl** Nick White is represented by Heart Agency – www.heartagency. com / **pp.216–217** All images courtesy Nobrow. Studio photography by Michael Bodiam.

The author would like to thank the following in particular:

Steve Aldridge, Sion Ap-Tomos, Jessica Barlow, Douglas Bevans, Coralie Bickford-Smith, David Blamey, Marc Boutavant, Mark Brooks, Clive Challis, Debbie Cook, Faye Dowling, Andy Forshaw, Neal Fox, Jennifer Hall, Kelly Hall, Simon Hall, John Hamilton, Joel Harrison, Timon Harrison, Jamie Hewlett, Ryu Itadani, Nicola Jenkins, John Jervis, Garth Lewis, Angelina Li, Simone Lia, Josie Lynwode, Cecilia Mackay, Martin McGrath, Mus Mehmet, Roderick Mills, Russell Mills, Sara Morrissey, Patrick Morrissey, Paul Neale, David Oscroft, Guy Parker-Rees, Alice Rawsthorn, Howard Read, Darrel Rees, Paul Rennie, Paul Ryan, Dani Salvadori, Iain Simons, Alex Spiro, Kam Tang, Anne Townley, Ben Ward, Andrew Whittle, Wilfrid Wood and Bill Wright.